Accounting for Business Activity

Accounting for Business Activity

Case scenarios in accounting

David Hatherly BSc(Econ), MAcc, FCA

Professor of Accounting
The University of Edinburgh

PITMAN PUBLISHING
128 Long Acre, London WC2E 9AN

A Division of Longman Group UK Limited

© Longman Group UK Limited 1993

First published in Great Britain 1993
Reprinted 1993

British Library Cataloguing in Publication Data
A Catalogue record for this book is available from the British Library.

ISBN 0 273 60115 6

Typeset by Mathematical Composition Setters Ltd, Salisbury, Wiltshire

Printed by Bell and Bain Ltd, Glasgow

CONTENTS

PREFACE

Accounting is a control mechanism or control 'technology' which enables one party to monitor and evaluate the performance of another. In this way it has facilitated the separation of ownership (shareholders) from management (directors) necessary for the growth of capital intensive industry and commerce. Thus accounting information provides the basis for measuring financial performance and it is also used explicitly or implicitly in specific decisions such as the level of dividends, taxation, investment, and product prices. The theme of this book, however, is not the use of accounting for control or for specific business decisions, but the relevance of accounting to an 'understanding' of business, such an understanding being the essential background to any business decision. What becomes clear is that not only is accounting essential to an understanding of business activity, but understanding business is essential to an understanding of accounting. It is the two-way linkages between business activity and accounting information which provide the primary focus of this book.

The first chapter of the book introduces accounting as being the preparation of financial statements from transactions (a transactions perspective). It also gives an introduction to the financial ratios which can be derived from the financial statements. Such ratio analysis is a necessary prerequisite for understanding the linkages between financial statements and business activity.

Business activity may be viewed from many different perspectives and each perspective can give a different insight. For example, business activity may not only be viewed as a set of transactions, but also as a set of projects, a set of organizational processes or a set of functions. Whilst traditional financial statements have evolved as a means of recording and summarizing complete or partially complete transactions, investment appraisal has developed on a project by project basis around techniques such as discounted cash flow. These two perspectives are exhaustively covered in nearly all current introductory texts and provide much of the intellectual base for current thinking in the accounting profession. The ideas with which the trainee accountant is first presented retain a profound influence. There is, however, a growing awareness that these perspectives provide only a very limited understanding of business. For this purpose the most insightful perspectives are the organizational and the functional.

The organizational perspective considers the implications of different organizational processes and structures for the relationships between, and interests of, stakeholders in the business. Such stakeholders include shareholders, other financiers, managers, other employees, suppliers, customers and regulators. Much recent and important research has investigated both the implications of organizational issues for accounting and the influence of accounting on organizations. Organizational issues, however, are not the primary focus of this book which takes a functional perspective. It is based around the model given as Exhibit 2.1 in Chapter 2. This lists the operational functions as marketing, sales, product development, production, purchasing, personnel, finance and asset management. However, each function has a strategic as well as an operational dimension, and the book proceeds in Chapters 3 to 17 through a series of brief case studies which illustrate the linkages between different strategic/operational considerations and accounting measures. The 'business' settings covered by the case studies include financial services, heavy industry, regulated business and the public sector. A list of the case studies and the functions considered by each are given in Exhibit 2.4 of Chapter 2. The last section of that chapter briefly discusses each case study in turn. Chapter 2 provides an integrating framework for the case studies and provides the cohesion and the rationale for the book.

The book is designed as an introduction to accounting for business students. It also provides an excellent introduction to accounting for specialist accounting students since the important linkages between business and accounting are clearly established from the start. Since understanding business activity is essential to both investor and managerial decision-taking, the book sits astride the traditional categorization of accounting into financial and management. It therefore provides an overall introduction to accounting which can later be built upon by a more traditional study of financial and/or management accounting. I have used the case studies at Edinburgh University with great success on both MBA and first-year undergraduate courses. I have also used the case studies on a selective basis for the second and third years of the accounting degree. Thus the case study presentation has proved highly flexible. Chapters 3 and 4 cover different stages of the same case study and, with the exception of Chapter 13 which contains two cases, Chapters 5 to 17 each contain one case study. Chapter titles reflect an important feature of the business setting for the case. Case exercises to be attempted by the reader (self-study exercises) are included either at the end of each chapter, or on occasions they are embedded at the relevant stage within the chapter itself.

This is not a radical book. It does not directly challenge the existing structure of limited companies or the various modes of the 'capitalist' system which presume particular patterns of privileges and responsibilities for the various stakeholders. Similarly it does not directly challenge current accounting ideas which have largely evolved from a transactions perspective. The main theme is to take an existing organizational structure – predominantly the limited company – and show how business activity carried out impacts on the accounting numbers derived either by current practice or by ideas well covered in the accounting literature. Having said that, I believe that the functional perspective of the book generates a host of novel insights with significant implications for the future development of accounting and the way it is taught.

The case study for Chapter 1, the Wooden Stool Company, is based on a case developed by my colleague Falconer Mitchell. The self-study exercise for Chapter 13 was prepared by another colleague, Tom Brown. I am grateful to them for allowing me to incorporate their material. Finally I am most grateful to Caroline Hall for typing the manuscript.

Accounting for transactions

INTRODUCTION

The Wooden Stool Co. Ltd is a case study to illustrate how business trans-actions are recorded in the accounts. Book-keeping developed as a way of recording and keeping track of transactions. From these basic records balance sheets, profit statements and cash flow statements can be prepared to summarize the assets, liabilities and transactions of the business. These financial statements provide the basis from which the business's financial position and performance can be analysed.

THE WOODEN STOOL COMPANY

On 1 January 19X1 the Wooden Stool Co. Ltd was set up to produce and sell three-legged stools. During their first year in business the following transactions and events take place:

1 £40,000 of share capital is raised from investors.

2 A bank loan of £60,000 is obtained.

3 Purchase of equipment by cheque £20,000. This equipment has a four-year life.

4 Purchase of premises by cheque £50,000. The premises have a ten-year life.

5 Purchase of wood on credit £60,000.

6 Use of £40,000 of wood to produce 4,000 stools.

7 Incurrence of further production costs:
Wages for labour £25,000
Other production costs/payments £25,000

8 Sale of 3,000 stools on credit at £50 each.

9 Payments by cheque to suppliers of wood £20,000.

10 Received cheques from customers £50,000.

11 Tax of £30,000 due on company profits but not yet paid.

12 A capital equipment replacement reserve of £10,000 is created.

13 A dividend of £20,000 is proposed but not yet paid.

14 Interest of £6,000 on the bank loan is paid.

The case provides the above list of the Wooden Stool Company's transactions/events which have then to be detailed in the basic accounting records. Each of the listed transactions impacts on the assets and/or liabilities of the business. A list of these assets and liabilities for the Wooden Stool Company is included in Exhibit 1.1.

Assets and liabilities

An asset provides access to a future economic benefit which can be used by the business. Hence assets include a positive bank balance and stocks and debtors which will ultimately be turned into cash. Also included are the equipment and premises of the business which, although the company may not intend to sell, will benefit the business by allowing the process of manufacture to take place. A liability is the business's obligation to transfer economic benefits away from the business at a future date. Hence liabilities include negative bank balances together with dividends payable, tax payable, creditors and loans, all of which must be paid from the bank balance at a future date.

Equity

Underneath the liabilities section of Exhibit 1.1 is a section headed equity. Equity represents the ownership interest in the business. It is the residual amount found by deducting all liabilities of the business from the assets of the business. The Wooden Stool Company's equity is subdivided into capital, retained profit and reserves. Capital is the amount paid by the owners to the business in return for shares. Retained profit is the cumulative amount of profit which the business has not yet paid or proposed to pay as dividends. The owners of the business are entitled to have an amount equivalent to the profits of the business paid to them as dividends. It is, however, unusual for all the profits of a business to be paid as dividends. The meaning of reserves is addressed later in the chapter. It is akin to retained profit and hence part of the ownership interest.

Assets			Liabilities		
Transactions £		*Total £000*	*Transactions* £		*Total £000*
Bank			Tax payable		
			Creditors		
Equipment			Dividend payable		
Premises			Loan		
Raw material stock			**Equity**		
			Capital		
Finished goods stock			Retained profit		
Debtors			Reserves		

Exhibit 1.1 Assets and liabilities of the Wooden Stool Company

Recording the transactions/events

1 £40,000 of share capital is raised from investors

This transaction impacts on the cash and capital accounts in Exhibit 1.1 as follows:

Assets	Equity
Bank	Capital
(1) £40,000	(1) £40,000

The reader can start to build up a set of accounting records by putting these entries into the appropriate accounts (boxes) in Exhibit 1.1. It should be noted that the transaction gives rise to *two* entries in the accounts and that these are of equal amounts. It is this duality or double entry which keeps the books in balance. After the first transaction, assets = equity, and the books balance.

2 A bank loan of £60,000 is obtained

This transaction impacts on the cash (i.e. bank) and loan accounts in Exhibit 1.1 as follows:

Assets	Liabilities
Bank	Loan
(2) £60,000	(2) £60,000

These entries should be added by the reader to those already contained in Exhibit 1.1 from the first transaction. Exhibit 1.1 now shows:

Assets	Liabilities
Bank	Loan
(1) £40,000	(2) £60,000
(2) £60,000	
	Equity
	Capital
	(1) £40,000

The second transaction gives a double entry of £60,000, allowing the assets of £100,000 to equal the sum of the liabilities and equity. Assets = Liabilities plus Equity is known as the accounting equation and is an artefact of double-entry book-keeping. As a result of this equation the books continue to balance.

3 Purchase of equipment by cheque £20,000. This equipment has a four-year life.

The purchase of equipment impacts on the bank and equipment accounts:

Assets	
Bank	
(3.1) £(20,000)	
Equipment	
(3.1) £20,000	

This is an example of a double entry where both entries impact on asset accounts. The transaction reduces the bank balance by £20,000, and the fact that this is a reduction is shown by putting brackets around the £20,000. The bank balance is now £80,000 (60 + 40 − 20).

The equipment is expected to provide four years of economic benefit. It is accounting practice to allocate the original cost of £20,000 as £5,000 of benefit receivable in each year from the use of the machine. Hence at the end of the first year £5,000 of economic benefit from the machine has expired, leaving £15,000 for the three remaining years. The expiry of the first year's £5,000 allocation is recorded in the books by the entries (tagged 3.2) as follows:

Assets	
Equipment	
(3) £(20,000)	
(3.2) £(5,000)	
Finished stock	
(3.2) £5,000	

The cumulative total or 'balance' on the equipment account at the end of the year now stands at £15,000 (20 − 5) reflecting the three remaining years of economic benefit. The loss during the year of one year's economic benefit from the machine is called the 'depreciation' cost suffered through the use of the machine. This cost has been suffered in order to produce the finished stock of stools. Since the use of the machine is a cost of *production* it is included in the finished stock account. Hence the double entry to the £5,000 reduction in the equipment is to be found in finished stock.

The reader should continue to update Exhibit 1.1 for this and all the remaining transactions. A completed set of accounts for the first year is given later as Exhibit 1.2.

4 Purchase of premises by cheque £50,000. The premises have a ten-year life

The entries for this transaction follow the pattern of those for transaction 3:

Assets	
Bank	
(4.1) £(50,000)	
Premises	
(4.1) £50,000	
(4.2) £(5,000)	
Finished goods stock	
(4.2) £5,000	

The annual depreciation of £5,000 is obtained by taking the original cost of the premises and dividing by its expected ten-year life. Assuming the premises house the productive equipment, then the first year's depreciation of the premises is a cost of production and hence included in finished stock.

5 Purchase of wood on credit £60,000

This transaction impacts on the stock (of wood) and creditors accounts. Wood is the raw material for the production process.

Assets	Liabilities
Raw material stock	Creditors
(5) £60,000	(5) £60,000

6 Use of £40,000 of wood to produce 4,000 stools

This transaction, like the depreciation of the equipment and the premises, is internal to the business and does not involve any outside parties. The wood is transferred out of raw material stock and becomes part of the stock of finished stools. The entries are:

Assets	
Raw material stock	
(6) £(40,000)	
Finished goods stock	
(6) £40,000	

7 Incurrence of other production costs:

Wages for labour	£25,000
Other production costs	£25,000

To manufacture the stools takes raw materials, labour, other production costs (such as the electricity and rates for the factory) and the use of premises and equipment. Since these are all costs of *producing* the stools they are all included in the cost of the finished stock and collected in the finished stock account. The raw materials cost has already been collected by the entries for transaction 6. The use of the equipment and premises has already been collected by the inclusion of their depreciation costs in the finished stock account entries for transactions 3 and 4.

Assuming that wages and other production costs are paid in cash, the entries for transaction 7 are:

Assets	
Bank	
(7) £(50,000)	
Finished goods stock	
(7) £50,000	

The cumulative total in the finished goods stock account is now £100,000, being:

	£
Use of equipment	5,000
Use of premises	5,000
Use of wood	40,000
Use of labour	25,000
Other production costs	25,000
	100,000

Production volumes are stated in transaction 6 as being 4,000 stools and hence £100,000 must be the total production cost for 4,000 stools, giving a unit cost of £25. This unit production cost can in general be derived from the accounts provided the number of units produced is known. It is an important piece of management information.

8 Sale of 3,000 stools on credit at £50 each

A sale transaction sets up two double entries. The first reflects the creation of sales revenue and the establishment of a debtor. Sales revenue is collected in the retained profit account. The first double entry is as follows:

Assets	Equity
Debtors	Retained profit
(8.1) £150,000	(8.1) £150,000

The second double entry reflects the fact that the sales revenue has been obtained by transferring finished stock to the customer. The loss of this finished stock is a cost (of sale) to be subtracted from sales revenue in the calculation of profit. The double entry (8.2) is:

Assets	Equity
Finished goods stock	Retained profit
(8.2) £(75,000)	(8.1) £150,000
	(8.2) (75,000)

The amount to be taken from finished goods and set against sales revenue £(75,000) is calculated as 3,000 stools sold at a unit production cost of £25 as previously calculated.

It should be noted that it is at the point of selling when traditional accounting recognizes the generation of profit. This is called the *recognition* concept. Until transaction 8 no profit had been recognized and the profit accounts did not contain any entries. It now shows a balance of £75,000, being sales revenue less the cost of those sales, and this £75,000 is known as the 'gross' profit.

9 Payments by cheque to suppliers of wood £20,000

This transaction reduces cash at bank and creditors:

Assets	Liabilities
Bank	Creditors
(9) £(20,000)	(5) £60,000
	(9) (20,000)

The balance on the creditors account of £40,000 (60 – 20) is the out-standing amount still owing to the business's supplier(s).

10 Received cheques from customers £50,000

This transaction increases cash at bank but reduces another asset, debtors:

Assets	
Bank	
(10) £50,000	
Debtors	
(8.1) 150,000	
(10) (50,000)	

The balance on the debtors account of £100,000 represents the amount still receivable at the year end from the business's customer(s).

11 Tax of £30,000 due on company profits but not yet paid

In general a company will organize its affairs to minimize its tax liability. Provided it is done legally this is a valid and important managerial activity. Of course it is a perspective which sees tax as a cost rather than as a contribution to the common good! The management of taxation is an intricate subject in its own right and is not a topic covered in this book which in general ignores taxation. However, transaction 11 serves as a reminder that tax is chargeable on company profits and hence £30,000 must be taken out of profit, reducing the ownership interest, and included in the tax payable account:

> *Liabilities*
>
> Tax payable
> (11) £30,000
>
> *Equity*
>
> Retained profit
> (8.1) £150,000
> (8.2) (75,000)
> (11) (30,000)

The assets of the business will be reduced in due course when the tax is paid. The balance on the retained profit account is now £45,000 being the gross profit (sales less cost of sales) of £75,000 less the tax charge.

12 A capital equipment replacement reserve of £10,000 is created

In law the owners of the company are entitled to receive in dividends an amount of cash up to the amount of profits which the business has earned. Retained profit therefore represents an ownership (or equity) interest which is returnable to the shareholders in the form of dividends at some as yet unspecified date. In practice it is seldom prudent for the business to distribute all its profits as dividends. By creating a 'reserve' of £10,000 the company is saying that £10,000 which might otherwise be paid as dividend is needed by the company for other purposes – in this case to pay for replacement of equipment. £10,000 is therefore transferred out of retained profit and into 'reserves'. This, however, is not a transfer of cash. It is a movement from one section of equity or ownership interest (retained profit) to another section of equity (reserves). The entries are as follows:

> *Equity*
>
> Retained profit
> (12) £(10,000)
>
> *Reserves*
>
> (12) £10,000

It should be noted that the double entry impacts on two equity accounts and that no asset or liability accounts are affected, since there is no transfer of assets and there is no liability to pay the £10,000 until a decision in the future is made to replace. What has happened is that the shareholder owners have received a signal that £10,000 of their ownership interest ought not prudently to be regarded as returnable to them in the form of dividend payments.

13 A dividend of £20,000 is proposed but not yet paid

This decision to pay £20,000 reduces the retained profit and increases the dividend payable accounts as follows:

	Liability
	Dividend payable
	(13) £20,000
	Equity
	Retained profit
	(13) £(20,000)

No asset account is affected until the dividend is paid, at which point cash is reduced and the liability for dividends payable extinguished.

14 Interest of £6,000 on the bank loan is paid

The interest on the bank loan is charged by the bank to the Wooden Stool Company's current account with the bank. This charge reduces the profits available to shareholders. The double entry is as follows:

Assets	*Equity*
Bank	Retained profit
(14) £(6,000)	(14) £(6,000)

PREPARING THE ANNUAL FINANCIAL STATEMENTS

Exhibit 1.2 shows the overall position in the accounts at the end of the first year, including the cumulative totals.

The cumulative total on each account is known as the account balance at the end of the year. It is seen that the sum of the asset account balances (£209,000) equals the sum of the liability and equity account balances (£209,000). The accounting equation (assets equals liabilities plus equity) holds and the accounts balance. The listing of accounts to make sure that they balance is known as taking a 'trial balance'. It is now possible to extract from the accounts the balance sheet given as Exhibit 1.3.

Assets			Liabilities		
Transactions £		*Total* £000	*Transactions* £		*Total* £000
Bank (1) £40,000 (2) 60,000 (3.1) (20,000) (4.1) (50,000) (7) (50,000) (9) (20,000) (10) 50,000 (14) (6,000)		4	Tax payable (11) £30,000		30
			Creditors (5) £60,000 (9) (20,000)		40
Equipment (3.1) £20,000 (3.2) (5,000)		15	Dividend payable (13) £20,000		20
Premises (4.1) £50,000 (4.2) (5,000)		45	Loan (2) £60,000		60
Raw material stock (5) £60,000 (6) (40,000)		20	**Equity**		
			Capital (1) £40,000		40
Finished goods stock (3.2) £5,000 (4.2) 5,000 (6) 40,000 (7) 50,000 (8.2) (75,000)		25	Retained profit (8.1) £150,000 (8.2) (75,000) (13) (20,000) (11) (30,000) (14) (6,000) (12) (10,000)		9
Debtors (8.1) £150,000 (10) (50,000)		100	Reserves (12) £10,000		10
		209			209

Exhibit 1.2 Accounts after recording year 1 transactions

WOODEN STOOL COMPANY LIMITED
Balance Sheet as at 31 December 19X1

	£	£	£
Fixed assets			
Premises			45,000
Equipment			15,000
			60,000
Current assets			
Raw material stock		20,000	
Finished goods stock		25,000	
Debtors		100,000	
Bank		4,000	
		149,000	
Current liabilities (due within 1 year)			
Trade creditors	40,000		
Tax payable	30,000		
Dividend payable	20,000	90,000	
Net current assets			59,000
			119,000
Long-term liabilities			
Bank loan			60,000
NET ASSETS			59,000
Represented by:			
Capital			40,000
Retained profits			9,000
Reserves			10,000
SHAREHOLDERS' FUNDS			59,000

Exhibit 1.3

It is seen from Exhibit 1.3 that this balance sheet divides assets into fixed assets which are held for the long term, and current assets which are *cash*, *debtors* to be converted shortly into cash, *finished goods* shortly to be sold, and *raw material stock* shortly to be processed into finished goods and then sold. The idea is that current assets have the ability to be converted into cash within a relatively short period, of say one year, from the balance sheet date. Furthermore, the balance sheet divides liabilities into short-term liabilities payable within one year and longer-term liabilities such as the bank loan. Having established these sub-classifications of assets and liabilities the particular balance sheet presentation given in Exhibit 1.3 rewrites the accounting equation as follows:

Assets = Liabilities + Equity

Fixed assets + Current assets =
Current liabilities + Long-term liabilities + Equity

Fixed assets + (Current assets − Current liabilities) =
Long-term liabilities + Equity

Fixed assets + Net current assets = Long-term liabilities + Equity

Fixed assets (£60,000) + Net current assets (£59,000)
− Long-term liabilities (£60,000) = Equity (£59,000)

Current assets less current liabilities is known as the company's net current assets (in a healthy company this will be a positive figure) and is shown as a separate section in the balance sheet. It should be noted that different presentations of the balance sheet are possible, following different versions of the accounting equation. Different presentations are employed throughout the book so that the reader's exposure is not limited to a single presentation.

The remaining financial statements, given in Exhibit 1.4, are the profit statement and the cash flow statement for the first year of business. These are an analysis of the retained profit and bank accounts in Exhibit 1.2. The reader should confirm this by tracing the entries in the retained profit account to the profit statement and the entries in the bank account to the cash flow statement. To enable this to be done easily, Exhibit 1.4 includes the retained profit and bank accounts in the sidelines.

Debits and credits

Traditional double-entry book-keeping describes each account entry as either a debit or a credit. Moreover each account is divided into two columns with debits being entered in the left-hand column and credits in the right-hand column. For assets, each increase in the asset is a debit

WOODEN STOOL COMPANY LIMITED
Profit and cash flow statements

Profit statement for the year ended 31 December 19X1

	£		Retained profit account
Sales	150,000	(8.1)	150,000
Cost of sales	75,000	(8.2)	(75,000)
Gross profit	75,000		
Interest	6,000	(14)	(6,000)
Profit before tax	69,000		
Taxation	30,000	(11)	(30,000)
Net profit	39,000		
Transfer to reserve	10,000	(12)	(10,000)
	29,000		
Dividend proposed	20,000	(13)	(20,000)
Profit retained	9,000		9,000

Cash flow statement for the year ended 31 December 19X1

Cash inflows	£	£		Bank account
Share capital contributed		40,000	(1)	40,000
Bank loan obtained		60,000	(2)	60,000
Receipts from customers		50,000	(10)	50,000
		150,000		
Cash outflows			(3.1)	(20,000)
Purchase of fixed assets	70,000		(4.1)	(50,000)
Payment to wood suppliers	20,000		(9)	(20,000)
Payment of wages and overheads	50,000		(7)	(50,000)
Payment of interest	6,000	146,000	(14)	(6,000)
Balance of cash 31/12/X1		4,000		4,000

Exhibit 1.4

entry and each reduction is a credit entry. Thus the bank account can be written:

	Bank		
(1)	£40,000	(3.1)	£20,000
(2)	60,000	(4.1)	50,000
(10)	50,000	(7)	50,000
		(9)	20,000
		(14)	6,000
Increases		Decreases	
= Debits		= Credits	

It should be noted that the brackets around those entries which are reductions have been dropped and the fact that they are reductions is now signalled by their appearance in the right-hand or credit column of the account. The debit column totals £150,000 and the credit column totals £146,000. It is said that the account has a debit balance at the end of the year of £4,000 since the debits exceed the credits by that amount. The balance on the account is shown as follows:

	Bank		
(1)	£40,000	(3.1)	£20,000
(2)	60,000	(4.1)	50,000
(10)	50,000	(7)	50,000
		(9)	20,000
		(14)	6,000
		Balance	4,000
	150,000		150,000
Balance	4,000		

For liabilities and equity accounts, each increase in the liability or ownership interest is a credit entry and each reduction is a debit entry. Thus the rule for liability and equity accounts is the reverse of that for assets. The retained profit account can be written:

	Retained profit		
(8.2)	£75,000	(8.1)	£150,000
(11)	30,000		
(12)	10,000		
(13)	20,000		
(14)	6,000		
Balance	9,000		
	150,000		150,000
		Balance	9,000

It should be noted that the £150,000 of sales revenue (8.1) is a credit entry whereas expenses such as the £75,000 of cost of sales (8.2) is a debit entry. The closing balance on the account is a credit balance (credits exceed debits) of £9,000 representing an ownership interest of that amount. In general, liability and equity accounts contain credit balances whilst asset accounts contain debit balances.

For the moment the idea of accounts having two columns, one for debits and one for credits, can be put aside, and the reader can continue to work with the accounts as a single column with reductions shown by the use of brackets.

PERFORMANCE ANALYSIS RATIOS

Traditionally the starting point for an analysis of the financial statements is the calculation of key financial ratios. These ratios are concerned with the company's profitability, liquidity and capital structure.

Profitability ratios

The main profitability ratios are illustrated in the pyramid of ratios given as Exhibit 1.5. Profitability is examined in the first instance by relating profit (after tax but before interest) with the total assets, both fixed and current, used to generate that profit. This ratio is the return on total assets (ROTA). For the Wooden Stool Company it is:

$$\frac{\text{Net profit plus interest}}{\text{Total assets}} = \frac{45}{60 + 149} \times 100 = 21.5\%$$

The pyramid shows that further analysis of how this ratio has been achieved is obtained by looking at profit to sales and sales to assets. The first of these ratios is known as the profit margin and the second as asset productivity. For the Wooden Stool Company:

$$\text{Profit margin} = \frac{45}{150} \times 100 = 30\%$$

$$\text{Asset productivity} = \frac{150}{209} \times 100 = 71.8\%$$

It should be noted that profit margin times asset productivity equals ROTA ($71.8\% \times 30 = 21.5$). Profit margin and asset productivity form the major twin branches of the pyramid in Exhibit 1.5. Each branch is

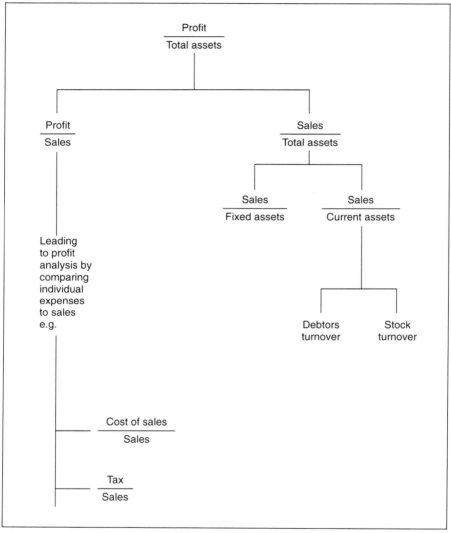

Exhibit 1.5 The pyramid of ratios

now followed in turn, starting with profit margin and following with asset productivity.

Profit margin

The profit margin is analysed by comparing each individual line of expense in turn to sales. For the Wooden Stool Company the expense lines are cost of sales and tax. This gives the following ratios:

$$\frac{\text{Cost of sales}}{\text{Sales}} = \frac{75}{150} \times 100 = 50\%$$

$$\frac{\text{Tax}}{\text{Sales}} = \frac{30}{150} = 20\%$$

Cost of sales account for 50% of sales revenue, whilst tax accounts for 20%.

Asset productivity

The pyramid shows that further analysis of asset 'productivity' looks separately at the 'productivity' of fixed assets and current assets. Asset 'productivity' can be examined through asset turnover ratios which can be expressed either as the number of times the asset divides into sales or as a percentage. For the Wooden Stool Company:

$$\text{Fixed asset turnover} = \frac{150}{60} = 2.5 \text{ or } 250\%$$

$$\text{Current asset turnover} = \frac{150}{149} = 1.01 \text{ or } 101\%$$

In general a company which works its assets very hard will have a higher asset turnover than one which does not.

Finally the pyramid shows that the productivity of current assets can be explored by looking at the performance of individual current assets such as debtors and stock. Debt collection can be examined in terms of debtors turnover, either through the number of times debtors divide into sales or as the number of days sales in debtors. The calculations are as follows in the case of the Wooden Stool Company:

$$\frac{\text{Sales}}{\text{Debtors}} = \frac{150}{100} = 1.5 \text{ times}$$

or

$$\frac{\text{Debtors}}{\text{Average daily sales}} = \frac{100}{150/365} = 243 \text{ days}$$

It should be noted that the first of these turnover ratios has debtors as a denominator and the second has debtors as a numerator. A company which is good at collecting its debts will 'turn over' its debtors many times and have a small debtors figure in terms of daily sales.

Stock turnover is normally calculated by relating total stock, both finished and raw material, to cost of sales rather than to sales. For the Wooden Stool Company:

$$\frac{\text{Cost of sales}}{\text{Stock}} = \frac{75}{45} = \text{a stock turnover of } 1.66$$

or in terms of the number of days cost of sales in stock:

$$\frac{\text{Stock}}{\text{Average daily cost of sales}} = \frac{45}{75/365} = 219 \text{ days}$$

A company which is experiencing high demand for its products relative to production will 'turn over' its stock many times during the year and have a relatively low stock figure in terms of daily (cost of) sales.

A further refinement is achieved by relating finished stock to cost of sales to give an idea of how many days sales can be met from finished stock, and by relating raw material stock to the daily consumption of raw material in production so as to give an idea of how many days of production can be met from raw material stock. These ratios are not calculated at this stage but they serve to indicate how the further refinement of ratios is always possible.

Creditors

Just as the management of debtors and stock can be investigated through ratio analysis, so can the management of creditors. In the case of creditors it is sensible to relate the balance on the account to purchases. For the Wooden Stool Company creditors are for the purchase of wood and so this balance is related to wood purchases. The relevant ratios are:

$$\frac{\text{Purchases}}{\text{Creditors}} = \frac{60}{40} = \text{a creditors turnover of } 1.5$$

or alternatively in terms of the number of days purchases in creditors:

$$\frac{\text{Creditors}}{\text{Average daily purchases}} = \frac{40}{60/365} = 243 \text{ days}$$

A company which pays its creditors promptly will turnover its creditors many times and have a relatively small creditors figure in terms of daily purchases.

Liquidity

A company's liquidity is generally investigated by comparing its current assets to its current liabilities. The current ratio for the Wooden Stool Company is:

$$\frac{\text{Current assets}}{\text{Current liabilities}} = \frac{149}{90} = 1.66$$

If this ratio is declining over time then the company is becoming less liquid. If it falls below 1 then its short-term liabilities exceed its short-term assets and it *may* have difficulty meeting its debts. However, a clearer idea of its ability to meet its liabilities is obtained via a cash flow forecast. If a company is experiencing difficulty in selling its stock then it may be prudent to exclude stocks from its current assets when comparing with current liabilities. If this is done the resulting ratio is called the quick ratio, and for the Wooden Stool Company it is:

$$\frac{\text{Current assets} - \text{Stock}}{\text{Current liabilities}} = \frac{149 - 45}{90} = 1.16$$

There are great variations between companies in respect of both current and quick ratios, depending upon the type of business the company undertakes. This serves to illustrate the importance of relating financial statement ratios to the nature of the business activity.

Capital structure

Whilst the current and quick ratios are concerned with the short-term asset and liability position, the company's long-term financial structure is generally investigated by examining the proportion of long-term finance (equity plus long-term loans) which is financed other than by the shareholders. In the case of the Wooden Stool Company the long-term non-shareholder finance is the loan of £60,000 and this accounts for $60/(60 + 59) \times 100\%$ of the long-term finance. This proportion is known as the company's gearing, and for the Wooden Stool Company it is 50.4%. It will be shown later that a company's gearing is important in assessing the stability of a company's profits over time, and is an important influence on the return which the profit gives to shareholders as a percentage of shareholder funds. The return on shareholders' funds (ROSF) is a measure of the profitability of the company from the perspective of shareholders. For the Wooden Stool Company:

$$\text{ROSF} = \frac{\text{Profits after tax and interest}}{\text{Shareholders' funds}} = \frac{39}{59} \times 100 = 66.1\%$$

SELF-STUDY EXERCISE 1.1

Exhibit 1.6 sets out the accounts of the Wooden Stool Company showing the balances on the accounts which were in place at the end of the first year.

These are the closing balances for the first year and they become the opening balances for Wooden Stool's second year in business. The entries for Wooden Stool's second year transactions are cumulatively added or subtracted from these opening balances. The Wooden Stool Company's second year (19X2) transactions are as follows:

Transactions/events in year 2, i.e. year to 31 December 19X2:

1 19X1 tax and dividends paid.

2 Expansion requires the purchase by cheque of equipment for £15,000. This equipment has a three-year life.

3 Wood purchased on credit £80,000.

4 Payments to wood supplier £50,000.

5 Use of £60,000 of wood to produce 6,000 stools.

6 Incurrence of production costs:
   Wages   £45,000
   Overheads paid   £30,000.

7 Depreciation is charged for the second year's use of the equipment and premises, including the equipment bought in year 2.

8 Sale of 5,000 stools on credit at £55 each.

9 Cheques from customers total £150,000.

10 Tax of £40,000 due on profits but not yet paid.

11 A transfer to replacement reserve of £10,000 is made.

12 A dividend of £25,000 is proposed but not yet paid.

13 Interest of £6,000 on the bank loan is paid.

THE WOODEN STOOL COMPANY
Opening account balances for 19X2

Assets			Liabilities		
Transactions £		*Total* £000	*Transactions* £		*Total* £000
Bank OB £4,000			Tax payable OB £30,000		
			Creditors OB £40,000		
Equipment OB £15,000			Dividend payable OB £20,000		
Premises OB £45,000			Loan OB £60,000		
Raw material stock OB £20,000			**Equity**		
			Capital OB £40,000		
Finished goods stock OB £25,000			Retained profit OB £9,000		
Debtors OB £100,000			Reserves OB £10,000		

Exhibit 1.6

Required:

1 Use Exhibit 1.6 to collect the entries for the 19X2 transactions.

2 Calculate the balances on each account at the end of 19X2 and take a trial balance.

3 Prepare the Wooden Stool Company's balance sheet at the end of 19X2 using the pro-forma given as Exhibit 1.7.

4 Prepare the Wooden Stool Company's profit and cash flow statements for 19X2 using the pro-formas given in Exhibit 1.8.

5 Prepare key financial ratios for 19X2 using the pro-forma given in Exhibit 1.9.

THE WOODEN STOOL COMPANY
Pro-forma balance sheet at 31/12/X2

			£000
Fixed assets			
Premises			X
Equipment			X
			X
Current assets			
Raw material stock		X	
Finished goods stock		X	
Debtors		X	
		X	
Current liabilities			
Bank	X		
Trade creditors	X		
Tax payable	X		
Dividend payable	X	X	
Net current assets			X
			X
Long-term liabilities			
Bank loan			X
NET ASSETS			X
Represented by:			
Capital			X
Retained profits			X
Reserves			X
SHAREHOLDERS' FUNDS			X

Exhibit 1.7

THE WOODEN STOOL COMPANY

Pro-forma profit statement for 19X2

	£000
Sales	X
Cost of sales	X
Gross profit	X
Interest	X
Profit before tax	X
Taxation	X
Net profit	X
Transfer to reserves	X
	X
Dividend proposed	X
Retained profit for 19X2	X
Retained profit brought forward from previous year	X
Retained profit carried forward	X

Pro-forma cash flow statement for 19X2

		£000
Cash inflows from operations		
Receipts from customers		X
Cash outflows from operations		
Payments to wood suppliers	X	
Payments of wages and overheads	X	X
Operating cash flow		X
Tax and finance payments		
Payment of tax	X	
Payment of dividends	X	
Payment of interest	X	X
Cash flow after finance payments		X
Purchase of fixed assets		X
Cash flow for 19X2		X
Opening balance		X
Balance carried forward		X

Exhibit 1.8

THE WOODEN STOOL COMPANY

Pro-forma for 19X2 financial ratios

ROTA $\qquad = \dfrac{\text{Net profit plus interest}}{\text{Assets}} \times 100 \quad =$

Profit margin $\qquad = \dfrac{\text{Net profit plus interest}}{\text{Sales}} \times 100 \quad =$

Asset productivity $\qquad = \dfrac{\text{Sales}}{\text{Assets}} \times 100 \quad =$

Expense analysis 1 $\qquad = \dfrac{\text{Cost of sales}}{\text{Sales}} \times 100 \quad =$

Expense analysis 2 $\qquad = \dfrac{\text{Tax}}{\text{Sales}} \times 100 \quad =$

Fixed asset turnover $\qquad = \dfrac{\text{Sales}}{\text{Fixed assets}} \quad =$

Current asset turnover $\qquad = \dfrac{\text{Sales}}{\text{Current assets}} \quad =$

Debtors turnover $\qquad = \dfrac{\text{Sales}}{\text{Debtors}} \quad =$

No. of days sales in debtors $\qquad = \dfrac{\text{Debtors}}{\text{Average daily sales}} \quad =$

Stock turnover $\qquad = \dfrac{\text{Cost of sales}}{\text{Total stock}} \quad =$

No. of days sales in stock $\qquad = \dfrac{\text{Stock}}{\text{Average daily cost of sales}} \quad =$

Creditors turnover $\qquad = \dfrac{\text{Purchases}}{\text{Creditors}} \quad =$

No. of days purchases in creditors $\qquad = \dfrac{\text{Creditors}}{\text{Average daily purchases}} \quad =$

Current ratio $\qquad = \dfrac{\text{Current assets}}{\text{Current liabilities}} \quad =$

Quick ratio $\qquad = \dfrac{\text{Current assets} - \text{Stock}}{\text{Current liabilities}} \quad =$

Gearing $\qquad = \dfrac{\text{Long-term loan}}{\text{Long-term loan plus equity}} \quad =$

ROSF $\qquad = \dfrac{\text{Net profit}}{\text{Shareholders' funds}} \quad =$

Exhibit 1.9

As a check for the reader, the completed accounts, financial statements and financial ratios for the second year are given in the appendix at the end of the book.

CONCLUSION

This chapter has served as an introduction to:

1 the way accounting records transactions;
2 the way financial statements are prepared from the accounting records; and
3 the way financial ratios can be calculated from those financial statements to provide insights on various aspects of the business.

The chapter is essentially traditional and backward looking in the sense that it is recording and analysing past transactions. It focuses on business as a set of transactions, whereas the next chapter focuses on business as a set of functions, and it is the next chapter which provides the springboard for the approach to financial analysis taken in this book. It is the following chapters which relate financial statements and financial statement ratios to the wider context of business activity. Nevertheless some insights on the Wooden Stool Company can be obtained from the financial ratios calculated thus far in the case exercises. Comparing 19X1 and 19X2 it is seen that return on total assets is improving. This reflects the fact that the fixed assets are being worked harder in year 2 (6,000 stools produced) than in year 1 (4,000 stools produced). Profit margin has also improved, reflecting the fact that costs have been held whilst prices have risen. The company has not improved its management of debtors and stock as illustrated by the falling debtors and stock turnovers. Liquidity has improved and the company's dependence on non-shareholder finance has fallen as shown by the lower gearing. However, the changes in the ratios should be seen in the context of a business start-up. In these circumstances it is likely that production (and possibly stocks) will increase as the business builds and that prices may have to be held down in year 1 in order to establish a foothold in the market. Similarly liquidity is likely to be lower in year 1 as the company invests in materials, labour, premises and equipment in order to facilitate production. Finally gearing improves as the company earns and retains profits, thus reducing its dependence on non-shareholder finance.

CHAPTER 2

A financial analysis framework

INTRODUCTION

This chapter provides the framework within which financial analysis can be conducted. Each of the case studies and exercises incorporated in the book can be related to this framework which therefore serves to integrate the various chapters of the book. The framework is set out in Exhibit 2.1. It places profitability in the context of the strategic and operational choices facing the business. The remainder of the book explores the linkages between profitability and these strategic and operational issues, and thus provides an understanding of how businesses work and measure their own performance in various different environments.

THE FUNCTIONS

Exhibit 2.1 sets out the main operational domains of business activity as being marketing, sales, product development, production, purchasing, personnel, finance and asset management. It is top management's task through an organizational process to bring these functions together in the creation of a successful, profitable business. Exhibit 2.1 shows that for each operational dimension there is an equivalent strategic dimension. For example, the operational function of *marketing* is equivalent to the strategic issue of deciding which *markets* to target. Thus within each domain the function is not only operational (are we doing things well?) but also positional or strategic (are we attempting the right things?). In the domain of markets, positional or strategic considerations dictate objectives with respect to target markets and market shares whereas operational marketing considerations dictate whether target markets are being penetrated, market shares achieved, and whether the cost of doing so is being minimized. This framework can be presented in the following terms:

Determining objectives (strategy – positional)
Meeting objectives (effectiveness – operational)
Minimizing cost (economy – operational)

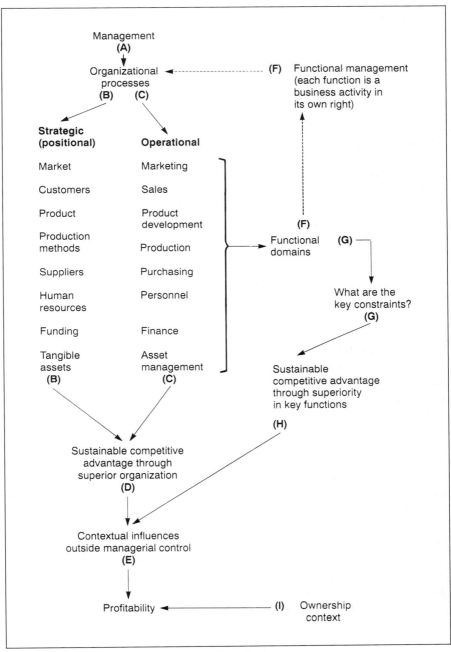

Exhibit 2.1 A framework for financial analysis

There are similarities with the economic ideas of allocative and productive efficiency. Allocative efficiency is concerned with the question 'are we making the right products in the right volumes?' and productive efficiency with whether we are making those products as inexpensively as possible. Whilst allocative efficiency relates to determining and meeting objectives regarding product choice and volumes, productive efficiency is more closely identified with minimizing cost.

SUSTAINABLE COMPETITIVE ADVANTAGE

For any company, a sustainable competitive advantage can be achieved through operational leadership and/or positional superiority, particularly in those key functions where the industry typically experiences constraints or bottlenecks (Exhibit 2.1, (G)). For example, if the constraint on a service business is the availability of suitably competent staff, then competitive advantage should be sought operationally by using staff efficiently, and positionally by adoption of superior staff selection, development and reward strategies. Alternatively, at the strategic level, the business may be conceived in ways which minimize reliance on the scarce resource (e.g. fast food eliminates a fully trained chef).

Each function may itself be regarded as a business activity in its own right (Exhibit 2.1, (F)) with its own organizational process, functional domains and positional and operational considerations. This can lead to conflicts of interest between functions and the company as a whole. For example, suppose success in terms of cost minimization for the function can be achieved by allowing the manager of that function to provide a service not only for the company but also for outside parties on a commercial basis. However, this may not be in the interests of the company as a whole if that function is a *key* function responsible for the company's overall competitive advantage. In these circumstances top management are unlikely to want to provide the service to competitors. For example, a large retailing organization with purchasing power would not wish its purchasing department to purchase, for a fee, on behalf of smaller competitors. Thus, whilst functional managers can be motivated by autonomy this needs to be set against the goals of the organization as a whole. It is important to encourage managers of key functions to share the goals and values of the organization as a whole.

Sustainable competitive advantage can also be achieved through superior organization. Organizational processes (Exhibit 2.1, (B) and (C)) should be designed to enable the right strategic decisions to be taken with respect to each function, for functions to be coordinated effectively, and for choices with respect to different functions to be consistent. Managers of key functions should be involved, along with central management, at the collective heart of the organization in framing the organization's strategy. Managers of non-key functions will be less involved in developing the organization's overall strategy but can be given more freedom by central management to develop strategy for their own specialist function. All functional managers are responsible for operational matters and accountable to top management for their operational performance. The degree of autonomy and decentralization is the key organizational issue, and organizational processes are at the two extremes characterized as organic or mechanistic. Mechanistic organizations are centralized with hierarchical accountability structures, whereas organic organizations are decentralized with more horizontal accountability. Ownership may be regarded as an organizational issue to the extent that different patterns of ownership set up different incentive and motivational structures. For example, an otherwise identical business might perform differently if established as a partnership, a cooperative or a management buy-out.

PROFITABILITY

Profitability is the result of a successful business, and the main accounting measures of profitability, introduced in Chapter 1, are profit margins, return on total assets (ROTA) and return on shareholders' funds (ROSF). Three points to consider when interpreting these measures are time lags, short-termism and contextual influences.

First, let us consider *time lags*. Current profitability reflects current operational success, but perhaps equally influential are strategic decisions taken in the past to develop markets, products, links with suppliers, etc. Hence an explanation of current profitability must assess both past strategic and current operational considerations. Similarly, in order to evaluate the future prosperity of a company it is necessary to assess current strategic decisions together with future operational performance.

Short-termism is a problem because it is possible to improve current profitability by, for example, cut-backs in investment, research, training or quality; but these actions can weaken the strategic positioning of the company and hence the prospects of future profitability. Most of the influences on profitability are included in the model as strategic or operational variables capable, to a greater or lesser extent and on various timescales, of being altered by management. However, macroeconomic considerations such as the level of demand in the economy are a significant influence on any business's profitability and yet lie largely beyond the influence of a company's management. The *macro economic environment* is therefore the main contextual influence outside managerial control (Exhibit 2.1, (E)).

A further consideration is the *ownership context* (Exhibit 2.1, (I)). Accounting practice considers profit to be earned for the owners of a business and hence payments to the owners such as shareholder dividends are not regarded as an expense of the business but as an allocation of the business profit. Hence payments to shareholders in return for finance provided are, unlike all other payments for services rendered, not treated as an expense. The effect of this is that both the absolute level of shareholder finance and the proportion of a company's financial needs met by shareholders affect accounting measures of profitability. In general a company's need for long-term finance is determined by the *capital intensity* of its production methods whereas the proportion of those needs met by shareholders is a reflection of its gearing. Profitability measures can also be affected by changes in shareholder interests following a *takeover or demerger*. Exhibit 2.2, bottom row, summarizes the main contextual influences on profitability.

In theory profitability can be segmented for any of the functions shown in Exhibit 2.1. Thus profitability can, for example, be reported separately by market, by customer, by product and by production process, although there may be difficulties in allocating all revenues and expenses. These difficulties can become acute if trying to segment by supplier, by people or groups of people, by funding source or by tangible asset.

POSITIONAL CHOICES

It would take a text on business strategy to cover all the strategic options, and only a selection of the main ones are covered here. The main variables are summarized in Exhibit 2.2, column 2, and the following paragraphs discuss each function in turn. As regards *markets* the main issues are market share, market growth and the market share of competitors. Market share should lead to economies of scale and give market dominance. However, market dominance in turn may lead to regulation and constraints on the opportunity to exploit such dominance. In general a company attempts to move out of low growth markets in which it has low market share towards high growth markets in which it seeks a high market share. Of course, such repositioning needs to be coordinated with other functions since it is likely to require changes in product, production, financing, etc. Smaller companies may seek to follow a market niche in which they exploit a small but neglected section of the market.

In general a company seeks good quality *customers* in terms of growth, and ability and willingness to pay. Customer loyalty is an important asset and where existing firms in the industry maintain good relationships with customers, new entrants may have to target lower quality customers if they

(1) Functional domains	(2) Variables	(3) Financial indicators
Markets	Growing Market share Dominance Competitiveness Regulation	Segmentation Marketing/sales turnover Operating profit margin
Customers	Quality Terms Relationships Delivery	Debtors turnover
Products	Differentiation Innovation High technology Specialized Lifecycle Design Development	Segmentation Stock turnover Stock write-offs R&D spend, advertising spend Sales volume Operating margin
Production methods	Volume Flexibility Technological change Efficiency Capacity Capital/labour intensity Stage in production process	Wages/sales turnover Fixed asset turnover Depreciation/sales turnover Expected remaining asset life Asset age ROTA/ROSF
Suppliers	Overseas/local Terms Relationships Delivery	Creditors turnover Materials/sales turnover
Human resources	Recruitment Training Development Organizational climate	Training spend Wages/sales turnover Numbers growth
Funding	Rent or buy Share or loan capital Cash flow equilibrium Investor	Gearing Interest/dividend cover Cash flows/forecasts
Tangible assets	Risk of obsolescence Capital appreciation	Expected remaining asset life Holding gains/losses

Accounting dimension	Context	Indicators

Profitability	Macroeconomy
	Ownership
	  – capital intensity
	  – gearing
	  – takeover, demerger
		ROTA
		ROSF
		Profit margin

Exhibit 2.2 Functional domains and financial indicators

are to break into the market. A company with good quality customers may try to exploit this asset by selling additional products to its existing customer base. Alternatively, if a company has low quality customers, and new customers for existing products are hard to find, then it may be necessary for the company to reposition itself through the development of new products and markets.

The matching of *products* to markets and customer requirements involves product development, design and differentiation. An innovative product can generate its own market and 'create' customer requirements. Products which are 'hi-tech' or 'specialized' may be easier to differentiate but hi-tech products in particular are susceptible to a short life cycle. New products and new *production methods* are intimately linked. New products will often require new production methods and a search for new production methods can inspire a radical rethink of the product. Thus positioning with respect to production methods requires careful attention to product market considerations. Highly automated, high volume production is associated with lower margin standard products, whilst more labour intensive and/or specialized technology production processes are associated with lower volumes but hopefully higher margins for a craft or specialized product. Investment in long lasting, capital intensive, high capacity plant may result in cost reductions through economies of scale but there is less flexibility to meet market changes and the plant may be susceptible to obsolescence through technological change.

There is increasing realization by management of the importance of relationships with *suppliers*. For many businesses it is essential to have access to suppliers capable of providing quality supplies at competitive prices and capable of meeting delivery and design requirements. More-over, suppliers must stay in business if continuity of supply is to be assured. Price is only one element here, the others being quality, delivery, design and continuity. The ability of the supplier to respond flexibly to volume or design changes may also be important. In essence, a company must decide which of the above elements are most crucial and choose its suppliers accordingly. There may be an important element of working with chosen suppliers in a longer-term relationship rather than the more traditional arrangement of playing suppliers off against each other in an open competition. As regards the choice of materials, management must keep one eye on the future and move towards the use of materials which are becoming more plentiful and less expensive. There are implications here for product design and development.

Building a sense of longer-term partnership with employees is also a policy issue for many businesses. *Human resources* are an important asset for all companies and, of course, crucially so for those providing services or using labour intensive production methods. It is necessary to take a position on such issues as recruitment, employment terms, training, development and on the organizational climate in which people have to work. This latter point serves to emphasize the links between people and the organizational processes and organizational structure. It is important that the organization and its people are in harmony. To an extent people are 'socialized' into accepting the cultural norms and behavioural culture of the organization. However, there is also a sense in which people will get the organization to work for them in the interests of their own aspirations.

Funding and *tangible assets* are the two functional domains covered by the accountant's balance sheet. As a result there is generally more information available to investors regarding these two, than there is regarding any of the other domains. Consequently it is possible that funding and tangible assets receive too much attention as against human resources, suppliers, etc. Important issues with respect to funding include policy on 'rent or buy', the balance between loan and share capital and the balancing of cash flows. It is generally undesirable to hold large liquid balances if these might be more profitably invested in non-financing activities. Equally it is undesirable to inhibit the business through cash shortage or to rely on expensive short-term funding such as bank overdraft.

Finance is needed for short-term purposes to fund purchases and employee salaries, but the majority of external finance is needed to provide long-term *tangible assets* such as plant and machinery. It is important to maintain good relations with providers of finance, and from a managerial perspective within a limited company, it is particularly important to maintain good investor relations with shareholders who have the legal right to remove directors. Finance requirements are heavily influenced by decisions to invest in plant and machinery. The choice of financial package normally involves an element of speculative risk-taking on future interest rate movements. The purchase and subsequent holding of assets is also a speculative risk-taking activity especially in technological or otherwise unstable markets. It is a matter of judgement whether it is better to purchase productive assets, thus carrying the risk of obsolescence, or to rent assets under an operating lease. In the latter case the risk is effectively carried by the lessor who presumably includes a premium in the rental in order to cover the risk. In effect holding assets is, more than for the other functional domains, a separable business activity in its own right. Although the above discussion focuses on the long-term holding of fixed assets, most businesses also hold, for a much shorter term, stocks. The holding of stocks is another business activity the performance of which should be monitored by management.

THE ULTIMATE STRATEGIC DECISION

The ultimate strategic decision facing management is the selection of business activities in which to engage. Essentially management will focus on those activities (the 'key' activities) in which the company has or feels able to develop some sustainable comparative advantage over its competitors. Management's primary concern is the selection of appropriate products and markets, but this selection may be crucially influenced by other functions in which the company has a comparative advantage. Non-key activities may be provided internally or purchased from outside. A company's decision to purchase a non-key activity from outside is influenced by the degree of difficulty in specifying contracts with a prospective supplier and installing suitable monitoring arrangements, as well as cost. It follows that, since each functional activity may itself be regarded as a distinct business activity, management must also decide in which non-key functions they wish the company to engage. Hence, for each function, in addition to the choices (variables) identified in Exhibit 2.2, column 2, there is the ultimate strategic decision of whether to engage in the particular function at all or whether to purchase the functional service from outside. A company can, for example:

1 Elect to use a marketing consultant.
2 Decide to deal with an agent rather than directly with its customers.
3 Become an agent for other companies' products rather than develop its own products.
4 Purchase from outside rather than produce within.
5 Use a purchasing agent.
6 Hire consultants rather than employ its own staff.
7 Rent rather than own its assets thus removing the need for long-term finance of asset-holding activity.

The ultimate strategic decision therefore relates to the existence of the company itself, being the identification of those activities in which it seeks to engage and the development of an appropriate organizational structure to facilitate its activities.

THE FINANCIAL INDICATORS

Exhibit 2.2, column 3, indicates financial indicators relevant to an assessment of each of the functional domains. Financial indicators are influenced by both strategic and operational considerations and hence their precise interpretation requires knowledge of the strategic intentions of management. For example, a low debtors turnover is a statistic which might indicate failure to vet or chase debtors (a poor operational performance) or a strategic decision to enter a market by taking on lower quality customers. In the latter case the low debtors turnover reflects the successful implementation of the strategy (an operational success) but not necessarily the success, or failure, of the strategy itself in terms of promoting business profitability.

Interpretation of financial indicators, therefore, remains problematic unless the interpreter has a good knowledge of the business, especially with regard to the strategic choices made by management. The following paragraphs briefly discuss the relevance of the financial indicators listed in Exhibit 2.2, column 3, for each of the functional domains in turn.

Markets

Where a company operates in different markets with different tastes, risks, prospects, etc., then the performance of the business in each market should be shown separately in the financial statements. Hence the segmentation of the company's results should indicate the range and diversity of the different markets in which the company operates. Information on market size, share and growth rates is necessary to judge how well positioned the company is. However, such information is not normally included in the financial statements which typically provide information of rather limited use in judging the company's strategic or operational success in this function. The ratio of marketing spend to sales turnover gives some indication of the sensitivity of the market to marketing spend. For many businesses marketing is a key functional activity matching the market, customer and product dimensions. A highly competitive market will normally lead to low operating margins. However, if a business is experiencing low margins then a competitive market is only one of a number of possible alternative explanations or contributing factors. For example, an alternative or contributory factor might be productive inefficiency leading to high costs. Hence low margins are a possible but not conclusive indicator of the high competition levels commonly associated with static or declining markets. Low margins may still lead to profitability if sales are increasing and may be a reflection of a strategic decision to increase market penetration through competitive pricing.

Customers

A high debtors turnover means quick paying debtors and is associated with good customer relations and quality customers in terms of ability and willingness to pay. A low debtors turnover is indicative of poor relations or of customers in financial difficulties or customers who exploit their bargaining position, or it may be a reflection of sloppy credit control. As previously discussed, it may also reflect a strategic decision to enter a market via the lower quality customers.

Products

A company's financial statements should show separately the performance of each major product or product group. Hence the segmentation should indicate the major product groups. The results for each product should indicate whether that product is in essence a 'standard' high volume, low margin product or a 'premium' low volume, high margin product. The latter category will tend to include products which are highly differentiated, specialized, 'hi-tech', etc. Products reaching the end of their lifecycle are often associated with low stock turnover, stock write-offs and high advertising to try and boost sales. At the same time there might be high research and development activity to bring on the next generation of products, especially if the product is 'hi-tech'. Ageing products pose a dilemma for management. Should their life be extended through advertising or their demise hastened through the development of replacement products? Strategically it is necessary to interpret products in terms of their point in the lifecycle, and the development of replacements. Expenditure on research and development reflects implementation of a particular strategy but not necessarily the ultimate success of that strategy in terms of a profitable new product.

Production methods

A high wages/sales turnover statistic indicates labour intensive production typically associated with service industries, whilst a high depreciation/sales turnover statistic indicates capital intensive production more typical of manufacturing. Hence these statistics determine the relative importance of the people and asset-holding dimensions. They also affect the relevance and interpretation of ROTA and operating margin as indicators of profitability. Generally speaking operating margin rather than ROTA is more relevant in judging the performance of service industries. For manufacturing businesses operating margins are influenced by that business's stage in the productive chain. Value added towards the end of the chain is a smaller percentage of the existing value and hence margins might be expected to decrease. This is not always so in practice since businesses at the end of the productive chain often have control of key functions such as product design and marketing.

For manufacturing business low fixed asset turnover suggests over-capacity and the need to improve efficiency through greater volumes. It also suggests that capacity cannot be flexed, and this is a particular problem in businesses where high technology may cause sudden shifts in product demand or provide opportunities for new entrants using the latest production facilities. The expected remaining asset life is a statistic indicating vulnerability to change. If asset lives are short or assets are reaching the end of their expected lives, then the company can, if necessary, replace assets without undue (unexpected) expense. It should, however, be noted that the replacement of assets can substantially affect depreciation when charged on a historical basis. Typically a modern plant is associated with higher (historical cost) depreciation, and this should be taken into account when comparing businesses with different fixed asset histories. Asset age is relevant in so far as a company which has old assets is probably not using the latest production methods and if so is open to challenge from a new entrant, which may take crucial market share and lead to productive overcapacity in the market.

Suppliers

The ratio of materials to sales turnover indicates the relative importance of material supplies to the business under examination. In the same way that debtors turnover can reveal the nature of relations with customers, creditors turnover can reveal the nature of relations with suppliers. Prima facie a low turnover reflecting slow payment would lead to poor relations with suppliers. However, some major manufacturers enter into long-term single supply agreements with suppliers on condition that payment is deferred. In effect there is a long-term partnership with suppliers in which suppliers participate in the financing of their customer's business. In these circumstances a low creditors turnover signifies a strategic decision 'to get closer to suppliers' rather than the existence of bad relations. Once again the possibility of a 'dual explanation' for a financial performance indicator is well illustrated.

Human resources

Wages to sales turnover, training spend and the number of employees are all indicative of the dependency of a business on its people. Financial statements seldom give much further information on the company's human resources. Non-financial information, however, will be available within the company and might include details of stoppages, staff turnover, educational achievements, next destination analysis, time lags in filling posts, etc. Once again there is a potential for dual explanation of the financial statistics. A high training spend may be associated with a high turnover of disaffected staff and the need to train replacements. Alternatively it may reflect a strategic decision to improve staff quality through training. A high training spend would indicate the implementation of such a policy but not necessarily its success in terms of the quality of the training or its benefit to the company.

Funding

A high gearing indicates a high level of dependency on non-shareholder finance. Interest payments on such finance must be met regardless of the profitability of the business and are therefore in the nature of a fixed cost. When business is doing badly there is no possibility of cutting back on this expenditure. When business is doing well there is no need to provide additional rewards above the interest payments. As a consequence profits after interest in a highly geared company fall disproportionately in bad times and rise disproportionately in good times. Profits available for shareholders in a highly geared company tend to be volatile. The level of gearing is therefore of great significance for shareholder returns. High gearing may be a conscious strategic decision or it may be the result of the need to increase borrowing in the wake of poor business results.

Interest and dividend cover are statistics which indicate the risk of the company being unable to meet respectively interest obligations or the payment of dividends at existing levels. These statistics can reflect the opportunities available to the company to raise further finance from non-shareholders and shareholders. Non-shareholders may be reluctant to provide further loans if the company is already stretched by current obligations. Similarly dividend cover may influence the take-up of new share issues. Once again 'duality' of explanation is present. Relatively low interest cover, rather than being a reflection of an unsuccessful business, may reflect a strategic decision to go for high gearing.

It should be noted that external finance is normally provided to the company as a whole and is not mandated for use on any particular business activity the company undertakes. A company raises finance to support its overall portfolio of business activities and subsequently allocates funds to meet the needs of individual activities. Thus there are two aspects to the finance function in a company, namely (1) the raising of finance externally and (2) the allocation of funds internally. In the short term some activities are cash generative whilst others are cash absorbing. The finance function must balance the demands of cash absorbing activities against cash generated internally and the ability of the company to raise cash externally.

Tangible assets

As previously discussed, the holding of assets, especially fixed assets, is a business activity in its own right and wherever possible the performance of this activity should be separately monitored. If there are markets for the sale of the assets and for the rental of the assets then holding gains or losses can be calculated. If there are no markets then it may be possible to provide surrogate market prices through the use of indices and imputed rentals. The risks associated with asset holding are greater if the assets are susceptible to technological change and if the assets have a long way to go before their expected life is complete.

TOWARDS A DETAILED MODEL

It is beyond the scope of this chapter to develop a detailed analytical model for appraising business activity. However, a pro forma for such a model is set out in Exhibit 2.3.

It is dependent upon a specific knowledge base for the business under investigation together with a general knowledge base for other businesses. In the *specific knowledge base* the analyst sets the status of the variables for the specific business under examination. These variables cover organizational process, functional domains, financial indicators, profitability and contextual influences on profitability as discussed previously. Output from the model is in the form of answers to *key questions* which provide the basis of any assessment of the future for the business concerned. A business with a really bright future should generate positive responses to all of the key questions. It should be noted that whilst operational efficiency is an important consideration, the balance of the questions are concerned with strategy (positioning) and in particular the need to develop and exploit comparative advantages. As an intermediate step between the questions and the knowledge bases the model needs rules. It is the *rules* which form the heart of a detailed model, and they need to be capable of answering the key questions on the basis of both the specific knowledge base and equivalent knowledge bases for other businesses. Development of the rules is a substantial task outside the scope of this book. The discussion in this chapter has only begun to scratch the surface, but the flavour of some of the rules may be apparent from the discussion which has covered, for example, the relationship between profitability and contextual influences, the possible association of financial indicators with both operational efficiency and strategic choices, and the implications of choices made for one functional domain on other functions.

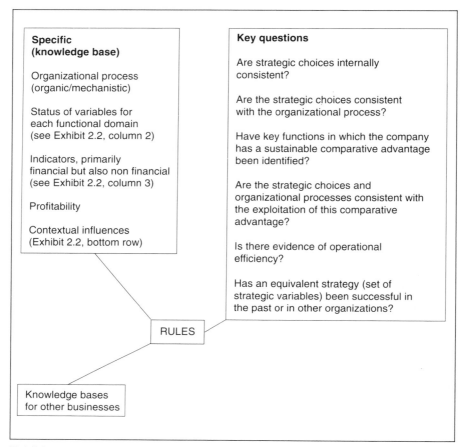

Exhibit 2.3 The scheme for a financial model

THE CASE STUDIES

The case studies covered in the book relate profitability and financial indicators to a variety of functional contexts. *Quickneasy* is the first case and it covers two chapters. Business activity may be regarded as a set of transactions, a set of projects or a set of managerial functions. Quickneasy provides a link between these three perspectives. It starts with the company undertaking a project for which forecast financial statements are prepared. As actual transactions and events unfold it traces how the actual financial statements compare with the forecast. Undertaking the original project is a crucial *strategic* decision. Monitoring the subsequent events and transactions is in essence *operational*. Both strategic decisions and operational control are important managerial activities and it is the notion of business as a set of managerial activities which ultimately develops, through the later case studies, into the functional model specified in this chapter.

Midlothian Zaibatsu looks at the cash flows associated with new, mature and retiring products. It demonstrates the importance of segmenting cash flows on a product basis as part of the process of product management, including innovation and development.

Whilst Midlothian Zaibatsu focuses on the product, *Manyhands/Lightwork* is a case concentrating on the closely associated issue of production methods. At a functional level it is a case which illustrates the impact of different production methods and stages of production on profitability. Manyhands has a labour intensive production process whilst Lightwork is capital intensive. As a further issue the case illustrates the impact of different shareholder stakes (the ownership context) on profitability. In terms of resource creation versus resource consumption the two companies exhibit equivalent 'real' profitability. However, the profitability measures for the two companies are shown to diverge due to the different interests of ownership. Being capital intensive Lightwork has the higher requirement for share capital and hence the owners of Lightwork have more at stake than the owners of Manyhands. This affects ROSF and ROTA. The case also investigates the influence on profitability measures of changing ownership interests caused by takeover and demerger activity. Takeovers are commonly used as a means of strategic positioning and from a functional perspective the accounting emphasis should be on this strategic repositioning rather than the ownership issue.

Mark Tips and *Sidney Widget* are cases concerned with tangible fixed assets from the perspective of treating the holding of fixed assets as a distinct business activity from operations. The primary focus is on the separate calculation of holding gains and operating profits. The distinction between the two cases is that for Sidney Widget, there is no rental alternative to the purchase of fixed assets and once purchased, there is no second-hand market in which the assets can be sold. As well as dealing with tangible fixed assets, Mark Tips also introduces the notion of intangible assets. When a business has a sustainable comparative advantage of any kind then that comparative advantage is regarded as an (intangible) asset which commands a price. If that price can be established with reasonable certainty then it becomes possible to include the intangible asset in the business's balance sheet. Mark Tips's intangible asset is a taxi licence giving a right to access a controlled market. The case study illustrates how the value of the licence is a reflection of market prospects.

Age and Beauty also focuses on the interaction of assets and market characteristics. Production requires long-term investment in fixed assets and is large scale relative to the size of the market which is static. Age fails to re-equip when technological advance renders its plant prematurely obsolete and this allows Beauty into the market, with fairly catastrophic results for Age. The strategic options for Age and Beauty are considered. *Bonnie and Clyde* maintains the theme of technological advance in production techniques but in the public sector where the type of market and financing arrangements are quite different to those of the private sector.

The principal focus in *Booze* and in *High Hopes and High Anticipation* (HHHA) is on stocks and their treatment in the financial statements. Booze highlights the distinction between the holding of (specialized) stocks as a separate business activity from routine trading activity. For 'fine wines' the key functions are stockholding and finance whereas for 'plonk' the key considerations are purchasing and the efficiency of operations. The different constraints experienced by the 'fine wines' and 'plonk' businesses influence their accounting treatment and the interpretation of profitability. Booze also looks at the balancing of cash flows between cash generating and cash absorbing activities. HHHA examines insights on the stock costing problem which may be gained by regarding fixed asset holding as a distinct though non-profit-making business activity which charges operations for use of the productive facilities. The impact of stockholding on profitability is examined through the comparison of High Hopes, which does not hold stocks, with High Anticipation, which does.

abcd Makes ZY and *Stock Maintains Delivery* (SMD) continue with stockholding as the main theme. In both cases the companies are moving towards a policy of much lower stockholding. Abcd Makes ZY serves to illustrate the point that such a strategic decision can only be implemented successfully at the operational level if there is a sophisticated and accurate production and stock control information system. Strategic decision-taking is important but successful implementation of strategy can be difficult. SMD serves to illustrate the importance of assessing the impact of suggested strategic change on the financial statements. SMD's proposal to discontinue sales of low volume items and hold lower stocks of high volume items does not appear to lead to improvement in the forecast profit. However, is the strategic change needed because of changes being made by competitors?

Easymoney is a bank providing a variety of different financial packages for its corporate clients. On the one hand Easymoney is a case which looks at different ways in which those client companies can finance their fixed asset purchases, and the impact of the company's funding choice on each company's profitability. This aspect of the case looks at funding from the perspective of Easymoney's corporate clients. From Easymoney's point of view the case examines the impact on Easymoney's profitability of product differentiation in the financial services industry. In Easymoney each product essentially delivers the same service but is differentiated through a different package of facilities. Profitability is segmented by product to demonstrate the performance of each package.

Faith, Hope and Charity is the most strategic of the cases since the three companies take differing positions on sales/marketing, product/production and finance. The case explores the impact of these strategic choices on profitability and prospects. All three companies manufacture the same product.

Gourmet and Formula are two companies which on the face of it are both in the hotel business, but on closer examination their two products and markets are clearly differentiated. This difference impacts on their organizational processes and on the marketing function. Future strategic options and prospects are discussed for each company. Current profitability is very similar for both companies and hence current stock market evaluations based on future prospects depend upon each company's strategic positioning and the potential for improved operating efficiency. Formula has a separate division marketing the hotels for weekends. The case invites discussion of the extent to which this separate division should be granted managerial autonomy. From an accounting perspective the case demonstrates how segmentation of the financial results improves the investor's ability to understand the two businesses. Segmentation can be performed via any of the functional domains specified in the Exhibit 2.1 model. Gourmet and Formula focus on segmentation via the strategic domains of market and product and the operational domain of marketing.

The final case study – *The University of ABC* – looks at the development of a budget as a planning vehicle for the implementation of strategy. It highlights the role of budgeting in the coordination of functional activities and mobilization of the efforts of functional heads. The development of the budget requires the participation of the functional heads and hence the case study is a role play. A university is chosen as the appropriate setting since it is an organization with which students will be familiar.

Exhibit 2.4 sets out the case studies' coverage of functions. Each column gives the principal functions and functional interactions on a per case basis with the ultimate objective in each case being the relationship between functions and profitability. Each row indicates the overall coverage of the case studies on a per function basis. The market/marketing function dominates and this reflects the strategic importance of this function. There is no substantial coverage of the human resources domain and little coverage of organizational processes. This should not be taken to reflect any lack of importance. It is rather a reflection of the fact that

Chapters	3, 4	5	6	7	8	9	10	11	12	13	14	15	16	17
Organizational process													X	X
Markets	X			X	X	X	X					X	X	X
Customers	X													X
Product		X						X		X	X	X	X	X
Production methods	X		X		X	X						X		X
Suppliers								X		X				
Human resources														X
Funding		X					X	X			X	X		X
Tangible assets				X	X			X	X	X				
Ownership context			X											
Profitability	X	X	X	X	X	X		X	X	X	X	X	X	
Case	Quickneasy	Midlothian Zaibatsu	Manyhands/Lightwork	Mark Tips	Sidney Widget	Age and Beauty	Bonnie and Clyde	Booze	High Hopes, High Anticipation	abcd makes ZY Stock Maintains Delivery	Easymoney	Faith, Hope and Charity	Gourmet and Formula	University of ABC

Exhibit 2.4 Case study coverage of functions

organizational processes and organizational climate are not the primary focus of this book which concentrates on the functions themselves rather than the organizational environment. This functional perspective provides important insights into many current accounting issues and provides the book's framework for understanding linkages between business activity and accounting.

SELF-STUDY EXERCISE 2.1

Ratio analysis is widely recognized as a useful tool for interpreting financial statements.

On 1 January 199X the Zoom Camera Company implemented a new strategy. Up to that date it had manufactured a high quality specialist camera (the Hi Zoom Special) which it had sold through specialist camera shops largely to the photographic profession. After that date it discontinued the manufacture of the Hi Zoom Special and instead assembled high volume, standard specification cameras. Parts were largely bought overseas and sales were through high street retail chains.

Required:

1 Discuss how you might expect the strategic change identified above to impact on the key company ratios as used in ratio analysis.

2 Briefly explain by reference to the Zoom Camera Company example why it is important to interpret ratios in the context of company strategy.

CHAPTER 3

Capital investment activity

INTRODUCTION

This chapter uses a simple business investment project – named Quickneasy – both to practise the modest level of skill in handling accounting numbers obtained in Chapter 1, and to provide an introduction to how those accounting numbers relate to the organizational, economic and business context. These are the basic skills of the accountant – the ability to handle and to interpret the financial data of a business. The basic handling skills covered in this chapter are:

1 the ability to prepare simple profit statements, cash flow statements and balance sheets;
2 an appreciation of how discounted cash flows are used to evaluate a business project; and
3 an appreciation of how a computer can assist in both the preparation of financial statements and in discounted cash flow calculations.

The basic interpretative skills covered are:

1 an appreciation of how accounting acts as both a feedback and a feedforward control in relation to economic activity;
2 an appreciation that different insights into a firm's activities are obtained through different accounting analyses;
3 an understanding of the key components of the financial statements and of the relationships between accounting profit, cash flows and discounted cash flows.

THE QUICKNEASY CASE STUDY

When setting up a business it is necessary to look forwards – at the profits and cash expected to flow from that investment. Consider the case of Quickneasy.

Quickneasy Limited is established as a company to provide agency typing. The major initial investment is £4,000 in a word processor and laser printer. It is estimated that the equipment has a life of four years during which time annual invoiced turnover is expected to be steady at £6,000 with £3,000 being paid to the typist, leaving a net operating cash flow of £3,000 per annum. It is company policy to ensure that work in progress and debtors are minimal at each year end.

Assume:

1 for computational convenience that each year's operational cash flows take place on the last day of the year;

2 Quickneasy's share capital is £100 and in Quickneasy's case this has been used to pay formation expenses; all other capital needs are financed by bank overdraft at an interest rate of 10%;

3 operational cash flows are used firstly to pay off the bank overdraft and then to provide a positive balance at the bank, on which the bank pays interest of 10%;

4 that expectations are realized (this is later relaxed in the next chapter);

5 no dividends are paid.

The initial investment

At the time of establishing the business the balance sheet of Quickneasy shows resources and sources of finance as follows:

Resources	£	Sources of finance	£
Equipment	4,000	Bank overdraft	4,000
Formation costs	100	Share capital	100
	4,100		4,100

The first year's operations

The first year's operating details are expected to be:

	£	£
Sales		6,000
Typist	3,000	
Depreciation	1,000	
		4,000
Operating profit		2,000

The operating profit matches the resources created during the year (sales revenue) and the resources consumed during the year (typist's labour and depreciation of equipment). It is important to understand the way depreciation has been treated. This is covered in the following section.

Depreciation

The purchase of a £4,000 word processor and printer represents a cash outflow of £4,000 recoverable against the cash inflows expected to be associated with the equipment's use. In historical cost accounting this recovery is made by charging the original expenditure against accounting periods in proportion to the benefit expected to be gained during the accounting period from the use of the equipment. Since the first four years are all expected to benefit equally, the original cost of £4,000 is charged as £1,000 depreciation to each year. This is an example of the *period matching* concept which attempts to match the benefits realized during an *accounting period* with the cost incurred. It should be distinguished from the lifetime matching concept which matches all the costs and benefits expected during the life of a project. The formation expenses of £100 represent an initial cash outflow of £100 recoverable against the lifetime cash inflows of Quickneasy. If Quickneasy is expected to have an indefinite life then the expenditure of £100 may be carried forward indefinitely as an asset. There is therefore no write-off of the formation expenses charged against accounting profits.

Financing costs

Operating profit ignores financing costs, which in Quickneasy's case is the interest charge on the bank overdraft. The first year's cash flows and profits are as follows:

Cash flows	£	*Profit*	£
		Sales	6,000
Received from customers	6,000	Typist	(3,000)
Paid to typist	(3,000)	Depreciation	(1,000)
Operating cash flow	3,000	Operating profit	2,000
Paid for equipment	(4,000)	Interest	(400)
	(1,000)	Net profit	1,600
Interest for year	(400)		
Closing overdraft	(1,400)		

It should be noted in this example that the interest charge of £400 is calculated on the opening overdraft of £4,000 created when the equipment is bought – no other receipts or payments take place until the end of the year. Having calculated the net profit for the year it is possible to complete the balance sheet at the end of the first year. In the balance sheet the year's net profit (£1,600) is included with the original share capital (£100) to give shareholders' funds (a source of finance for year 2) of £1,700. This figure would be reduced by dividends if dividends had been paid out of the first year's net profits.

Balance sheet – end of first year

At the end of the first year the resources and sources of finance for Quickneasy are as follows:

Resources	£	*Sources of finance*		£
Equipment				
Cost	4,000	*Bank overdraft*		1,400
Depreciation	1,000	*Shareholders' funds*		
	3,000	Share capital	100	
Formation costs	100	Retained profit	1,600	1,700
	3,100			3,100

You should now be in a position to work through the expected cash flow statement, profit statement and year end balance sheet for year 2 as shown in the pro forma shown in Exhibit 3.1. Having done that you should complete the pro forma for years 3 and 4.

SELF-STUDY EXERCISE 3.1

Complete the following pro forma financial statements in Exhibit 3.1 for Quickneasy in years 3 and 4 for:

1 Cash flow

2 Profit

3 Balance sheet

As the final test put the completed pro forma out of sight – can you reproduce the pro forma headings (without the figures!)?

Cash flows

	Years				
	1	2	3	4	Total
	£	£	£	£	£
Received from customers	6,000	6,000			
Paid to typist	(3,000)	(3,000)			
Operating cash flow	3,000	3,000			
Paid for equipment	(4,000)				
Cash flows before financing costs	(1,000)	3,000			
Interest	(400)	(140)			
	(1,400)	2,860			
Opening balance	Nil	(1,400)			
Closing balance	(1,400)	1,460			

Profit

	£	£	£	£	£
Sales	6,000	6,000			
Typist	(3,000)	(3,000)			
Depreciation	(1,000)	(1,000)			
Operating profit	2,000	2,000			
Interest	(400)	(140)			
Profit for year	1,600	1,860			
Opening balance	Nil	1,600			
Closing balance	1,600	3,460			

Balance sheets

	Year ends			
Resources	1	2	3	4
	£	£	£	£
Equipment cost	4,000	4,000		
Depreciation	(1,000)	(2,000)		
Book value	3,000	2,000		
Formation costs	100	100		
Cash		1,460		
	3,100	3,560		
Sources of finance				
Share capital	100	100		
Opening retained profit	Nil	1,600		
Profit for year	1,600	1,860		
Closing retained profit	1,600	3,460		
Shareholders' funds	1,700	3,560		
Bank overdraft	1,400			
	3,100	3,560		

Exhibit 3.1 Pro formas for self-study exercise 3.1

UNDERSTANDING PROFIT

Over the four years' life of the equipment expected profits and cash flows are:

Year	Operating profits £	Profits £	Operating cash flows £	Cash flows £
1	2,000	1,600	3,000	(1,400)
2	2,000	1,860	3,000	2,860
3	2,000	2,146	3,000	3,146
4	2,000	2,461	3,000	3,461
	8,000	8,067	12,000	8,067

It can be seen that total profits equal total cash flows at £8,067 but that the distribution over time is different. The following points should be noted:

1 *Operating* profits are constant. This reflects the expected constancy of sales and expenses.

2 *Operating* cash flows, like operating profits, are constant, but total operating cash flows exceed total operating profits by the amount of the capital investment in the typewriter.

3 Profits show a rising trend. This reflects the retention and investment of cash flows so that in years 1 and 2 interest charges are reduced whilst for years 3 and 4 the bank overdraft has been eliminated and interest is earned.

4 Cash flows are considerably lower than profits in the first year, being the year of the capital investment in the equipment.

5 Cash flows are considerably higher than profits in years 2–4. This is because through the depreciation charge, capital expenditure is recovered against profit equally from the four years expected to benefit. In cash flow terms the whole outlay falls in year 1.

Cash is something we are all familiar with. Businessmen in particular are comfortable with the notion of cash and cash flows. To them it is a kind of economic reality representing a claim against economic resources. Profit is *not* cash, although we see that in the long term profits and cash flows are equivalent, at least for the simple example of Quickneasy. Profits are a contrived performance measure and like all performance measures they need to be interpreted with care.

c

OPERATIONS AND FINANCING AS SEPARATE ACTIVITIES

In our example a little thought reveals that Quickneasy is really engaged in two businesses or business activities, namely:

1 the provision of typing services;
2 the investment of cash flows at the bank.

The return on typing activities

During the four years the typing operation converts the original equipment outlay of £4,000 into operating cash flows which total £12,000. This £8,000 surplus is £2,000 per annum in each of four years and equals the annual operating profit. It represents an annual return from the typing operation of 50% on the £4,000 outlay.

The return on the financing activity

The investment of cash flows at the bank provides a return of 10% − far less than is being achieved in the typing services business. The question has to be asked − why aren't the cash flows reinvested in the business where the far greater return is earned? There may be valid reasons why it is not being reinvested in the typing business. For example, managerial capacity might be constrained and unable to cope with expansion. Alternatively the size of the market might be limited and therefore the returns which can be earned at the margin by expansion are far lower than the returns earned on the existing volume of business.

Nevertheless, anyone in business needs to recognize that his or her business is really a combination of many different *business* activities − in our illustration an operating and a financing business − and he or she needs to be able to analyse and monitor the performance of each activity. It is then necessary to challenge the firm's involvement in each activity. In this way the firm develops its own optimum portfolio of activities. This is a recurring theme throughout the book ... accounting for business activities.

OPERATIONS AND FINANCING AS INTEGRATED ACTIVITIES

Of course many of the business activities are highly interdependent and the danger of looking at each activity's results separately is that the activity's effect on interdependent activities may not be fully appreciated. In our example the results of each year's operating activity – operating profits – do not reflect the ultimate consequences of those operations for the financing activity and interest charges. If the effects of operational activity on interest were taken into account then the operating profits over the four years might be rewritten (an explanation of the figures follows) as below:

	Years				
	1	*2*	*3*	*4*	*Total*
	£	£	£	£	£
Sales	7,986	7,260	6,600	6,000	27,846
Typist	3,993	3,630	3,300	3,000	13,923
Operating surplus before depreciation	3,993	3,630	3,300	3,000	13,923
Depreciation	1,679	1,527	1,388	1,262	5,856
Operating profit	2,314	2,103	1,912	1,738	8,067

The following discussion explains how these figures are calculated using period 1 as illustrative.

Sales in period 1 generate cash of £6,000 at the end of period 1. As a result interest totalling £1,986 can be earned during periods 2 to 4. The calculation is:

	£	£
Received end of year 1	6,000	
Year 2 interest	600	600
	6,600	
Year 3 interest	660	660
	7,260	
Year 4 interest	726	726
	7,986	1,986

If the sales (an operating activity) had not been made during period 1 then the subsequent interest could not have been earned. Period 1 sales therefore, inclusive of the subsequent interest effect, bring benefits of £7,986. Similarly the typist expense in period 1 absorbs £3,000 cash at the end of period 1 and interest on this cash is foregone for periods 2 to 4.

The typist expense inclusive of the interest effect is £3,993, calculated as follows:

	£
	£
Paid end of year 1	3,000
Year 2 interest	300
	3,300
Year 3 interest	330
	3,630
Year 4 interest	363
	3,993

Finally the payment of £4,000 for the equipment at the beginning of year 1 becomes £5,856 inclusive of the interest foregone during years 1 to 4. The calculation is:

	£
Paid beginning of year 1	4,000
Year 1 interest	400
	4,400
Year 2 interest	440
	4,840
Year 3 interest	484
	5,324
Year 4 interest	532
	5,856

The normal approach to allocating this total cost is to charge it against accounting periods in proportion to the benefit which each period has derived from the use of the asset. Thus the proportion charged to the first period might be £3,993/13,923, being the proportion of the operating surplus before depreciation earned in the first period. This proportion applied to total cost of the equipment gives a first year depreciation charge of £3,993/13,923 × 5,856 = £1,679.

Over the four-year period profits decline from £2,314 to £1,738 reflecting the fact that cash generated by operations in the earlier years is worth more than equivalent sums of cash generated in later years. The four year profit figures show the overall effect of operations in each of the four years including the 'knock-on' effect of operations on the financing activity. Such a method of accounting is known as 'interest adjusted' accounting. Although advocated by a number of academics, in practice profit figures are not normally prepared in this way. The purpose of the discussion in this chapter is to illustrate the interdependence of operating and financing activities, to demonstrate an accounting system which fully integrates operations and financing, and to introduce a managerial dilemma.

THE MANAGERIAL DILEMMA

Top management are responsible for the overall performance of the organization. They formulate strategy and policies for its implementation. Recognizing the interdependence of activities, they need to ensure that the different activities within the organization work together in the interests of the organization as a whole. At the same time top management need to motivate and to promote opportunity taking by functional/departmental managers in charge of each of the organization's various activities. This in turn requires freedom of action for functional managers and performance reward measures which reflect the economic performance of each individual activity. Thus within any organization there is a tension between the need for central control and the need for functional/departmental freedom of action. Getting the tension right is a key requirement for organizational success.

In general the organization's approach on this issue influences its choice of accounting procedures. At one end of the spectrum is the organization which gives managers little freedom of action at the level of individual activities. The profit focus is at the organizational level and a functional/departmental manager's performance tends to be assessed in terms of adherence to preset budgets and operational norms. At the level of individual activities such an organization runs the risk of reducing managerial initiative and innovation which might cause departures from the norms. At the organizational level it runs the risk of failing to achieve the most efficient allocation of resources between the various activities. This is because in the absence of suitable measures of economic performance for each individual activity, allocation of resources will tend to respond to the internal political processes of the organization rather than respond to any internal market process.

At the opposite end of the spectrum is the organization which gives a great deal of freedom of action to functional/departmental managers. The focus is on trying to assess the economic performance of each activity individually. Problems arise whenever, due to the interdependence of activities, maximization by the manager of one activity frustrates the economic performance of other activities in the organization, and is therefore not necessarily in the interests of the profitability of the organization as a whole. A simple example might be as follows:

Managers in charge of the finance function decide not to place incoming cash from operations at the bank where it is accessible and earns 10%. Instead it is invested in bonds which earn 15% but tie up funds for five years. This improves the reported performance of the finance function but frustrates operational management if the funds are essential for expansion of operations within the five year period. Moreover, the financial managers' decision might not be in the interest of the organization as a whole if the frustrated expansion in operations would have earned a return well in excess of 15%.

An organization is a set of activities tied together by a management structure. Ultimately top management in the organization is responsible for all its activities. Of course, it might be sensible for top management to take different approaches with respect to different functional activities, taking a close interest in those functions where the organization hopes to exploit its sustainable competitive advantage, but allowing greater freedom for managers of other functions. Whereas an organization is a set of activities, a national economy is a set of organizations tied together by allegiance to the same political structure. Just as organizational top management needs to motivate managers at the level of individual activities, so the national economy needs an environment which motivates managers of its constituent organizations whether they be in business or public service. In a capitalist system there is a great deal of freedom of action accorded to top management of individual business organizations. However, even in a capitalist system there are constraints on top company management. These constraints may be imposed by law which, for example, specifies the accountability of company directors to share-holders. Alternatively the constraints may result from freely negotiated contracts with financiers, employees, customers or other interested parties.

By comparison with socialist economies, the capitalist system appears to work well, at least in terms of economic performance. However, there are occasional circumstances when the attempts of individual business firms to maximize profits do not operate in the best interests of the economy as a whole. The perspectives of the business firm and the economy as a whole can and do differ — we shall return to these differing perspectives at various times during the following chapters. There are occasions where governmental coordination and motivation of firms within the economy might be desirable in the interests of the economy as a whole, just as the individual activities undertaken by each firm require coordination and purpose in the context of that firm's overall strategic objectives.

It is important to note that accounting does not stand in isolation. Within a business organization it is a reflection of, and supportive to, the management structure and style. Similarly the way a business 'accounts' to the external community is a reflection of, and is supportive to, the economic structure and style imposed by the political system.

MAKING THE INVESTMENT DECISION

Before making an investment a business manager will *forecast* the cash flows, profits and balance sheets associated with the investment. If the project, as is the case for Quickneasy, is to be financed by a bank then the bank will want to see the forecasts. Banks are increasingly willing to lend against projected cash flows rather than the security of a company's existing assets. Forecasting is an exercise ideally suited to the use of a spreadsheet.

SELF-STUDY EXERCISE 3.2

Prepare a spreadsheet to provide Quickneasy's four years of forecast cash flows, profits and balance sheets.

When making an investment it is that act of investing which is the critical activity to be evaluated. The evaluation needs to capture all the positive and negative consequences of the investment whether they be operational or financial. The evaluation ought, therefore, to focus on the effect on the organization as a whole, rather than individual activities. In Quickneasy's case the investment is expected to generate overall retained profits of £8,067 by the end of the project's four-year life. Positive lifetime net profits suggests that the project is worth undertaking. In practice, in order to allow for the uncertainty inherent in any forecast, management may require a substantial margin of forecast cumulative net profits before going ahead with a project.

In Quickneasy's project, all cash flows are to be invested at the bank. The cumulative net profit of £8,067 reflects in part the rewards from this financial activity. If Quickneasy had not invested all of its operating cash flow but had for instance distributed some of it as dividends to shareholders, then cumulative net profit would be lower than £8,067. However, the shareholders could take their dividend and invest it at the bank on their own behalf. It is apparent that if Quickneasy were to follow a policy of dividend distribution rather than investment at the bank then the investment project would be no less worthwhile even though forecast cumulative net profit would be lower. It follows that cumulative net profit does not provide a fully reliable basis for project evaluation.

Net present value

A more reliable method is to consider the project's net present value (NPV). The net present value is arrived at by 'discounting' all the cash flows associated with the project. The idea of discounting can be illustrated as follows:

Let us consider the £3,000 operating cash flow anticipated at the end of year 3. It can be shown that at an interest rate of 10%, £2,254 today (C_0) is equivalent to £3,000 in 3 years' time (C_3) since:

after 1 year C_0 becomes $C_1 = C_0 \dfrac{110}{100}$

after 2 years C_0 becomes $C_2 = C_1 \dfrac{110}{100} = C_0 (110/100)^2$

after 3 years C_0 becomes $C_3 = C_2 \dfrac{110}{100} = C_0 (110/100)^3$

Hence $C_0 = C_3 (100/110)^3$
$C_0 = 3,000 \times (100/110)^3 = £2,254$

In the above calculation it is said that the £3,000 cash flow in three years' time has been discounted using a discount rate of 10%. The £3,000 has been multiplied by $(100/110)^3$ which is known as the discount factor. The net present value of the £3,000 cash flow in three years' time is £2,254. The net present value of the project is as follows:

Year	Annual operating cash flow	Discount factor	Contribution to present value	
	£		£	£
1	3,000	$(100/110)$	2,727	
2	3,000	$(100/110)^2$	2,480	
3	3,000	$(100/110)^3$	2,254	
4	3,000	$(100/110)^4$	2,049	
			9,510	9,510
Less initial outlay				4,000
Net present value				5,510

A positive net present value implies that a project is worth undertaking. In the event of competing projects the one with the highest NPV is, prima facie, the more attractive. In calculating the NPV the discount rate should equate to the company's overall cost of capital. In practice, where a company is financed by a variety of shares and loan capital as well as overdraft, it may be difficult to determine the cost of capital. In Quickneasy's case the cost of capital is easily determined since the company is almost wholly financed by the bank and hence cost of capital equals the bank's interest rate.

It should be noted that the NPV of the project is unaffected by whether or not the incoming cash flows are reinvested at the bank. If the £3,000 operating cash inflow at the end of year 3 was invested at the bank for year 4 then in effect the £3,000 cash inflow (C_3) is replaced by a £3,300 cash inflow (C_4) at the end of the fourth year. When discounted, a £3,300 cash flow at the end of year 4 is equivalent to a £3,000 cash flow at the end of year 3. Hence the reinvestment of a cash flow at the bank leaves the NPV of the cash flow unaltered.

The discount factors serve to weight cash received in earlier years more highly than cash received in later years irrespective of whether and how such cash is reinvested.

Two exploratory exercises

SELF-STUDY EXERCISE 3.3

Below is a simple program to calculate the NPV of Quickneasy's forecast cash flows for different interest rates (i). Load this program (or similar) on your computer. In this program the symbol ∗ stands for multiplication.

```
IN
PRINT   "Input a value for i"
INPUT  i
Let     a = i
Let     b = 100/(100 + i)
Let     c = 3000 ∗ b
Let     d = c ∗ b
Let     e = d ∗ b
Let     f = e ∗ b
Let     g = (c + d + e + f) − 4000
PRINT   "The NPV = ", g
GO TO IN
```

Use this program to complete the following table:

i	NPV	Remarks
0		1 When the interest rate is zero, the return on financing
5		activity is zero and the project's NPV equals cumulative
10		operative profits.
20		
30		2 When the NPV approximates to zero, the interest (discount)
40		rate is called the internal rate of return (IRR). The IRR for
50		Quickneasy's project is expected to be approximately 65%.
60		The IRR is the highest possible interest rate at which it is
65		still worthwhile to go ahead with the project.

SELF-STUDY EXERCISE 3.4

Below is a simple program to calculate Quickneasy's forecast cumulative profits after four years for different interest rates (i). Load this program (or similar) on your computer. In this program the symbol $\wedge$ means 'to the power of'.

```
IN
PRINT   "Input a value for i"
INPUT   i
Let     a = i
Let     b = (100 + i)/100
Let     c = -4000 * (b ∧ 4)
Let     d =   3000 * (b ∧ 3)
Let     e =   3000 * (b ∧ 2)
Let     f =   3000 * b
Let     g =   3000 + (c + d + e + f)
PRINT   "Cumulative profit is", g
GO TO IN
```

Use this program to complete the following table:

i	Cumulative profit	Remarks
0		Cumulative profit rises slowly as the interest rate
1		increases from 0% to 7%. This demonstrates that
2		increasing the interest rate is not necessarily bad for
3		business! The best interest rate for Quickneasy is 7%.
4		At higher rates the expected cumulative net profit at the
5		end of the project falls, reaching zero with an interest
6		rate equal to the IRR (approximately 65% for
7		Quickneasy).
8		
9		
10		
20		
30		
40		
50		
60		
65		

These exploratory exercises show that Quickneasy's project has an expected NPV of £5,510 and an internal rate of return of approximately 65%. At the internal rate of return, expected cumulative net profits – assuming no dividends – at the end of the project are zero. With an interest rate of a little under 65%, cumulative operating profits of £8,000 are exactly cancelled out by cumulative financing charges of £8,000, based on a return to financing activity of 65%. Since the operating and financing activities cancel out at an interest rate of 65%, it can be said that the operating activity generates a 65% return over the life of the project. It should be noted that the IRR does not equal the 50% return given by the annual operating profit (£2,000) on the initial capital outlay (£4,000). The latter return is a measure of operating performance during a year and can be used for year-by-year comparisons. The IRR represents a measure of operating performance over the entire life of the project and, like NPV, can be used for project v. project comparisons.

UNDERSTANDING THE BALANCE SHEET

Let us look at Quickneasy's balance sheet at the end of year 1. It is:

Resources	£	Sources of finance		£
Equipment cost	4,000	Share capital		100
Depreciation	(1,000)	Opening retained profit	Nil	
		Profit for year	1,600	
	3,000	Closing retained profit		1,600
		Shareholders' funds		1,700
Formation expenses	100	Bank overdraft		1,400
	3,100			3,100

The following points should be noted:

1 The net book value of the equipment (£3,000) is an unexpired cost. It does not represent either the selling price or replacement cost of a one-year-old word processor and printer.

2 The law allows companies to pay to shareholders dividends up to the amount of profits earned. If profits, as in the case of Quickneasy, are not paid to shareholders then they become retained profits and part of shareholders' funds. Since profit is a contrived performance measure it follows that shareholders' funds is also a contrived figure.

3 Share capital is permanently provided by shareholders and is not normally paid back. Retained profits may, however, be paid as dividends at a future date.

4 The bank overdraft represents 'hard' cash due to the bank. However, many bank overdrafts continue for years without ever being recalled by the bank, provided the company remains profitable.

5 No figure on the balance sheet represents the value of the company. At the end of year 1 (T_1), assuming expectations for the first year are realized, the investment in the typewriter has an NPV of approximately £6,061. You can check this figure by discounting to T_1 the expected cash flows in years 2, 3 and 4 and adding the present value of those cash flows to Quickneasy's existing cash balance at T_1. You will find that it comes to £6,061 which also equals £5,510 (NPV at T_0) plus 10%. Presumably any bidder for the company would have to offer at least £6,061 to tempt the current owners to sell. £6,061 does not relate to any figure on the balance sheet. In fact the bidder might have to bid more than £6,061 since the company will presumably continue in business and continue to generate cash flows beyond the four-year life of the typewriter – these subsequent cash flows have not been included in the NPV calculation giving £6,061.

ACCOUNTING AS AN ECONOMIC SYSTEM CONTROL

There are essentially two types of system control – feedback and feedforward. In an economic system a feedback control provides 'after the event' (ex post) information on the consequences of economic activity so that the activity can be modified in future. On the other hand, a feedforward control provides 'before the event' (ex ante) information for the planning process on the likely consequences of a proposed pattern of economic activity. It therefore allows economic activity to be modified before it actually takes place. In this chapter we have been looking at accounting as a feedforward control providing information on the likely outcome of Quickneasy's project. Such information can take the form of projected cash flows, accounting profits and balance sheets. The likely performance of operating and financing activities can be examined separately, with projected operating returns being examined on a period-by-period basis (operating profit as a percentage of capital outlay) or on a project basis through the IRR.

It should be noted that whilst NPV/IRR are important as feedforward controls, their role in feedback is limited since for many 'multi-project' businesses it is difficult to allocate subsequent operating cash flows to individual projects. It should also be noted that there are risks in placing too great an importance on one year's accounting profits as a feedback control since accounting profits relate only to a relatively short period in an organization's or project's life and do not necessarily indicate longer-term progress by the organization or project.

The significance of feedforward and feedback controls in the form of performance indicators should not be underestimated. The existence of such performance indicators facilitates economic activity. In Quickneasy's case it is the existence of suitable indicators such as profits and cash flows which enables Quickneasy to persuade the bank to agree finance (an economic agreement) and this allows the project to go ahead (economic activity). The outcomes of this activity are subsequently monitored − again through performance indicators. Without suitable monitoring arrangements it is again doubtful whether the bank would agree finance. Financial statements are a crucial element in these monitoring arrangements.

Economic activity is multi-dimensional and multi-faceted. It is difficult for any concise set of accounting data to reflect all the different aspects of economic activity and therefore published accounting data tend to be partial and selective. Many commentators have regretted this partiality and argued that accounting should reflect many insights on economic activity. For example, our introduction has introduced two possible aspects of a business's economic activity. One view focuses on the distinction between operating and financing activities divided into discrete accounting periods. The second view looks upon business activity as a set of individual projects each of which is multi-period and involves both operations and financing. Thus economic activity is at least two-dimensional as follows:

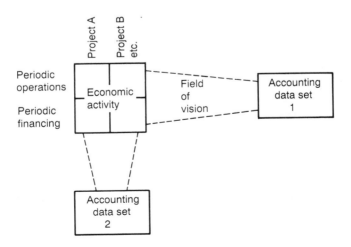

For Quickneasy, accounting data set 1 comprises the annual profits, cash flows and balance sheets. Accounting data set 2, however, comprises the net present value of the investment in the word processor and printer (Quickneasy only has the one project).

In fact as we go through the chapters, we shall discover other important dimensions of a business's economic activity giving further possible insights. There has been a tendency for accounting to attempt to give a clearer picture of economic activity by magnifying or providing high resolution pictures from one vantage point. Thus we find more and more detailed disclosure of the view from the vantage point of financial statements based on historical cost. This is not altogether an efficient or effective way of improving our insight and understanding of economic activity. Instead of greater resolution from a single vantage point a far more promising approach is to multiply the vantage points.

Hence this book explores a variety of insights on business activity. No single vantage point is imposed.

Representational faithfulness

Within the context of a given vantage point it is necessary for the financial statements to provide a faithful representation of the aspects of economic activity on view. For example, suppose periodic operational activity is on view and such activity is expected to be stable throughout the life of the project. In these circumstances the expected stability of operating activity should be reflected in stable projected operating profits and operating cash flows. Quickneasy's expected financial activities, however, are not stable since Quickneasy expects to vary the amount of its bank lending. Hence interest and profits net of interest are not expected to be stable during the four years. The stability of the operating activities is illustrated below:

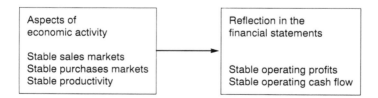

The direction of the arrow is important. Whilst stable operational activity should be reflected in stable operating profits, it does not follow that stable operating profits always imply stable economic conditions. For example, a company can maintain its profits in a declining market through increased productivity, thus achieving stable profits in unstable conditions. It follows that if profits or cash flows are being used to assess *management's operational performance*, it is necessary to look at the market conditions in which those profits or cash flows are achieved. All performance measures must be studied in context ... profits and cash flows are no exception.

CONCLUDING COMMENT

This chapter is neither quick nor easy! It takes a long time to develop a genuine understanding of accounting and its relationship with its organizational, business and economic setting. However, a good understanding of this chapter will provide a solid foundation for the adventures to come!

CHAPTER 4

Monitoring activities

INTRODUCTION

In the previous chapter forecasting Quickneasy's results for the four years involves the following steps:

1 *Forecasting sales.* This requires a study of Quickneasy's product and its position in the market, and consideration of market developments including market growth and the likelihood of new entrants into and exits from the market. In addition to these issues concerned with the product and its markets, sales success also depends upon the day-to-day activities of the sales function. Quickneasy is too small a business to have a separate sales department, but most businesses of any size will. If the sales department is good then, other things being equal, sales will benefit. It is of course important that the day-to-day experience of the sales department, especially with regard to product acceptability, is fed to those responsible for longer-term product development decisions. Strategic decision-taking should be informed by day-to-day experience.

2 *Forecasting variable expenses.* The ratio of variable expenses to sales is used to calculate variable expenses. This ratio is a function of the production techniques used and of the day-to-day efficiency with which production operations are conducted. In Quickneasy's case the only variable expenses are the wages of the typist who is engaged on the basis of the number of hours worked. Typist costs are 50% of sales. This ratio can be regarded as a measure of efficiency with respect to the use of variable expenses.

3 *Forecasting depreciation.* This involves an assessment of the cost and of the longevity and possible obsolescence of the fixed assets necessary to cope with the volume of sales. More efficient use of fixed assets is achieved by generating increased sales volume from the same fixed assets. Thus the ratio of sales to fixed assets is a measure of efficiency with respect to the use of fixed assets.

4 *Making finance assumptions.* Assumptions need to be made regarding the way in which fixed assets are financed and the cost of such finance. This includes the level of dividends considered necessary to reward capital provided by shareholders. In Quickneasy's case a nil dividend has to date been presumed as the basis of the forecasts. Assumptions must also be made regarding the level of so-called working capital items of debtors, creditors and stock. In Quickneasy's case it is assumed for convenience that the working capital will be nil. Hence sales are cash receipts and purchases/expenses are cash payments.

The order in which the above steps are carried out assumes that the key constraint is sales and hence the forecast (and the company) is sales driven. Once the sales are forecast, then the expenses associated with those sales are calculated. If, however, the key constraint on the company were access to a typist or to word processing facilities or to finance, then that matter would have to be considered first. Managing the key constraint is a primary issue for management, and it is the assumptions regarding the management of that constraint which drives the forecast.

The four steps are identifiable with important aspects of management relating to (1) market position, (2) day-to-day operations, (3) capital investment, and (4) financial management. Each of these represents an important managerial activity which is reflected in the financial statements. Thus the financial statements − along with other information − can be used to help monitor such managerial activities. Managing the product's position in the market, capital investment decisions and decisions about the way capital investment should be financed are essentially long-term, judgemental and strategic. They cannot be changed on a day-to-day basis. Much more immediate and under the day-to-day control of management are selling and production activities and the control of working capital items such as debtors, creditors and stock. Both strategic and the more immediate managerial activities impact on the financial statements, and it is important that these impacts are understood. When analysing changes in the financial statement figures, it will be necessary to identify those changes with one or more of the different managerial activities. However, it is not always possible on the strength of the financial statements alone to identify whether a change in the accounting figures is attributable to day-to-day management or longer-term strategic management or both. A certain amount of narrative explanation accompanying the financial statements is usually necessary.

In the previous chapter it was assumed that the expectations and forecasts on which the decision by Quickneasy to invest in the word processor was based were subsequently realized. Hence no distinction was made between the expected (ex ante) cash flows and profits anticipated at time point zero for the first four years of operations and the actual (ex post) cash flows and profits for those four years. This chapter investigates the effect on Quickneasy's profits and cash flows if, as is nearly always the case in practice, those expectations are not realized. Three categories of 'changed expectations' are considered:

1 Unexpected difficulties in obtaining cash from debtors (managing the debtors).

2 The unexpected entrance into Quickneasy's market of a competitor (new competitors).

3 The unexpected development of a superior word processor rendering Quickneasy's equipment uncompetitive (technological advance).

In addition to these changes, in this chapter it is assumed that Quickneasy reverses its intended policy on dividends. Instead of paying no dividends during the four years of the project, it pays dividends each year right up to the legal maximum – the computed net profits for the year being operating profits less interest paid (net of interest received). Under a full dividend policy, dividends equal operating profits less interest paid. Or, to look at it another way, dividends plus interest paid equals operating profits. Of course, in practice the nil dividend and full dividend policies are the two extremes, with most companies being somewhere in between.

Consequences of the new dividend policy

Dividend policy is a financial rather than an operations issue. The effect of Quickneasy's radical change of policy is to radically change the expected financing results – expected operating profits remain unchanged at £2,000 per annum. Under the new policy and before allowing for any other changing expectations, the anticipated results from financing activities – the interest charges – are shown below:

| | Year | | | |
| | 1 | 2 | 3 | 4 |
	£	£	£	£
Opening cash balance	(4,000)	(3,000)	(2,000)	(1,000)
Cash from operations	3,000	3,000	3,000	3,000
Interest	(400)	(300)	(200)	(100)
Dividends paid	(1,600)	(1,700)	(1,800)	(1,900)
Closing balance	(3,000)	(2,000)	(1,000)	Nil

Operating profit	2,000	2,000	2,000	2,000
Interest	(400)	(300)	(200)	(100)
Dividends paid	1,600	1,700	1,800	1,900

A comparison can be made between these interest charges and the anticipated financial results under a no dividend policy, as follows:

		Interest			Total
	£	£	£	£	£
No dividend policy	(400)	(140)	146	461	67
Full dividend policy	(400)	(300)	(200)	(100)	(1,000)

MANAGING THE DEBTORS

Managing the extent of credit granted to Quickneasy's debtors is an important task for Quickneasy's management. It is therefore important to recognize the effect of any unexpected difficulty in obtaining cash from debtors.

The unexpected event

It is Quickneasy's company policy to have no work in progress (i.e. unbilled work) or debtors (i.e. work that is billed but unpaid) at each year end. Suppose that at the end of year 1, in spite of Quickneasy's attempt to reduce debtors to zero, debtors of £500 are still outstanding. The customer is experiencing trading difficulties and at the end of the first year (time point 1) when the first year's financial statements are prepared, it is anticipated that the outstanding £500 will not be received until the end of year 2 (time point 2). It is still expected that debtors will be zero at the end of years 2, 3 and 4.

Consequences

The £500 debtors at the end of year 1 cause the actual cash flows for year 1 to reduce by £500 and for year 2 the expected cash flows increase by £500. The revised figures are as follows:

	Year 1 expected £	Year 1 actual £	Year 2 expected £
Operating cash flow	3,000	2,500	3,500
Accounting profit from operations	2,000	2,000	2,000

The illustration shows that a change in the level of debtors causes turbulence in cash flows but not in accounting profit. Similarly, any changes in creditors or stock levels would cause turbulence in cash flows and hence interest charges, but would not affect *operating* profit.

At the end of year 1 Quickneasy's balance sheet will include debtors of £500. In historical cost accounting debtors is a monetary asset corresponding to an expected future cash inflow and creditors is a 'monetary' liability corresponding to an expected future cash outflow. Both the future cash outflow and cash inflow must be the result of a past transaction or event. In the case of a debtor it is generally a sale and delivery of goods or services. In the case of a creditor it is generally a purchase and receipt of goods or services. An accounting concept called 'prudence' requires a very high expectation of a cash inflow to recognize a monetary asset and a somewhat lower expectation of a cash outflow to recognize a monetary liability. Accounting does not attach precise probabilities to these expectations. Recognition of debtors and creditors is a matter of judgement and provides considerable difficulty for the accountant when there are uncertainties.

Since under a full dividend policy, dividends and interest paid each year total profits from operations (£2,000), then the revised interest can be calculated as in Exhibit 4.1. This calculation assumes that interest is paid each year on the opening bank overdraft.

It is seen that although the accounting profits from operations are unaffected by the introduction of debtors, the interest charge in year 2 to be paid by Quickneasy is expected to rise from £300 (original expectation under a full dividend policy) to £350 (revised expectation). Thus,

	Year 1 expectations £	Year 2 original expectation £	Year 1 actual £	Year 2 revised expectation £
Opening cash balance	(4,000)	(3,000)	(4,000)	(3,500)
Cash from operations	3,000	3,000	2,500	3,500
Dividends paid	(1,600)	(1,700)	(1,600)	(1,650)
Closing cash balance	(2,600)	(1,700)	(3,100)	(1,650)
Interest paid	(400)	(300)	(400)	(350)

Exhibit 4.1 Original and revised results for year 2

additional debtors impose additional financing costs and year 2 expectations for profit net of interest are reduced as follows:

	Original expectation £	Revised expectation £
Operating profit	2,000	2,000
Interest	300	350
Profit after interest	1,700	1,650
Dividends	1,700	1,650
Retained profit	0	0

It is important that operating profit is distinguished from interest (paid to service bank overdraft), and dividends (paid to service share capital). The distinction is between *operations* and *financing*. It should be noticed that whilst operating profit is not revised, profit net of interest is revised downwards to reflect the higher borrowing (gearing). The company is expected to perform just as well in terms of operations (purchases, sales and production) but less well in terms of financial management.

The distinction between 'operations' and financing is one traditionally adhered to by accountants in the preparation of profit statements. It distinguishes the function of financing a business from all other business functions which for purposes of the profit statement are generically termed 'operations'. This distinction should not be confused with the quite different distinctions highlighted in Chapter 2, Exhibit 2.1, between the operational and strategic dimensions of functional activities. This latter distinction applies to all functions, including the finance function.

NEW COMPETITION

Unexpected event

At the beginning of year 3 a competitor, Suretype, unexpectedly starts business, driving down expected sales for years 3 and 4 to £4,000. Associated typist costs are £2,000.

Consequences

Anticipating the extent and timing of increased competition is an important task for Quickneasy's management. It is important therefore to monitor the effect of Suretype's unanticipated entrance into the market.

The revised expected operating cash flow and operating profits for years 3 and 4 are as follows:

	Year 3		Year 4	
	Original	Revised	Original	Revised
	£	£	£	£
Operating cash flow	3,000	2,000	3,000	2,000
Operating profit	2,000	1,000	2,000	1,000

As a result of the new competitor, expected cash flows over the four years of use of the word processor and laser printer are expected to drop by £2,000, from £8,000 to £6,000, the shortfall being experienced over years 3 and 4.

The operating profit has been revised downwards for year 3 (and 4) and this reflects the decline in the business conditions facing Quickneasy. The nature of the problem can be seen more clearly from the following analysis of the 'contribution' from operations towards the 'fixed' cost of depreciation:

	Year 3	
	Original	Revised
	£	£
Sales	6,000	4,000
Variable cost of sales	3,000	2,000
Contribution	3,000	2,000
Depreciation	1,000	1,000
Operating profit	2,000	1,000

The ratio of variable cost of sales (typist) to sales has remained at 50% whilst the ratio of sales to depreciation has fallen from 6 to 4. This implies that expectations of purchase costs and productivity have remained constant and that the problem lies in the company's selling markets.

TECHNOLOGICAL ADVANCE

Unexpected event

At the end of year 3 a new advanced technology combined processor and printer renders the existing word processor and printer obsolete. Suretype has invested in the new equipment which gives a faster service and better print. Quickneasy decides to follow suit in order to retain its market share.

Assume the new combined machine costs £4,000 and is bought on the first day of year 4. Annual sales and costs continue at £4,000 and £2,000 respectively. The new machine is expected to last four years.

Consequences

The expected and actual accounting profits for year 3 are as follows:

	Year 3	
	Expected	Actual
	£	£
Sales	4,000	4,000
Typist	(2,000)	(2,000)
Depreciation	(1,000)	(2,000)
Operating profit	1,000	Nil

At the beginning of year 3 the balance sheet includes the equipment at £2,000, being its original cost (£4,000) less two years' depreciation (£2,000). The balance of £2,000 is expected to be recovered from net cash inflows in years 3 and 4. At the end of year 3 it was expected that the balance sheet would show the equipment at £1,000 (£4,000 – 3,000). However, we now know that this amount is not recoverable in year 4 from net cash inflows associated with the use of the equipment, although it is recoverable from cash inflows expected to be generated by its replacement. Current practice in these circumstances is to write the equipment down to zero at the end of year 3, generating £2,000 of depreciation to be charged against year 3 sales.

Year 3's actual operating result is the sum of two parts. First there is the operating profit of £1,000 which would have been earned if expectations had remained unchanged. Secondly there is a loss of £1,000 caused by the change in expectations for the fixed asset. A better understanding of what has happened during year 3 can be obtained by showing these two parts separately in the profit statement. In particular it would provide a better basis for comparing years 3 and 2 as follows:

	Year 2	Year 3	Notes
	£	£	
Sales	6,000	4,000	1
Cost of sales	4,000	3,000	
Operating profit	2,000	1,000	
Revised expectations		(1,000)	2
All inclusive operating profit		Nil	

Notes
1 Drop in sales due to new entrant to the market.
2 Revised expectations regarding the longevity of existing equipment due to technological development.

Such a presentation serves to distinguish the effects of two separate environmental risks faced by the company, namely (1) the risk of increased competition and (2) the risk of equipment obsolescence. It is, however, a presentation seldom adopted under current standards.

So far our treatment of the change in expectations has been ex ante., i.e. the change in expectations is used to revise depreciation for the current year (up from £1,000 to £2,000) and for future years (effectively year 4 depreciation for the old equipment is reduced by £1,000), but it is not used to go back and revise depreciation charges in the past (years 1 and 2). If this were done our treatment of the change in expectations would be ex post. With the benefit of hindsight the original equipment should have been written off over three years to give the following results:

	'Ex post' operating results			*Anticipated result*
	Year 1	*Year 2*	*Year 3*	*Year 4*
	£	£	£	£
Sales	6,000	6,000	4,000	4,000
Typist	(3,000)	(3,000)	(2,000)	(2,000)
Depreciation	(1,333)	(1,333)	(1,333)	(1,000)
Operating profit	1,667	1,667	667	1,000

This approach divides the £4,000 depreciation charge equally between years 1–3. It could, however, be argued that the three years do not benefit equally from the use of the equipment and that years 1 and 2 should bear higher depreciation charges than year 3 to reflect the higher benefits obtained in those years due to the greater use of the equipment in more favourable market conditions.

A striking feature of the ex post approach is that profit for any given period is revised in subsequent periods as a result of new information being received. Thus year 2 operating profits are thought to be £2,000 at the end of year 2 but by the end of year 3 this has been revised to £1,667. This continuing revision of profits is perfectly logical but neither preparers nor users may feel comfortable with such a visible exposition of unachieved expectations. The ex post treatment is not allowed under current accounting standards. It is thought to give management too much opportunity to improve current profits by attributing expenses to prior years.

There is a third way to treat expectation changes – ignore them. Such a treatment continues to charge depreciation on the basis of the original expectation of the four years irrespective of what happens thereafter. On this basis the year 3 and 4 results are as follows:

	Year 3 £	Year 4 £
Sales	4,000	4,000
Typist	(2,000)	(2,000)
Depreciation	(1,000)	(1,000)
Operating profit	1,000	1,000
Loss associated with discontinued use of equipment		(1,000)
All-inclusive profit		Nil

Such a treatment may be regarded as the 'pure' historical approach since it retains not just the historical cost but also the historical expectations which led to that historical cost being incurred.

SPECULATIVE ASSET-HOLDING ACTIVITIES

The sudden obsolescence of Quickneasy's equipment brings home the point that any investment in fixed assets is a risky activity. Therefore, whenever fixed assets can be rented rather than bought, any purchase of those assets is a speculative activity, distinguishable from the other activities of the business. In effect renting gives Quickneasy the option of transferring the risk, for a premium, to the supplier which rents out the assets.

Let us suppose that both the original word processor/printer and the new advanced technology processor/printer could be hired for £1,462 per annum with the option of return to the hirer at the end of each year. It is possible to divide Quickneasy's actual operating performance during years 1–3 (given that Quickneasy elected to buy rather than rent) into (1) the results from its speculative investment in the word processing equipment and (2) the results from its other activities. The split is as follows:

	Years			
	1	2	3	Total
Operations	£	£	£	£
Sales	6,000	6,000	4,000	
Typist	(3,000)	(3,000)	(2,000)	
Notional rental	(1,462)	(1,462)	(1,462)	
	1,538	1,538	538	3,614

Investment in equipment

Notional rental	1,462	1,462	1,462	
Depreciation	(1,000)	(1,000)	(2,000)	
	462	462	(538)	386
Total operating profit	2,000	2,000	Nil	4,000

It is possible to go a stage further and to identify those interest costs in years 1–3 which result from the speculative investment in the equipment as follows:

	Years		
	1	*2*	*3*
	£	£	£
Opening balance	(4,000)	(2,938)	(1,770)
Notional rental	1,462	1,462	1,462
Interest	(400)	(294)	(177)
Closing balance	(2,938)	(1,770)	(485)

The overall performance of the investment in the equipment – the speculative asset-holding activity – is:

	1	*2*	*3*	*Total*
	£	£	£	£
Operating profit before interest	462	462	(538)	386
Interest	(400)	(294)	(177)	(871)
	62	168	(715)	(485)

Over the three years as a whole the decision to invest has not proved successful and shows a total loss of £485. This is attributable to losses in year 3, when news of the equipment obsolescence was first received. Speculative gains and losses are normally associated with new information which changes market expectations regarding future profitability.

CONSEQUENCES OF A FULL DIVIDEND POLICY

One of the consequences of following a full dividend policy in an uncertain environment is that adverse developments can easily make a firm legally insolvent. In Quickneasy's case it will be shown that it becomes technically insolvent at the end of year 3. The calculation of the bank balance at the end of year 3 is as follows:

Quickneasy's bank balance
Year

	1	2	3
	£	£	£
Opening balance	(4,000)	(3,500)	(2,000)
Operations	2,500	3,500	2,000
Interest	(400)	(350)	(200)
Dividends	(1,600)	(1,650)	Nil
	(3,500)	(2,000)	(200)

Quickneasy's balance sheet at the end of year 3 thus shows:

Quickneasy's balance sheet:	*Beginning year 3*	*End year 3*
	£	£
Intangible assets:		
Formation costs	100	100
Tangible assets:		
Equipment	2,000	Nil
	2,100	£100
Creditors due within 1 year:		
Bank overdraft	(2,000)	(200)
Total assets less current liabilities	100	(100)
Capital and reserves:		
Share capital	100	100
Profit and loss account		(200)
		(100)

As the law stands at the moment a company is insolvent if *either* (1) it cannot pay its debts as they fall due or (2) its liabilities exceed its assets. At the end of year 3 Quickneasy's liabilities exceed its assets and the company is therefore insolvent. This insolvency is the result of paying dividends instead of building up retained profits in years 1 and 2, followed by accounting policies in year 3 which have resulted in insufficient 'profits' to cover the interest charge. It is illegal for the directors to carry on trading whilst knowing that the company has an 'insolvent' balance sheet. The problem would be resolved by paying in a further £100 of share capital. There is little doubt that the company can meet its debts as they fall due given that it expects to have a healthy cash inflow in year 4 and that the bank overdraft has virtually been eliminated.

If the legislation regarding insolvency encourages companies to build up retained profits at the expense of high dividend payouts then that might disadvantage shareholders. The point is that when profits are paid out as dividends it is the shareholders who decide whether and where to reinvest. If profits are retained by the company it is company management who control the reinvestment.

The legislation should focus on the ability to pay debts as they fall due as the *only* primary test of insolvency. A deficit on the balance sheet does not *necessarily* imply future default on payments, as our example indicates. Nevertheless it is not uncommon for legal agreements, or the law itself, to specify dire consequences if accounting numbers (or some combination or ratio of accounting numbers) offends a stated limit. Such an arrangement provides significant incentives for management to choose courses of action, including the selection of accounting policies, which avoid offending the specified requirement.

CLOSING COMMENTS

This chapter has identified some important managerial activities. Several of these activities are strategic whilst others are more routine. Among the strategic considerations are management of the company's market position, capital investment and financing of that capital investment. More routine activities include controlling working capital and the day-to-day efficiency of sales, purchasing and production. This chapter has indicated how success or failure in these managerial activities impacts on the numbers in the financial statements. In particular the chapter has explored the impact of (1) problems in controlling working capital (debtors higher than expected), (2) a deteriorating market position (due to a new entrant) and (3) unexpected technological development generating a capital investment decision. The chapter has also illustrated the impact of financial decisions such as those relating to dividend policy on the company's financial position.

It should be noted that the decision to scrap the original equipment at the end of year 3 and replace it with the new advanced technology combined processor and printer was unaccompanied by any net present value calculations to justify the investment in terms of expected cash flow. The investment should have been accompanied by a net present value justification. Nevertheless the motive force behind the investment was not net present value, but the strategic need to maintain quality and market share and not to concede further competitive advantage to Suretype. In practice, capital investment is a strategic decision committing the company to certain products, supplies and production methods. The decision should be supported by a net present value calculation, but future cash flows are uncertain and dependent upon future developments, including the response of competitors and changes in technology. To a significant extent, investment remains an act of faith!

SELF-STUDY EXERCISE 4.1

Switch plc

Switch plc manufacture training shoes at a factory in the United Kingdom. Two years ago, at the beginning of 19X1, they invested heavily in capital equipment for the factory. The equipment cost £3,200 and had an expected life of four years. The company's profit statements for the last two years are as follows:

		19X1		19X2
		£		£
Sales		5,000		3,500
Production costs				
Materials and labour	3,000		2,100	
Factory rental	350		350	
Depreciation	800	4,150	800	3,250
		850		250
Administration and marketing		100		100
Operating profit		750		150

It is seen that 19X2 has been a bad year. The company has come under pressure from competitors sporting new designs manufactured in the Far East. The board of directors meets on the last day of 19X2 to discuss whether to abandon UK manufacturing and switch to Far East sourcing of the finished product. Switch would concentrate on design and marketing. It is estimated that if Switch continues with its UK manufacturing for the next two years (i.e. it does *not* switch), it can repeat the 19X2 results during 19X3 and 19X4. Materials and labour together are currently accounting for 60% of sales. It is anticipated that a switch to Far East sourcing would reduce these costs to 55% of sales and there would be no factory rental or depreciation. It would, however, be necessary to make a 'one-off' £500 redundancy payment to production employees on the first day of 19X3. It would also be necessary to write off the fixed assets. It is considered that a doubling of the annual expense on administration and marketing would be necessary to counter adverse publicity associated with closure of the UK factory and allow turnover to continue at £3,500.

Assume:

1 Switch has no debtors, creditors or stocks at each year end;

2 the cost of capital is 10%;

3 cash flows take place on the last day of each year except with respect to the redundancy payment;

4 if any switch to Far East sourcing is delayed two years until the end of 19X4, then redundancy costs are avoided.

Required:

1 Assuming the switch to Far East sourcing takes place, discuss the appropriate accounting treatment of the £500 redundancy cost, i.e. in what year(s) should it be expensed?

2 Revise the 19X2 operating profit on the assumption that the switch to Far East sourcing does take place.

3 Prepare forecast operating profit statements and cash flows for 19X3 and 19X4 on the assumption that the switch does take place.

4 Compare the net present values (at the end of 19X2) of the 19X3 and 19X4 cash flows, (a) assuming the switch, and (b) assuming the switch does *not* happen.

5 Advise the directors on whether the switch should take place at the end of 19X2. What difference would it make if redundancy costs were £1,000?

6 Assuming the switch does take place, compare the operating profit figures for the four years 19X1, 19X2, 19X3 and 19X4. Discuss whether these figures give an appropriate impression of Switch's profit trend during the four years. Suggest how operating profits might be recalculated to give a more appropriate impression of each year's relative performance.

7 What do you anticipate would be the effects on the United Kingdom economy of any decision to switch manufacture to the Far East?

CHAPTER 5

Cash generating and absorbing activity

INTRODUCTION

Cash is the lifeblood of the business organization. Business activity absorbs cash to purchase productive assets, hire staff and purchase raw materials. It subsequently generates cash when its products are paid for by the customers. Cash may also be raised by issuing share capital and loan stock or by selling fixed assets. It is absorbed by dividend and interest payments and by the repayment of loans. Since cash is so crucial to business life, its control and management is an important managerial activity. The purpose of this chapter is to provide an understanding of how cash flows link to the other activities of the business. This is done in parallel with an explanation of the cash flow statement and how it relates to statements (accounts) of movements in the other assets and liabilities of the business. In the process the reader is reintroduced to the conventions of double-entry book-keeping.

Three important perspectives on cash flow are covered in this chapter. One such perspective is obtained by linking it to the cycle of production operations during which cash is expended for the purchase of materials and labour and generated by the sale of products to customers. The payment of dividends and interest can be subtracted from operating cash flow to show the net cash flow after servicing the finance of the third factor of production (capital).

A second perspective links cash flow to the investment cycle which is concerned with the raising/redemption of funds for the purchase of fixed assets. The production and investment cycles intersect when cash from operations is used to fund the purchase of fixed assets.

A third perspective links cash flow to the product lifecycle. Cash generated by mature and ageing products is used to support the development, launch and production of new and replacement products. The segmentation of cash flow by product also provides important insights in the Booze case study (Chapter 11) where it is seen that the cash flows generated by 'plonk' were applied to the longer-term investment in fine wines. The product lifecycle perspective has close links with the production perspective whenever it is the production of one product which generates the cash for the launch and production of other products. It also links with the investment cycle when cash from one product is used to purchase fixed assets for additional or replacement products.

The production, investment and product lifecycles and their inter-sections are represented diagrammatically as follows:

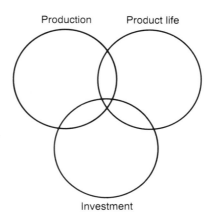

Production   Product life

Investment

The first part of this chapter looks at a cash flow statement for a company (Midlothian Zaibatsu). The particular presentation covers the cash flows associated with the production and investment cycles, and the intersection of the two cycles is discussed. The second part of the chapter looks at Midlothian's cash flows from a product cycle perspective.

THE PRODUCTION AND INVESTMENT CYCLES

Suppose that Midlothian Zaibatsu (Mid Z) is a company with the cash flows shown below during 199X.

An analysis of a company's cash flows normally focuses on its cash from operations before (line 4) and after (line 10) paying for financing costs and tax. It will also examine whether cash paid for assets (line 13) is derived from operations or borrowing. Mid Z has a healthy cash flow from operations, being £150 before and £100 after paying for financing costs and tax. Of Mid Z's £90 cash investment in fixed assets, £20 is funded by loans leaving £70 to be funded by cash from operations. Any company which is consistently borrowing not to finance fixed assets but to cover a deficit in its operating cash flows is likely to be in trouble.

Statement of cash flows: 199X

Line		£	£
1	Opening cash balance		20
2	Cash received from customers	232	
3	*Less*: Cash paid for materials and wages	82	
4	Cash from operations	150	
5	*Less*: Loan interest paid	5	
6	Pre-tax cash flow	145	
7	*Less*: Tax paid	25	
8	Distributable cash flow	120	
9	*Less*: Dividends paid	20	
10	Operating cash flow after distribution	100	
11	*Add*: Long-term loans received	20	
12	Total cash flow available for investment	120	
13	*Less*: Cash payments for assets	90	
14	Increase in cash resources during year		30
15	Closing cash balance		50

DOUBLE-ENTRY BOOK-KEEPING

As discussed in Chapter 1, double-entry book-keeping is a record-keeping system which maintains accounts in two columns: increases in assets on the left (the debit column) and decreases on the right (the credit column). Mid Z's cash account would look as follows:

Cash

	£		£
Opening balance	20	Materials, labour	82
Customers	232	Loan interest	5
Loans	20	Tax	25
		Dividends	20
		Fixed assets	90
		Closing balance	50
	272		272

The figures in this cash account are identical to those in the statement of cash flow. It is important to keep detailed breakdowns of the figures in the accounts. Hence a back-up computer listing should be kept showing the detail of the individual receipts which collectively generate the £232 received from customers and the individual payments which make up the £82 absorbed by materials and wages. Similar detailed breakdowns should be kept for other accounts.

The other asset accounts

Just as the cash account provides a record of the flow of cash during the year, so the account for any other asset provides a record of that particular asset's movements. Some important assets apart from cash are fixed assets (such as plant and machinery), stock and debtors. Midlothian's fixed assets are increased by the purchases during the year and reduced by the depreciation of the assets due to their consumption through the manufacturing process. Suppose that the fixed asset account for 199X is:

Fixed assets

	£		£
Opening balance	112	Depreciation	22
Cash purchase	90	Closing balance	180
	202		202

The cash purchase of £90 also appears in the cash account. 'Double'-entry book-keeping requires that every transaction or recognized event is recorded twice – once as a debit entry and once as a credit entry. In this case it appears as a £90 credit entry in the cash account and a £90 debit entry in the fixed assets account. It will be seen shortly that the £22 depreciation credit in the fixed assets account also appears as a debit in the stock account. The opening balance represents the unexpired cost of fixed assets at the beginning of the year and the closing balance represents the unexpired cost of fixed assets at the end of the year. For all asset and liability accounts the closing balance of one year becomes the opening balance of the next. Thus the closing balance of £180 becomes the opening (debit) balance for 199X + 1's fixed asset account as follows:

Fixed assets

	£		£
199X Opening balance	112	Depreciation	22
Purchases	90	199X Closing balance	180
	202		202
199X +1 Opening balance	180		

Stocks are increased by the materials purchased, by the expenditure of labour used in manufacturing, and by the depreciation of the machine through usage. Stock is reduced by the proportion of collected costs which are attributed to the units sold (the cost of sales). Mid Z's stock account for 199X is:

Stock

	£		£
Opening balance	27	Cost of sales	72
Materials purchased	55	Closing balance	54
Labour	22		
Depreciation	22		
	126		126

The total of materials (£55) and labour (£22) collected in the stock account does not equal the amount paid for materials and wages (£82). This is because the stock account 'collects' the cost of materials received irrespective of whether or not they have been paid for by the year end. £55 of materials have been received and therefore 'collected' in the stock account. However, £60 has been paid to trade creditors in respect of materials during 199X. This includes monies paid during 199X for materials purchased on credit during 199X – 1. The £60 paid to trade creditors plus the £22 paid as wages totals the £82 shown in the cash account.

At any point in time the balance on the debtors account represents the amount owing from customers. Debtors are increased by sales and reduced by the amounts received from customers. Midlothian's debtors (accounts receivable) account during 199X is:

Debtors

	£		£
Opening balance	20	Cash received	232
Sales	247	Closing balance	35
	267		267

The current liability accounts

At the end of the year a company may not have paid its suppliers in full for all materials received. Secondly, it may not have paid the Revenue in full for the tax payable on the profits for the year. Thirdly, it might not have paid its shareholders in full for the dividends declared in respect of the profits for the year. These amounts due are called 'current' liabilities since they are amounts which will have to be paid by the company in the near future. In double-entry book-keeping, liabilities are treated in the reverse manner to assets. Hence increases in liabilities are included on the right (the credit column) and decreases in liabilities on the left (the debit column).

During 199X Midlothian's trade creditors (accounts payable) account is increased by the purchase of materials and reduced by payments to suppliers as follows:

Trade creditors

	£		£
Cash payments	60	Opening balance	30
Closing balance	25	Stock purchases	55
	85		85

It should be noted that whereas an opening balance on an asset account appears in the debit column (a debit balance), an opening balance on a liability account appears in the credit column (a credit balance). The opening trade creditors balance for 199X + 1 is £25 and it appears as a credit balance at the beginning of the 199X + 1 trade creditors account.

The tax payable account is increased by tax payable (chargeable) on the profits for 199X and reduced by any amounts actually paid to the Revenue as follows:

Tax payable

	£		£
Cash paid	25	Opening balance	25
Closing balance	30	199X tax charge	30
	55		55

The amount paid during 199X is the opening balance of £25 which is the tax charge on the 199X − 1 profits.

The dividends payable account is increased by the dividends declared on the 199X profits and reduced by any dividends paid, as follows:

Dividends payable

	£		£
Dividends paid	20	Opening balance	20
Closing balance	25	Dividends on 199X profits	25
	45		45

The amount paid during 199X is the opening balance of £20 which is the dividend declared in respect of the 199X − 1 profits.

Midlothian has paid all the interest due on its loan and therefore has no liabilities at the end of 199X in respect of interest.

Midlothian's balance sheet lists the balances on the asset and current liability accounts and shows one figure for the 'total assets less current liabilities'. This figure equates with the total figure for shareholders' funds plus loans. Midlothian's balance sheets at the beginning and end of 199X are as follows:

		199X					
		Opening				Closing	
	£	£	£	£	£	£
Fixed assets			112				180
Current assets:							
Stocks	27			54			
Debtors	20			35			
Cash	20			50			
		67			139		
Current liabilities:							
Trade creditors	(30)			(25)			
Tax payable	(25)			(30)			
Dividends payable	(20)			(25)			
		(75)			(80)		
Net current assets			(8)				59
Total assets less current liabilities			104				239
Share capital		50			50		
Retained profit		54			169		
Shareholders' funds			104				219
Loan							20
			104				239

Stocks, debtors and cash are regarded as 'current' assets since the intention is that stocks and debtors should be converted into cash within a short space of time. Current liabilities are subtracted from current assets to give net current assets. A company with negative net current assets might have difficulty in meeting its short-term commitments. However, although Midlothian starts 199X with negative net current assets, its positive cash flows during 199X mean that in the event it has no difficulty in meeting its commitments.

Cash

	£			£
Opening balance	20	(3)	Materials, labour	82
(1) Customers	232	(4)	Interest	5
(2) Loans	20	(5)	Tax	25
		(6)	Dividends	20
		(7)	Fixed assets	90
			Closing balance	50
	272			272
Opening balance (199X + 1)	50			

Fixed assets

	£			£
Opening balance	112	(8)	Depreciation	22
(7) Cash purchase	90		Closing balance	180
	202			202
Opening balance	180			

Stock

	£			£
Opening balance	27	(10)	Cost of sales	72
(9) Materials	55		Closing balance	54
(3) Labour	22			
(8) Depreciation	22			
	126			126
Opening balance	54			

Debtors

	£			£
Opening balance	20	(1)	Cash	232
(11) Sales	247		Closing balance	35
	267			267
Opening balance	35			

Trade creditors

	£			£
(3) Cash payments	60		Opening balance	30
Closing balance	25	(9)	Purchases	55
	85			85
			Opening balance	25

Tax payable

	£			£
(5) Cash	25		Opening balance	25
Closing balance	30	(12)	Tax charge	30
	55			55
			Opening balance	30

Dividends payable

	£		£
(6) Paid	20	Opening balance	20
Closing balance	25	(13) 199X Dividend	25
	45		45
		Opening balance	25

Share capital

	£		£
Closing balance	50	Opening balance	50
	50		50
		Opening balance	50

Loan

	£		£
		Opening balance	Nil
Closing balance	20	(2) Cash	20
	20		20
		Opening balance	20

Retained profit

	£		£
		Opening balance	54
(10) Cost of sales	72	(11) Sales	247
(4) Interest	5		
(12) Tax	30		
(13) Dividends	25		
Closing balance	169		
	301		301
		Opening balance	169

Note:
The debit side of entry number 3 is in two parts as follows:

		£	£
Credit	Cash a/c		82
Debit	Stock a/c	22	
Debit	Trade creditors a/c	60	
		82	82

Exhibit 5.1 The complete set of Midlothian's accounts for 199X

Midlothian's profit statement for 199X is as follows:

Profit for 199X

	£
Sales	247
Cost of sales	72
	175
Interest	5
	170
Tax	30
	140
Dividends	25
Retained profit	115
Opening retained profit	54
Closing retained profit	169

Profits are increased by resources created during 199X (sales revenue) and decreased (1) by resources consumed (cost of sales), (2) by charges for interest and tax, and (3) by profits allocated to shareholders (dividends).

The sales revenue of £247 is a credit balance and forms the double entry to the debit balance in the debtors account. The sales figure (£247) represents the selling value of goods delivered and since goods are sold on credit it differs from the cash received from customers during 199X. This latter figure is £232 as shown in the cash and debtors accounts. All expenses are debit balances within the profit account and the double entries (credits) are in the stock (£72), cash (£5), tax payable (£30) and dividends payable (£25) accounts. In each case the reader should check the double entry. The recognition of expenses corresponds to the consumption of resources rather than the payment of cash. For example, cost of sales is charged when the goods are sold and not when the materials and other constituent costs (labour, fixed assets) are paid for.

Exhibit 5.1 provides the complete set of Midlothian's accounts for 199X and indicates the pairing entries (double entries) by the use of numbered 'tags'. It also shows the opening balances for 199X + 1.

THE PRODUCT LIFECYCLE

The statement of cash flows given earlier in this chapter provides an analysis showing cash generated by operations and how that cash is used to pay for financing costs, tax and investment in fixed assets. However, an equally revealing analysis is provided by looking at cash flows on a product-by-product basis. At any point in time a company has products which are nearing the end of their useful life, new products, and established products in mid-life. New products are cash absorbing since they require new production facilities and marketing support. To a significant extent the cash needs of the new products may have to be met from cash generation by the more mature products. Management must judge how much of the cash generation from mature and ageing products should be reinvested into supporting and lengthening the lives of those established products and how much should be diverted to new products. It is not necessarily a good idea to allow a brand manager to plough back all the cash generated by the brand into sustaining that brand. A cash flow analysis by product provides an insight into product management and how mature products are helping to foster their replacements.

MIDLOTHIAN'S PRODUCT CASH FLOWS

The remainder of this chapter continues with Midlothian Zaibatsu to illustrate cash flow analysis on a product-by-product basis. Relevant information on Midlothian and its three products A, B and C is given below:

1 Movements in working capital during 199X are as follows:

	Opening £	Closing £	
Cash	20	50	
Trade creditors	30	25	
Trade debtors	20	35	
Stocks:			
Material	15	30	(55.6% of stock cost)
Labour	6	12	(22.2% of stock cost)
Overhead (depreciation)	6	12	(22.2% of stock cost)
	27	54	

This shows the breakdown of opening and closing stocks into their constituent 'collected' costs of materials, labour and overhead.

2 Stocks have built up during 199X in anticipation of a new product (product C) to be launched early in 199X + 1. The stock figures can be analysed across the company's three products (A, B and C) as follows:

	A	B	C	Total
Opening	18	9	0	27
Closing	9	9	36	54

3 All products have the same cost structure of materials, labour and overheads. Of the closing creditors of £25, £10 relates to the new product C and £15 to products A and B. During 199X management have had a policy of reducing the stocks held for product A. Trade debtors have increased in order to allow terms of trade to keep in line with those of competitors. Creditors are having to be paid more quickly in order to retain discounts on purchases.

4 In all respects other than those mentioned above Midlothian has been experiencing steady business conditions with no growth or decline or change in production costs.

Operating cash flows for the old/new products

In order to calculate operating cash flows separately for the new/old products separate debtors, creditors and stock accounts can be opened for the new product (C) and the existing products (A and B). The opening (OB) and closing (CB) balances can be entered from information given above as follows:

A and B debtors				C debtors			
	£		£		£		£
OB	20	CB	35	OB	Nil	CB	Nil

A and B creditors				C creditors			
	£		£		£		£
CB	15	OB	30	CB	10	OB	Nil

A and B stock				C stock			
	£		£		£		£
OB	27	CB	18	OB	Nil	CB	36

Since C has not yet been launched its debtors balance is zero and it is assumed that its creditors are all incurred during 199X. The C stock has the same breakdown of materials, labour and depreciation as the other products and its account for the year can thus be completed:

C Stock

	£		£
OB	0	Cost of sales	0
Purchases	20	CB	36
Labour	8		
Depreciation	8		
	36		36

The labour charge of £8 has its double entry in bank, whilst the double entry for the purchases of £20 is in creditors. The depreciation in stock of £8 is the recovery of fixed assets and does not involve cash. The C creditors account can now be completed:

C Creditors

	£		£
Cash payments	10	OB	0
CB	10	Purchases	20
	20		20

It follows that the operating cash flow associated with product C is as follows:

	£
Receipts from customers	0
Payments to suppliers	(10)
Payments for labour	(8)
	(18)

The operating cash flows for A and B must be £168, being the overall operating cash flow of £150 plus £18 used to cover C's needs. This can be checked by completing the 'T' accounts for products A and B.

	A and B debtors		
	£		£
OB	20	Cash receipts	232
Sales	247	CB	35
	267		267

	A and B 199X operating cash flow
	£
Cash from customers	232
Paid to suppliers	(50)
Paid to labour	(14)
	168

	A and B creditors		
	£		£
Payment	50	OB	30
CB	15	Purchases	35
	65		65

	A and B stocks		
	£		£
OB	27	Cost of sales	72
Purchases	35	CB	18
Labour	14		
Depreciation	14		
	90		90

During 199X the old products (A and B) have generated operating cash flow of £168 of which £18 has been absorbed by C which has negative operating cash flow. It can also be assumed that the cash flows from A and B have been used to fund new machinery required by product C, or at least that part of the new machinery (£70) not funded by the new loan.

Forecasting 199X + 1 cash flows

Suppose you are informed that the directors estimate positive cash flows of £70 in 199X + 1 in respect of operations concerning the new product C. Assume that the sales for the old products (A and B) remain the same in 199X + 1 as for 199X, and that there is no change during 199X + 1 in the levels of stocks, debtors and creditors or in unit production costs. It is required to estimate operating cash flows for 199X + 1.

The 199X + 1 cash flows for A and B can be estimated by forecasting the 199X + 1 'T' accounts for A and B debtors, creditors and stock as follows:

A and B debtors	£			£
OB	35	Cash receipts		247
Sales	247	CB		35
	282			282

A and B 199X + 1 operating cash flow	£
Cash from customers	247
Paid to suppliers	(40)
Paid to labour	(16)
	191

A and B creditors	£		£
Cash payments	40	OB	15
CB	15	Purchases	40
	55		55

A and B stock	£		£
OB	18	Cost of sales	72
Purchases	40	CB	18
Labour	16		
Depreciation	16		
	90		90

The estimated 199X + 1 operating cash flow for A and B is £191 and this can also be calculated by adjusting A and B's 199X cash flow for movement during 199X in creditors, debtors and stock. These movements are as follows:

		£
199X decrease in creditors		15
increase in debtors		15
A and B stocks, material and labour		
opening	21	
closing	14	
decrease		(7)
		23

If creditors had not been reduced by £15 during 199X, cash flow would have been £15 higher. Similarly if debtors had not increased by £15, cash flow would be £15 higher. Finally if stock levels had been maintained it would have been necessary to invest £7 in materials and labour and hence cash flow would have been £7 lower.

Thus the 199X cash flow under conditions of unchanging levels of debtors, creditors and stocks would have been £168 + £23 = £191. These unchanging conditions are expected for 199X + 1 in respect of A and B and therefore the expected cash flows for A and B in 199X + 1 is £191 subject to any anticipated changes in markets or production costs.

Total cash flows

The directors' estimate of operating cash flows to be generated by C during 199X + 1 is £70. It follows that total estimated operating cash flow for 199X + 1 is £191 + £70 = £261.

Assuming that sales of products A and B continue to hold up, and if cash flows from product C are expected to remain steady at £70 per annum, then the launch of C is a critical event which has caused an upward shift in operating profit and cash flows. If cash flows from product C grow steadily then the launch of C is a critical event which has caused a static situation to change into a growth situation.

However, suppose you are advised that product C is to replace product B as from the first day of 199X + 1. Stocks of B held at the end of 199X therefore have no sales value. What information would you need in order to revise your estimate of 199X + 1 operating cash flows?

It now becomes necessary to know the 199X operating cash flows separately for products A and B. The repeatable cash flow should be calculated for product A, and used by the investors as the basis for anticipated cash flows from A. Anticipated cash flows for B are limited to cash receivable from year end debtors in respect of B and any scrap values in respect of B stock. It follows that to assist in forecasting, the 199X financial statements should show:

1 repeatable cash flow for product A;

2 anticipated cash flows for B;

3 directors' estimate of future cash flows for C.

CONCLUDING COMMENT

The study of Midlothian has focused on the retirement and birth of products – two aspects of a business which critically affect operating cash flow and which should therefore be highlighted for management and investors via a cash flow statement segmented according to three categories of product (emerging, continuing and retiring). Such a cash flow statement segments products according to their position on the product lifecycle. It provides a valuable perspective on operating cash flow in addition to the more traditional production cycle and investment cycle perspectives. In essence the production cycle requires a company to control its debtors so as to maximize cash receipts, control its creditors so as to minimize cash outflows to creditors and to control its investment in stocks. The investment cycle requires a company to match its internally and externally generated finance with its programme of fixed asset purchases. The product cycle requires a company to balance the cash needs of its new products with those of its existing products.

SELF-STUDY EXERCISE 5.1

Two companies – Livenow plc (LN) and Payofflater plc (POL) – are in direct competition. During the five years 19X1 to 19X5 the two companies generate identical cash flows from operations as follows:

19X1	2	3	4	5
£150	£50	£120	£170	£170

Further investigation reveals that these operating cash flows are before paying the following sums for product development (PD) and advertising (AD):

	19X1		2		3		4		5	
	PD	AD	PD	AD	PD	AD	PD	AD	PD	AD
LN	30	15	30	15		40		40		40
POL	30	15	30	15	50	15	30	15	20	40

Expenditure such as product development and advertising have a benefit which potentially lasts beyond the period in which the expenditure is incurred. However, this benefit is difficult to quantify and so in the profit statement these cash expenditures are normally treated as an expense of the period in which they are incurred. Such expenditure is known as 'deferred revenue expenditure'.

Required:

What difference does knowledge of LN and POL's deferred revenue expenditure make to your assessment of LN and POL's future prospects? Discuss.

SELF-STUDY EXERCISE 5.2

You are now advised that during the five years both LN and POL have manufactured two products (A and B). In addition during 19X1 and 19X2 both companies were developing a new product (C). However, at the end of 19X2, LN abandoned the development programme, but POL continued and launched the new product C at the beginning of 19X5. The operating cash (OC) flows and deferred revenue expenditures on a product basis are shown below:

	19X1 OC £	19X1 PD £	19X1 AD £	19X2 OC £	19X2 PD £	19X2 AD £	19X3 OC £	19X3 PD £	19X3 AD £	19X4 OC £	19X4 PD £	19X4 AD £	19X5 OC £	19X5 PD £	19X5 AD £
LN															
A	80		10	20		10	50		30	100		30	100		30
B	70		5	30		5	70		10	70		10	70		10
C		30			30										
	150	30	15	50	30	15	120	Nil	40	170	Nil	40	170	Nil	40
POL															
A	80		10	20		10	40		10	75		10	35		
B	70		5	30		5	80		5	95		5	75		
C		30			30			50			30		60	20	40
	150	30	15	50	30	15	120	50	15	170	30	15	170	20	40

Required:

Discuss these cash flow patterns from a product lifecycle perspective.
   What difference does the product cash flow information make to your earlier assessment of prospects for LN and POL?

SELF-STUDY EXERCISE 5.3

You are now given the operating profits for LN and POL with depreciation on a product basis, for each of the five years, as follows:

	19X1 LN £	19X1 POL £	19X2 LN £	19X2 POL £	19X3 LN £	19X3 POL £	19X4 LN £	19X4 POL £	19X5 LN £	19X5 POL £
Operating cash	150	150	50	50	120	120	170	170	170	170
Product development	(30)	(30)	(30)	(30)		(50)		(30)		(20)
Advertising	(15)	(15)	(15)	(15)	(40)	(15)	(40)	(15)	(40)	(40)
	105	105	5	5	80	55	130	125	130	110

Depreciation										
for A	(10)	(10)	(10)	(10)						
B	(10)	(10)	(10)	(10)	(10)	(10)	(10)	(10)	(10)	(10)
C										(30)
Total depreciation	(20)	(20)	(20)	(20)	(10)	(10)	(10)	(10)	(10)	(40)
Operating profit	85	85	(15)	(15)	70	45	120	115	120	70

You are told that the machines used to make product A are fully depreciated by the end of 19X2 and hence, although the machines continue to be used during 19X3 to 19X5, no depreciation is charged. Full depreciation occurs when a machine lasts for its expected useful life. At the end of 19X4 POL invested £300 in new equipment for the manufacture of product C. The new equipment has an expected useful life of ten years.

Required:

1 To what extent does the operating profit record of LN reflect its past performance and future prospects? Discuss.

2 To what extent does the operating profit record of POL reflect its past performance and future prospects? Discuss.

3 To what extent do the relative operating profits each year of LN and POL fairly reflect their relative performance and progress? Discuss.

CHAPTER 6

Changing patterns of production and ownership

INTRODUCTION

This chapter looks at how two key profitability ratios – return on capital and return on resources consumed – are influenced by the way the business carries out its production. In any study of business performance it is important to identify the extent to which differences in profitability reflect differences in the nature of the production process. It will be shown that differences in profitability can occur due to fundamental differences in the way two products are provided (e.g. capital intensive as against labour intensive) and/or because two activities occupy different positions in the chain of production (e.g. manufacture of parts as against assembly of finished product).

The chapter's case study – Manyhands and Lightwork – highlights a crucial difference between return on capital and return on resources consumed. Whereas return on capital is concerned with the performance of the business from the point of view of the providers of capital, return on resources consumed is concerned with the wider economic question of a return on all resources used by the business, including labour and materials as well as capital. This difference between shareholder and economy-wide perspectives on the business is a major focus of the chapter. This distinction carries into the later stages of the case study when shareholder (ownership) interests are changing due to first demerger and then takeover activity. This demerger and takeover activity is designed to achieve strategic changes in which the ownership of the production processes is altered. Hence the case study provides the chapter's two major themes – how apparent 'profitability' is affected by (1) changing patterns of ownership and (2) changing patterns of production.

In summary, the chapter proceeds through a study of two competing manufacturing companies – Manyhands and Lightwork. Whereas Manyhands is labour intensive, Lightwork is capital intensive. There follows a discussion of how the returns of Manyhands and Lightwork reflect their respective productive processes. Subsequently Lightwork demerges into two companies – Lightwork A and Lightwork B – which are engaged in cooperative rather than competitive activities. The impact of this on the returns of Lightwork A and Lightwork B is studied. Finally Lightwork A takes over Lightwork B and a set of 'consolidated accounts' is prepared. In the case study this takeover is assumed to have no short-term effect on productivity or product volumes and so any effect of the figures in the 'consolidated accounts' on the returns can be attributed to the takeover. Thus the ability of takeovers to 'confuse' the financial returns is highlighted.

INTRODUCING MANYHANDS

Manyhands is engaged in manufacturing. Manyhands' manufacturing facility can operate at three output levels – 4 units, 7 units or 10 units per annum. The costs associated with each of the three levels are as follows:

	Output (units)		
	4	*7*	*10*
	£	£	£
Labour costs	5	10	17
Materials	2	5	11
Depreciation	5	5	5
	12	20	33

These costs assume that, given each level of output, production is carried out within the existing manufacturing facility in the most cost effective manner possible. Thus there is an assumption of *productive efficiency* at whatever level of output is chosen.

If output is increased it is necessary to reduce the selling price in order that the output is sold. The best selling prices that can be achieved at each level of output (and still sell all the annual production) are:

	Output (units)		
	4	*7*	*10*
Unit selling price	£5	£4.29	£4

Assume that whichever annual production level is chosen, fixed assets are £50 and are financed by shareholders' funds. There are no other assets or sources of finance.

Required:

At which annual production level does Manyhands perform best? Discuss from the point of view of:

1 shareholders;

2 the economy as a whole.

Discussion of Manyhands

There is an important distinction between productive efficiency and allocative efficiency. *Productive efficiency* is concerned that for any given level of output, cost is kept to a minimum. *Allocative efficiency* is concerned that greater overall benefit could not be obtained by shifting moveable resources to or from other activities. Thus allocative efficiency requires the level of output of each product or service to be optimum. We are told that Manyhands is productively efficient and the question is therefore one of allocative efficiency — which output level is optimal?

The financial statements corresponding to the different output levels are as follows:

	Output (units)				
	4	*7*	*10*		
	£	£	£		
Shareholders' funds	50	50	50	}	Balance
Assets	50	50	50	}	sheet
Sales turnover	20	30	40	}	
Labour costs	(5)	(10)	(17)	}	Profit
Materials	(2)	(5)	(11)	}	statement
Depreciation	(5)	(5)	(5)	}	
Accounting profit	8	10	7		

Shareholder perspectives

An output of 7 units gives the highest accounting profit, and since the amount of shareholders' funds invested is £50 at all three output levels, an output of 7 also gives the highest return on shareholders' funds, being 20% (10/50). Hence an output of 7 is the most advantageous from the point of view of shareholders in Manyhands. An increase from this output level to 10 units will create further resources of £10 (marginal sales revenue) but absorb further resources of £13 (marginal costs). Since marginal costs would exceed marginal revenue, such an increase is disadvantageous. Similarly a decrease in output to 4 units would reduce sales (from £30 to

£20) by more than it would reduce costs (from £20 to £12) and is also unprofitable.

The lesson to be learned is a familiar one from the economist's theory of the firm, namely that output levels should be established by reference to the marginal effects of increasing or decreasing output. The optimum output is achieved when both an increase or a decrease in output would result *at the margin* in losses.

Thus an output level of 7 yields the highest accounting profits, provides the largest return on (shareholders') capital and is *allocatively efficient* in its use of resources from a shareholder perspective.

The 'economy-wide' perspective

Subject to the caveats discussed in the next section, it is reasonable to approximate sales turnover with the 'value' of resources released into the economy by the production process and the various costs reported in the profit statement with the 'value' of resources consumed or taken out of the economy by the production process. If these assumptions hold, an output level of 7 gives the largest surplus of resources created over resources consumed, but an output level of 4 units gives a better return on resources consumed (8/12 as against 10/20). In so far as the economy benefits by encouraging business activity to maximize on the use of resources, then 4 units, rather than 7 units, may be the preferred output level. Much depends upon whether the additional consumption of labour and materials necessary to move from 4 to 7 units of output could be put to better use elsewhere in the economy.

Caveats

This simple example serves to illustrate how the quest for accounting profits and the highest possible return on capital will not necessarily lead to allocative efficiency from the point of view of the economy as a whole. There are a number of other well-known problems with the identification of profitability with economic efficiency. Problems might arise, for instance, if Manyhands were a monopoly supplier or purchaser or if Manyhands' production processes create environmental problems. A monopoly has the power to dictate prices in a way which those who operate in competitive markets cannot. It can therefore artificially restrict output and compensate by raising its prices. If so, the relationship between profit and allocative efficiency becomes problematic from an economy-wide perspective. Another issue relates to environmental problems. The difficulty arises when environmental costs of production – pollution etc.

– are not included as costs in the profit statement which therefore gives an incomplete record of the costs of production.

INTRODUCING LIGHTWORK

Manyhands Limited has a competitor, Lightwork Limited. The two companies are producing the same product by two different production methods. Whilst Manyhands is labour intensive, Lightwork has invested heavily in capital equipment. Key figures from the 199X balance sheets and profit statements of the two companies are as follows:

	Manyhands £	Lightwork £	Total £
Shareholders' funds	50	100	150
Fixed assets	50	100	150
Turnover	30	30	60
Labour costs	(10)	(3)	(13)
Materials	(5)	(2)	(7)
Depreciation	(5)	(10)	(15)
Operating profit for 199X	10	15	25
Dividends	10	15	25
Retained profits	0	0	0

If it is assumed that the shareholders' funds have an opportunity cost of 5% per annum then the operating profit can be divided into two parts: (1) 'notional interest' necessary to cover the opportunity cost of the shareholders' funds, and (2) 'superprofits' earned in excess of notional interest. Notional interest and superprofits are as follows:

	£	£	£
Notional interest (say 5%)	2.5	5	7.5
Superprofit	7.5	10	17.5
	10.0	15.0	25.0

Required:

Which of the two companies has performed best from the point of view of:

1 the shareholders;

2 the economy as a whole?

Assume that both companies are *allocatively* efficient from a shareholder perspective.

Discussion of Lightwork and Manyhands

Since the case study specifies that Manyhands and Lightwork are both allocatively efficient, the following discussion is concerned with an assessment of their relative productive efficiency.

The shareholder perspective

From the point of view of share capital Manyhands has generated a return on capital (investment) of 20%, being profit of £10 divided by shareholders' funds of £50. Lightwork, however, has only managed a return on capital of 15%. In a system where any surpluses revert to the shareholders then, *from a shareholder perspective*, Manyhands has performed well. In so far as management's performance is judged in terms of the returns for shareholders, the management of Manyhands will also be judged to have done well. Generally speaking the capitalist system works by judging performance in terms of returns on capital.

From a shareholder perspective it is the superprofits − what has been earned over and above the cost of capital − which represents the true benefit of investing in the company. On this basis the performance gap between Manyhands and Lightwork is wider still. Manyhands' superprofit is 15% of capital whereas Lightwork's is 10%. Assuming that the shareholders' own cost of borrowing is also 5% then Manyhands' shareholders receive £7.5 of superprofits for each £2.5 of interest paid on their borrowings − a return of three times on outlays. However, Lightwork's shareholders receive £10 of superprofit for each £5 of interest paid − a smaller return of two times on outlays.

The 'economy-wide' perspective

The effect of all this on the economy as a whole depends, in large measure, upon the sophistication of the stock market. In a longer term strategic sense Lightwork may be able to exploit its better margins to maintain a sustainable advantage, and this may be reflected in the relative stock market ratings of the two companies. However, if the stock market focuses primarily on short-term shareholder returns then the effect will be to force Lightwork's management to adopt the productive processes of Manyhands in order to match Manyhands' return on capital. Suppose that as a result, Lightwork's financial statements in a future time period became equivalent to those of Manyhands and that Lightwork and Manyhands are the economy's only two producers, so that:

	Manyhands £	Lightwork £	Economy wide £
Shareholders' funds	50	50	100
Fixed assets	50	50	100
Turnover	30	30	60
Labour costs	(10)	(10)	(20)
Materials	(5)	(5)	(10)
Depreciation	(5)	(5)	(10)
Operating profit	10	10	20
Dividends	10	10	20
Retained profit	0	0	0
Notional interest	2.5	2.5	5
Superprofit	7.5	7.5	15
	10	10	20

It is instructive to compare the economy-wide performance before and after any such change in Lightwork's production processes. The comparative 'total' figures for the economy as a whole are:

	Before £	After £
Shareholders' funds	150	100
Fixed assets	150	100
Turnover	60	60
Labour costs	(13)	(20)
Materials	(7)	(10)
Depreciation	(15)	(10)
Operating profit	25	20
Notional interest	7.5	5
Superprofit	17.5	15

Return on capital improves from 25/150 (16.7%) to 20/100 (20%), thus pleasing the financial community. However, in terms of its use of physical resources the economy has become less efficient. Before the change the economy absorbed £35 of physical resources (£13 labour, £7 materials and £15 depreciation) to create £60 of product. After the change the physical resources consumed increases by £5 to £40. Moreover, this increase in the use of physical resources is not fully compensated by savings in the use of capital since the notional interest charge – the opportunity cost of capital – only falls by £2.5 from £7.5 to £5.

The lesson to be learned is that when two companies are producing directly competitive products, the capitalist system is optimal from the perspective of capital but not necessarily from an economy-wide perspective. From the latter perspective performance measures should relate profit to all resources consumed – physical as well as financial. Such an analysis can be applied to the 199X results of Manyhands and Lightwork and it reveals that Lightwork's productivity during 199X has been superior to that of Manyhands. The analysis is:

		Manyhands £	Lightwork £
Accounting profit		10	15
Resources consumed:			
Labour	10		3
Materials	5		2
Depreciation	5		10
		20	15
Accounting profit as % of resources consumed		50%	100%

This shows Lightwork's productivity as double that of Manyhands.

A more complete picture of the relative productivities of the two companies during 199X is obtained by recognizing notional interest. Such a detailed productivity analysis would be as follows:

	Manyhands	Lightwork
Superprofit	£7.5	£10
As a percentage of:		
1 Labour	75%	333%
2 Materials	150%	500%
3 Depreciation	150%	100%
4 Notional interest	300%	200%
5 Overall costs	33%	50%

Lightwork is the more efficient in terms of its use of labour (line 1), materials (line 2) and overall costs (line 5). Manyhands is the more efficient in terms of its use of fixed assets (line 3) and capital (line 4). In effect Manyhands has made itself efficient in terms of capital by substituting labour for capital.

It is this profitability analysis − relating superprofit to overall costs (financial and physical) − which reveals that Lightwork is the more efficient in its overall use of resources and that productive efficiency is best served through Manyhands adopting Lightwork's productive methods and not the reverse. It is important to recognize the potential conflict between such productive efficiency − using the least resources to create a given output − and indicators of financial capital efficiency such as return on capital. Whereas financial efficiency is important to shareholders, productive efficiency is important to the performance of the economy as a whole and hence in the long term to the well-being of all interest groups.

The importance of shareholders as an interest group and hence financial efficiency as a performance indicator, derives from the fact that, legally, company directors are appointed by shareholders and that superprofits revert to shareholders. In a different scenario − for example, if all finance was bank finance on which interest was paid but superprofits reverted to labour − then other indicators (for example superprofits as a percentage of labour) would assume importance. Such an indicator should in any case assume importance in service industries where the key resource being used is highly skilled labour.

Service companies vs. manufacturing companies

It has been shown that Manyhands achieves a higher return on capital than Lightwork by substituting labour for capital investment. However, its return on labour is far lower than that achieved by Lightwork. The distortion which can be caused through excessive concentration on capital returns when deciding upon the appropriate productive process for a given product (as illustrated in the Manyhands vs. Lightwork example) is mirrored on a bigger scale in the performance comparisons of capital intensive manufacturing industry as against skilled labour intensive service industry. At the economy-wide level, excessive concentration on capital returns as *the* performance measure could well favour the service sector which has a smaller capital base thus, potentially at least, promoting de-industrialization.

THE CHAIN OF PRODUCTION

This next section examines the effect which the position in the chain of production has on the profitability ratios.

Processes A and B

Suppose Lightwork's production requires two different processes – A and B. Process A manufactures the key components whereas process B assembles the finished product. Process B must be carried out after process A. However, the two processes are identical in terms of the value which they add to the product. The financial statements of the separate processes for 199X were as follows:

	Process A £	Process B £
Shareholders' funds	50	50
Fixed assets	50	50
Turnover	15	30
Labour costs	(1.5)	(1.5)
Materials	(1)	(16)
Depreciation	(5)	(5)
Operating profit	7.5	7.5
Dividends	7.5	7.5
Retained profit	0	0
Notional interest	2.5	2.5
Superprofit	5	5
	7.5	7.5

The above financial statements assume that A passes its output to B at a notional transfer value of £15 based on the market value of the manufactured components produced by A.

Required:

Discuss how process A and process B have performed during 199X from the point of view of:

1 the shareholders;

2 the economy as a whole.

Discussion of process A and process B

Shareholder perspectives

The return on capital is 15% for both process A and for process B, being a 5% notional interest and a 10% return on capital in the form of 'superprofits'. From a shareholder perspective, therefore, there is nothing to choose between the two processes.

Economy-wide perspectives

An operational profitability analysis of the two sets of financial statements (for process A and process B) would suggest that B was the less efficient. Its operating profit as a percentage of turnover is 25% (7.5/30) as against 50% (7.5/15) for A. Profit as a percentage of costs is 33% (7.5/22.5) for B as against 100% (7.5/7.5) for A.

However, these figures are misleading because A and B's activities are *cooperative* rather than *competitive*. A 'sells' its output to B which then performs further work on that product before it is sold to the public. In such circumstances it is necessary to relate B's profit to the *additional* or *marginal* costs added to the product through B's activities. The marginal costs incurred by B are:

	£
Labour	1.5
Materials	1
Depreciation	5
Notional interest	2.5
	10.0

Of process B's material costs of £16, £15 represents purchases from A and only £1 represents additional materials added by B.

A detailed profitability analysis for A and B based on marginal costs is:

	A	*B*
Superprofit	£5	£5
As a percentage of:		
1 Labour	333%	333%
2 Materials	500%	500%
3 Depreciation	100%	100%
4 Notional interest	200%	200%
5 Overall costs	50%	50%

These figures are identical to those of Lightwork as a whole in 199X, and they show the two processes as being equally efficient. The important point to remember is that the cooperative nature of A and B's activities requires that their performances be judged on profitability related to *marginal* costs. The lower operating profit/turnover percentage for process B reflects its position in the productive chain rather than any inherent inefficiency.

THE DEMERGER

The way Lightwork has perfected its process A for the manufacture of key components represents a major advance on previous technology. It is felt by the Lightwork board that the value of this process would best be released for the Lightwork shareholders by establishing process A and process B as two separately quoted companies – Lightwork A and Lightwork B. This is a demerger with Lightwork's original shareholders being allocated shares in both companies. The demerger takes effect at the beginning of 199X + 1. Lightwork A's shares immediately outperform Lightwork B's shares on the stock market due to its better prospects, even though in 199X process A and B showed identical profitability. During each of the four years 199X + 1 to 199X + 4 the financial results of the two companies are as follows:

	Lightwork A	Lightwork B
	£	£
Shareholders' funds	50	50
Fixed assets	50	50
Turnover	15	30
Labour costs	(1.5)	(1.5)
Materials	(1)	(16)
Depreciation	(5)	(5)
Operating profit	7.5	7.5
Dividends	7.5	7.5
Retained profit	0	0
Notional interest	2.5	2.5
Superprofit	5	5
	7.5	7.5

Intercompany sales from A to B remain at £15. The results reveal that the demerger has not released its intended benefits. Lightwork B's performance has not suffered and has matched that of process B in 199X. However, Lightwork A has not been able to increase its volume of business or its margins on the strength of its innovative manufacturing process. Lightwork A's business has remained with Lightwork B. By the end of 199X + 4, Lightwork A's management is under pressure for not realizing the intended benefits of the demerger. Lightwork A's share price has slipped back. Moreover, there are rumours of a takeover bid for Lightwork B from Manyhands, causing Lightwork B's share price to move ahead. Such a takeover would place A's principal customer in the 'hands' of a major competitor. Lightwork A decides to make a pre-emptive takeover bid for Lightwork B. It is a cash offer and this is accepted by B's board and shareholders.

THE TAKEOVER

Suppose that at the beginning of 199X + 5 Lightwork A buys Lightwork B at a valuation of 20 times Lightwork B's profits of £7.5. It therefore pays £150 for B's shares being:

£	
50	fixed assets
100	goodwill, being 20 times superprofits
150	

Goodwill equals the difference between the £150 paid for B's shares and the £50 book value of B's assets.

To finance the purchase of B's shares, Lightwork A issues £150 worth of shares to its existing shareholders for cash.

Required:

Discuss the impact which the takeover would have on Lightwork B's performance measures for 199X + 5 from the point of view of:

1 B's new shareholders
2 the economy as a whole.

Assuming:

The takeover makes no difference in 199X + 5 to the efficiency of Lightwork A or B's productive processes or to the volumes or margins of the businesses which remain as per previous years.

Discussion: impact of the takeover on the performance measures

Shareholder perspectives

From the point of view of B's new shareholders they have invested £150 in purchasing Lightwork B on which they receive profits of £7.5. This covers the notional interest of 5% on the £150 invested but gives no superprofits. The return on investment is 5% (7.5/150). Lightwork A's shareholders, therefore, have two investments:

1 a direct investment of £50 in the old Lightwork A which earns a return of 15%, and

2 an indirect investment of £150 in Lightwork B which earns a return of 5%.

The overall return is 7.5%, being £15 profit on £200 invested. From a shareholder perspective financial statements (called consolidated financial statements) which combine the two investments into a single set of financial statements should reflect the combined effect of these two investments and a return on capital of 7.5%. There are a number of ways in which such consolidated financial statements can be produced. One possibility is shown in Exhibit 6.1.

Full understanding of the consolidation process is difficult and outside the scope of this book. However, some appreciation may be gained by commenting on the five consolidation adjustments shown in column 3 of Exhibit 6.1. The first adjustment of £150 represents the issue of £150 share capital by Lightwork A to its existing shareholders. The second adjustment of (£50) represents the extinction of Lightwork B's share capital when its shares are purchased by Lightwork A. The third adjustment of £100 recognizes the purchase by Lightwork A of Lightwork B's goodwill for £100. The fourth adjustment of (£15) recognizes that the £15 sales of Lightwork A to Lightwork B now take place within the Lightwork group of companies and cannot be regarded as external sales of the Lightwork group. Similarly the final adjustment of £15 to materials purchases recognizes that £15 of Lightwork B's materials purchases come from Lightwork A and also therefore cannot be regarded as external purchases of the Lightwork group. Only external sales and materials purchases (i.e. sales and materials purchases to/from non-group companies) are shown in the group's consolidated financial statements. The consolidated figures in column 4 of Exhibit 6.1 are arrived at by cross adding columns 1 to 3, with the exception of notional interest and superprofit. The consolidated notional interest of £10 is arrived at by taking 5% of the consolidated shareholders' funds of £200. The consolidated superprofits of £5 is arrived at by subtracting the consolidated notional interest from the consolidated operating profit.

The consolidated financial statements show the appropriate overall return on investment of 7.5% (15/200) being 15% on £50 invested in A and

LIGHTWORK GROUP (LIGHTWORK A AND LIGHTWORK B)
Consolidated financial statements for 199X + 5

	Lightwork A £	Lightwork B £	Consolidation adjustments £	Consolidated figures £
Shareholders' funds	50	50	150 (50)	200
Fixed assets	50	50		100
Goodwill			100	100
Turnover	15	30	(15)	30
Labour costs	(1.5)	(1.5)		(3)
Materials	(1)	(16)	15	(2)
Depreciation	(5)	(5)	—	(10)
Operating profit	7.5	7.5		15
Dividends	7.5	7.5	—	15
Retained profit	0	0		0
Notional interest	2.5	2.5		10
Superprofits	5	5	—	5
	7.5	7.5	—	15

Exhibit 6.1

5% on the £150 invested in B. However, as discussed in the next section, such consolidated financial statements do not comply with the accounting standard in respect of goodwill.

Treatment of goodwill

Accounting Standard 22 prohibits the permanent retention of goodwill in the balance sheet and states that it should normally be immediately written off against shareholders' funds. If the standard were followed the balance sheet would show:

	£
Shareholders' funds	100
Fixed assets	100

Profits are unchanged at £15. Such a set of financial statements show a return on capital of 15% – far higher than the actual rates being achieved.

If an ability to reflect performance for *shareholders* is to be a test of an accounting standard, then this standard is a dismal failure! From the viewpoint of shareholders, performance of their investment has declined as a result of the takeover, but this is not reflected by the returns on capital shown in financial statements which follow SSAP 22. Lightwork management, however, will be keen to follow SSAP 22 since they will not want any fall in shareholder returns, as a result of the takeover, to be apparent.

Accounting Standard 22 permits an alternative to the immediate write-off of goodwill. It is that goodwill may be written off against profit over its expected useful life. However, the determination of the useful life of goodwill is to say the least problematic. In our example £100 has been paid for goodwill on the expectation that it will earn £5 superprofits indefinitely. If goodwill were written off over, say, five years and yet the anticipated superprofits continued, then capital returns would once again be distorted.

Economy-wide perspectives

From an economy-wide perspective the productive efficiency of the use of resources remains the same before and after the takeover. Lightwork has now gone full circle, starting life as a single entity, splitting into two (Lightwork A and B) at the start of $199X + 1$ and reunifying at the beginning of $199X + 5$ through the takeover. In our case study these corporate changes have left the processes, products, margins and volumes of business unaffected. From an economy-wide perspective nothing has changed from $199X$ to $199X + 5$.

Productivity is best measured by the ratio of profit to total resources consumed rather than by return on capital invested. Based on operational profit the consolidated accounts of Lightwork show such productivity at $15/15 = 100\%$ and this is equivalent to before the takeover and indeed is equivalent to Lightwork's profit to resources consumed for $199X$ (also $15/15$).

Care needs to be taken in interpreting the effect of the takeover on superprofits. Before the takeover Lightwork A and B both earn superprofits of £5 each, giving combined superprofits of £10. After the takeover Lightwork's (consolidated) superprofits (Exhibit 6.1) are £5. Thus, based on superprofits, there appears to be a decline in (economy-wide) performance due to the takeover. This, however, is deceptive. What has happened is that A's shareholders have purchased the stream of £5 per annum superprofits generated by B from B's shareholders for £100. The effect of this in the consolidated accounts has been to convert B's superprofits of £5 into £5 of notional interest for A's shareholders on their (indirect) £100 goodwill investment. One group of shareholders (A's) has effectively purchased

E

a stream of superprofits from another group of shareholders (B's). This, however, is of no consequence to the economy as a whole.

A more appropriate economy-wide (as opposed to shareholder) perspective is gained by following SSAP 22 and writing off goodwill against shareholders' funds in the consolidated accounts which then show:

	£
Shareholders' funds	100
Fixed assets	100
Turnover	30
Labour costs	(3)
Materials	(2)
Depreciation	(10)
Operating profit	15
Notional interest	5
Superprofit	10

Consolidated superprofits are then restored to £10 since notional interest reduces to £5, being based on the reduced shareholders' funds. This is equivalent to the combined superprofits achieved by both Lightwork A and Lightwork B before the takeover.

It has previously been remarked that SSAP 22 is unable to reflect performance from a shareholder point of view. However, it may provide a reflection of performance from an economy-wide perspective. Total superprofits are seen to be unmoved by the takeover, reflecting the fact that the takeover has so far proved to be of no consequence to the 'real' economy in terms of volumes, costs or value added.

Goodwill as a measure of inefficiency

There is further important economy-wide significance to goodwill. Lightwork A preferred to buy Lightwork B rather than establish its own plant performing B's processes and competing with B. This presumably is because B has an established plant with its own management and worker skills and customer base, and possibly with its own brands which may have been built up with advertising. The amount which Lightwork A is prepared to spend, over and above the cost of B's plant, is called goodwill (£100 in our example). Clearly if Lightwork A were to set up in competition to B it must feel that it would have to spend at least £100 over and above the cost of the plant in order to get established and achieve a market share equal to B's. Otherwise it would not make sense to pay £100 for B's goodwill. There is, in effect, an entry barrier of at least £100 for anyone entering Lightwork B's market. Thus the amounts spent on goodwill are market valuations of entry barriers and since entry barriers are generally associated with market inefficiency/uncontestability then the value of goodwill possessed by firms in the economy can be taken as *one* measure of that economy's 'entry barrier' inefficiency.

Goodwill epitomizes the difference between the interests of the shareholders and the economy-wide perspective. From the latter point of view it represents an (undesirable) entry barrier. For the shareholders, however, it represents the company's success in increasing its value over and above the value of its tangible assets. It is the opportunity to build up goodwill which provides the incentive to invest.

SUMMARY

The two key ratios to look at for an initial assessment of a business's performance are return on capital and return on resources consumed. Greater efficiency – allocative or productive – will, other things being equal, improve both returns. However, the two returns are not necessarily in harmony with each other. Return on capital reflects the capital intensity of the business. Hence two companies which provide equal returns on resources consumed can have different returns on capital if one has higher capital requirements than the other. The Manyhands versus Lightwork case shows that a business can improve its return on capital by moving to less capital intensive methods or activities but this does not necessarily benefit the economy as a whole. Neither does it necessarily help the strategic positioning of the company if it leads to lower margins or volumes. Too much emphasis on return on capital as *the* measure of performance would be detrimental to capital intensive businesses.

Return on resources consumed is the more reliable measure of the performance of a business over time from an economy-wide perspective. As shown by the Lightwork A and B case, it is, however, influenced by the stage in the production process at which the business operates. Two companies giving the same return on capital can exhibit different returns on resources consumed with that operating at the earlier stage of production showing the greater return. Thus a company can improve its returns by concentrating on the earlier stages of production. This does not help the performance of the economy as a whole if the later stages of production are essential in order to complete the product. Neither does this necessarily help the strategic positioning of the company if control of the later stages of production leads to control of key functions such as marketing or design of the finished product.

Return on capital is also influenced by takeover activity. The takeover case study shows that if goodwill arising on the takeover is written off immediately against shareholders' funds then return on capital will, from a shareholder perspective, be distorted. If goodwill is written off over an arbitrary number of years, then return on capital is distorted from both a shareholder and economy-wide perspective. If goodwill is not written off, then return on capital is distorted from an economy-wide perspective. The policy implication is that there should be two separate treatments of the goodwill to satisfy both shareholder and economy-wide perspectives. Although takeovers can lead to either favourable or unfavourable changes in operational performance, much of the motivation for takeover (or demerger) activity is strategic. Takeovers can secure new markets, suppliers, customers or human resources, to name just a few possible motives. It is therefore important that takeover activity is judged not only on profitability measures in the short term but also with regard to longer-term opportunities. In a takeover the acquisition or creation of a sustainable strategic advantage usually involves an inducement to the shareholders of the target company. This is the essence of purchased goodwill. The question to be addressed by the stock-market (a shareholder perspective) is whether or not the price paid for this strategic advance represents good value in terms of its likely eventual profit generation.

SELF-STUDY EXERCISE 6.1

Bliss and Sunstroke

On 1 January 19X2 the Bliss Corporation, a leading brewer, purchased the international hotel group, Sunstroke. Sunstroke's assets and liabilities were as follows:

	£
Fixed assets (hotels)	150
Net current assets	20
	170
Shareholders' funds	170

Sunstroke was making annual profits of £25. Bliss paid £250 for the share capital of Sunstroke. At the takeover date Bliss's balance sheet was summarized as follows:

	£
Fixed assets (brewery)	200
Net current assets	50
	250
Shareholders' funds	250

Bliss had for some years been making annual profits of £25. Bliss financed the takeover by taking out a long-term loan of £250 at a 10% interest rate. During 19X2 the takeover made no difference to the volumes, prices, margins or productive efficiency of either the hotel or brewing business. There is no trading between Bliss and Sunstroke.

Required:

1 Prepare the consolidated accounts for the Bliss/Sunstroke group for 19X2 showing fixed assets, net current assets, loan, shareholder funds and annual profit. Assume (a) goodwill is written off against shareholders' funds, and (b) all annual profits are paid as dividends for the year.

2 Compare the return on total assets (ROTA) for the Sunstroke and Bliss businesses taken together before the takeover versus after the takeover.

3 Compare the return on shareholders' funds (ROSF) for the Bliss shareholders before and after the takeover. Provide a brief explanation for any change.

4 During 19X3 the two businesses remain unchanged except that there is a change in the interest rate payable on the loan. The rate is increased to 15%. Compare the ROTA and ROSF for 19X3 with the equivalent in 19X2. What is the significance of the increased interest rate from (a) a shareholder perspective, and (b) an economy-wide perspective?

5 At 1 January 19X4, the group directors decide to sell the hotel properties of Sunstroke to a property company for £250 and to lease them back for £40 per annum. The £250 cash receipt is used to pay back the loan. Prepare the consolidated accounts for 19X4. Assume that profits other than those arising from property sales are paid as dividends.

6 Assume that apart from the property sales, business conditions and performance in 19X5 are identical to 19X4. Prepare ROTA and ROSF for 19X5, compare with 19X3 and provide a brief explanation for any change. Assume that annual profits continue to be paid as dividends.

CHAPTER 7

Holding and operating activities

INTRODUCTION

Any business which holds its own stock or owns rather than rents its assets is actually involved in two distinct activities – holding and operating. This chapter explores the significance of this distinction in the context of Mark Tips Limited, a simple taxi business. The crucial point about Mark Tips's business is that not only are its assets marketable but such assets can be obtained by either rental or purchase. It will be shown that this highly market-oriented environment allows holding gains or losses to be measured separately from operations. The separate identification of gains from holding and operating activities comes after an introduction to the alternative ways in which profit may be measured for Mark Tips's business as a whole.

THE MARK TIPS CASE STUDY

Mark Tips runs a taxi business. He has a car which serves as the taxi and a taxi licence issued by the local authority. The licence runs indefinitely provided the various conditions are met. The number of licences is controlled by the local authority but there is a market for the taxi licence which may be sold by the existing licensee to a new entrant with council approval.

At the beginning and end of 199X the (realizable) market values of the car and licence are as follows:

	Market value at 1.1.9X	Market value at 31.12.9X
Taxi licence	£1,400	£1,200
Car	480	240

There are no transaction costs associated with the transfer of a licence. Hence the realizable value (selling price) of a licence equals its replacement (purchase) cost. However, the realizable value of the taxi represents the price Mark Tips could obtain by selling to a dealer. The dealer then normally adds a mark-up of 25%. Hence the replacement cost of a second-hand taxi is 25% higher than its realizable value.

Mark Tips's business started on 1.1.9X − 2. £100 share capital was used to pay for formation costs. Thereafter the business has been financed by a bank overdraft on which interest is payable at 15% per annum. At 1.1.9X − 2 the overdraft was £3,500 being created by the purchase of the taxi and licence. Since 1.1.9X − 2 the net cash inflow after allowing for interest and dividends has been £700 and so at 1.1.9X the overdraft stands at £2,800.

During 199X his net cash inflow from operations (before interest) was £3,000. For convenience, it is assumed that this cash inflow takes place on the last day of the year. The assets were both purchased two years before the start of 199X. The licence cost £1,500. The car cost £2,000 and has an expected life of five years. Mark Tips expects to replace the taxi on 1.1.9X + 3 with a new taxi costing £2,000. Mark Tips is a cash business and there are no year end debtors or creditors.

The fall in value of the car during 199X is due to wear and tear and its market value represents its value in an alternative use as a private car. The fall in value of the licence during 199X reflects the fact that during 199X the local authority announced its intention to issue a significant number of new taxi licences. Its fall thus reflects less favourable prospects for Mr Tips's business.

During the year 199X +1 the local authority renounces its intention of issuing any additional taxi licences. As a result the market value of Mr Tips's licence is enhanced. Details of value changes during 199X + 1 are as follows:

	Market value at 1.1.19X + 1	Market value at 31.12.9X + 1
Taxi licence	£1,200	£1,800
Car	240	Nil

In 199X + 1 the net cash inflow from operations remained at £3,000. No dividends are paid during 199X or 199X + 1.

Alternative profit calculations

Mark Tips's profits during 199X and 199X + 1 can be calculated on at least four different bases, namely:

1 historical cost (HC);

2 future (replacement) cost (FC);

3 deprival value (DV);

4 realizable value (RV).

A crucial difference between each of the four is the way depreciation is treated. Exhibit 7.1 gives the profit figures under each basis in 199X and 199X + 1.

Depreciation under historical cost

Under historical cost, fixed assets with a *finite* useful life such as the taxi should, according to SSAP 12, be depreciated on a basis which allocates cost as fairly as possible over the periods expected to benefit from the use of the asset. If the level of business activity is variable then it could be argued that those accounting periods with higher activity levels benefit more and should bear a correspondingly higher depreciation charge. At the end of 199X it is expected that activity will drop in future due to the anticipated issue of new licences. There might therefore be an argument for recognizing this expectation in calculating the depreciation charge for 199X. However, the case specifies that depreciation is charged on a straight line basis and hence the assumption is that each period during the life of the taxi benefits equally. This would be a common assumption in practice. The car cost £2,000 and has an expected life of five years. Under straight line depreciation this results in a charge of £400 for 199X and 199X + 1. The licence has an *infinite* life subject to any change in the regulatory process for taxis. Under HC there is no requirement to charge depreciation for assets with an infinite life. In effect spreading the cost over an infinite period generates an annual depreciation of zero.

Depreciation under future replacement cost

Under future replacement cost, depreciation is charged over the life of an asset with a view to providing an amount capable of paying for a replacement. In the case, prices of new cars are constant and therefore the total amount required as the depreciation charge over the life of the taxi is £2,000 (equivalent to the cost of a replacement). This could be generated by charging the future replacement cost equally over the five years to give an annual charge of £400. Once again the principle of equal allocation applies and assumes that each period benefits equally from use of the car. It is assumed that the car will be retained for five years and replaced at the end of its useful life.

In our question historical cost and replacement cost of new taxis are the same since new car prices are constant. It follows that historic cost and

(a) *Profit for year 199X*

	Historical cost	Future replacement cost	Deprival value	Realizable income
	£	£	£	£
Operations	3,000	3,000	3,000	3,000
Depreciation:				
licence			(200)	(200)
car	(400)	(400)	(300)	(240)
	2,600	2,600	2,500	2,560
Interest*	420	420	420	420
Net profit	2,180	2,180	2,080	2,140

Operating cash flow of £3,000 less interest of £420 reduces the overdraft by £2,580 to £220 at 1.1.9X + 1.

(b) *Profit for year 199X + 1*

	Historical cost	Future replacement cost	Deprival value	Realizable income
	£	£	£	£
Operations	3,000	3,000	3,000	3,000
Depreciation:				
licence			600	600
car	(400)	(400)	(300)	(240)
	2,600	2,600	3,300	3,360
Interest*	33	33	33	33
Net profit	2,567	2,567	3,267	3,327

* 15% of the opening bank overdraft.

Exhibit 7.1 Mark Tips's results

replacement cost depreciation are the same. The taxi licence has an infinite life and does not therefore need replacement. Hence under future replacement cost accounting there is no need to provide for a replacement licence and no depreciation charge is necessary.

Depreciation under deprival value

The deprival value of an asset to Mark Tips is what he would lose if he were suddenly 'deprived' of the asset. Mark Tips is generating healthy operating cash flows and if he were suddenly deprived of the assets generating these cash flows it would be well worth his while to reinstate those assets by purchasing replacements. At any point in time the deprival value of the licence is what it would cost to purchase a replacement licence and the deprival value of the car is what it would cost to purchase a replacement car of equivalent age and condition. In most circumstances the deprival value of an asset is the *current* replacement cost of the asset. For deprival value accounting, depreciation is based upon movements in the deprival value of the assets. Thus depreciation of the car in 199X is the fall in its current replacement market value from £600 (480 + 25%) to £300 (240 + 25%) and similarly 199X +1 depreciation is the fall from £300 to zero. The taxi licence depreciates from £1,400 to £1,200 in 199X and appreciates (reverse depreciation) in 199X + 1 from £1,200 to £1,800.

Depreciation under realizable value

The realizable value of an asset is its net sale proceeds on the basis of an orderly disposal. There are no selling costs associated with the licence but there are selling costs for the car. Mr Tips could dispose of his car to a dealer who would add 25% to cover his expenses. This means that if Mr Tips wants to sell his car he will receive 20% less than what it would cost to buy the car from the dealer. Net realizable value is 20% less than market replacement value. For realizable value accounting, depreciation is based upon movements in realizable value of the assets. Thus depreciation of the car in 199X is the fall in its realizable value from £480 to £240. Similarly depreciation of the car in 199X + 1 is the fall from £240 to zero. The taxi licence depreciates from £1,400 to £1,200 in 199X and appreciates in 199X + 1 from £1,200 to £1,800.

Discussion of the historical cost results

Exhibit 7.1 shows that the historical cost profits (before interest) for 199X and 199X + 1 remain constant at £2,600 per annum. This reflects the constancy of the operating performance of Mark Tips's business during these two years. Thus historical cost profits are associated with operating activities. They do not reflect gains or losses on holding the taxi or the licence as reflected by changes in the market value of these assets. It is, however, possible to present changes in such market prices alongside historical cost profits as shown in Exhibit 7.2.

In comparing performances between 199X and 199X +1, the equivalent profit figures of £2,600 (Exhibit 7.2) reflect the fact that the underlying productivity of operations and market conditions have remained constant

---

Mark Tips 199X results

HC profit before interest
(repeatable assuming continuation of market conditions)   £2,600

Effect of future issue of licences on market value of the taxi
licence   £(200)

The equivalent statement for 199X + 1 would be:

Mark Tips 199X + 1 results

HC profit before interest
(repeatable assuming continuation of market conditions)   £2,600

Effect of withdrawal of notice to issue new licences on the
market value of the taxi licence   £600

Exhibit 7.2 Enhancing the HC results

between the two years. The movement on the taxi licence (199X = £(200), 199X + 1 = £600) reflects the changing outlook for the future. In a pure HC framework these movements are not regarded as profits or losses. However, although not included in the profit statement they should be disclosed and properly explained elsewhere in the financial statements. In practice, pure historical cost accounting is modified so that any permanent diminution in the value of an asset is charged against HC profit. Thus in 199X (modified) HC profit is reduced to £2,400 to reflect what is thought at that time to be a permanent drop in the value of the licence. Such a modification does not help interpretation of the profit figure which is now a combination of two quite different elements – current operations and the outlook for the future.

It is possible to regard the holding of the taxi licence and the operation of the taxi as different business units. For example, if a suitably interested party could be found, Tips could either:

1 hold the licence but allow someone else to run the taxi for an appropriate rental, or
2 sell the licence on the understanding that he (Tips) continued to operate the taxi, whilst paying an appropriate rental to the licence holder.

Since either 'holding the licence' or 'operating the taxi' could be disposed of, they can properly be regarded as different businesses. The two businesses do not altogether spread Mark Tips's business risk since a worsening of current market conditions for taxi operations may also cause the value of the taxi licence to fall. There might therefore be something to be said for Tips disposing of one of the businesses, even if it is doing well, and reinvesting the proceeds in a different business altogether as an exercise in risk spreading. The important point to note is that the presentation of Mark Tips's results suggested in Exhibit 7.2 goes some way towards highlighting separately the performance of the two business units. The performance of taxi operations is shown in pure HC profit terms and the performance of holding the taxi licence is in terms of realizable income. What is missing is any recognition of the rental which would have to be paid by the taxi operator to the licence holder should the two businesses be under separate ownership.

The car and the taxi licence

There is an important distinction between market prices which *influence* and those which are *influenced by* the prospects for a business. In our example the market price of the car is largely determined by its alternative use as a private vehicle. The market price is scarcely influenced by the prospects for the taxi industry. However, the taxi business needs to replace its cars. Thus, the prospects for the taxi industry are influenced by the price of cars. Car prices *influence* the prospects of a taxi business which uses cars.

An existing taxi business does not need to replace its licence and therefore the price of the licence, once purchased, no longer influences the prospects for the business (as opposed to the prospects for the proprietor who may wish to sell the licence). However, the market value of the licence is heavily *influenced by* the prospects for that taxi business. Other examples of prices influenced by a business's prospects are its goodwill and its share price.

The distinction between influencing and being influenced is a crucial one for financial statements. Generally speaking financial statements should show separately an 'operating profit' derived from prices which influence the business's prospects rather than prices which are influenced by the business's prospects. The idea is that such an operating profit can then help the investor to assess business prospects which in turn determine, where applicable, the value of licences, goodwill and the company's share price. It follows that the value of the licence, goodwill or share price should not influence the calculation of 'operating profit'. This is the principle being observed in the case of pure historical cost, keeping licence value changes out of the calculation of profit from operations.

Such an approach ties 'profits' as a measure of operating performance since 'profit' does not include changes in corporate wealth.

Future replacement cost

The crucial distinction between historical cost and future replacement cost is that historical cost looks backwards to the original cost of purchase whereas future replacement cost looks forwards to the expected cost of replacing the existing assets at the time of replacement. One system is historical and the other futuristic and neither is concerned with *current* costs or values. As a result historical cost and future replacement cost are more concerned with profit or income measurement than they are with the balance sheet. In historical cost the balance sheet assets represent unrecovered past cash outlays, and in future replacement cost balance sheet assets represent future cash outlays yet to be provided for. These balance sheet amounts are not easy for the uninitiated reader of financial statements to comprehend.

In Mark Tips's case the price of new cars is remaining constant. It follows that both historical cost and anticipated replacement cost of the taxi is £2,000 and that therefore the figures appearing in the financial statements under the two systems are the same. However, the meanings attributable to the two sets of figures are quite different. It is the replacement cost profits which are more conservative in the longer run assuming that Tips remains in the taxi business and replacement costs tend to rise.

Deprival value

Deprival value profit is £2,500 for 199X and £3,300 for 199X + 1. Unlike historical and future replacement cost profits using straight line depreciation this does not reflect the consistency of productivity and market conditions during the two years as evidenced by the consistency of operating cash flows. This consistency is reflected in the historical and future replacement cost profits. Under both deprival value and realizable value accounting the emphasis is on the balance sheet which gives in each case *current* values of the assets and is therefore more understandable to the uninitiated reader of the financial statements. In the case of deprival value Mark Tips's balance sheet shows *current* entry costs and in the case of realizable value it is *current* exit values. In the case of deprival value and realizable value it is the income figures, with depreciation based upon movements in deprival value and realizable value, which are harder to interpret.

From the point of view of the firm deprival value may be thought to be a notional concept since a firm does not expect to be suddenly and involuntarily deprived of its assets unless there is a catastrophe in which case deprival value is clearly relevant for insurance purposes. Deprival value makes more sense when looked at from the point of view of firms who have stayed out of the taxi business. Can they justify the decision to stay out? By staying out during 199X, for instance, a firm would have missed £3,000 of cash from operations and it would cost £1,500 to enter the business at the end of the year as opposed to £2,000 at the beginning – a net opportunity foregone of £2,500, being the deprival value income before interest of Mark Tips for 199X. Delaying the entry for one year would also save £300 in interest (15% of £2,000), so that the net opportunity foregone is worth £2,200.

Realizable value

As explained already, a period's *deprival* value income for Mark Tips and other taxi firms allows those firms who have decided *not* to enter the taxi business during that period to monitor the success of their decision. Mark Tips's realizable value income for that period allows him to monitor the success of his decision to stay in the taxi business. Whenever there are well developed markets for a company's assets, that company can dispose of its assets at one point in time and buy back equivalent assets later. For example, if Mark Tips had disposed of the car *and* taxi licence at the beginning of 199X and bought them back at the end of that year, he would have foregone a wealth increase of £2,560, being the lost realizable income excluding interest. This figure needs to be adjusted by the £282 saving in interest charges which could be achieved by selling the assets at the beginning of the year for £1,880 and using the proceeds to reduce the overdraft. Re-entry costs must also be taken into account and at the end of 199X these amount to 25% of £240 = £60, being the car dealer's gross profit. Finally, costs of disruption and non-continuity might be significant and should also be considered when assessing the wisdom of 'stay' versus 'get out/buy back' decisions.

Thus the quantifiable cost of a decision to leave the taxi business for 199X is as follows:

	£
Realizable income before interest	2,560
Interest saving	(282)
Re-entry costs	60
	2,338

This calculation suggests that it was well worthwhile for Mark Tips to stay in the taxi business during 199X.

HOLDING VS. OPERATING ACTIVITIES

It should be noted that it is staying in the whole business which has been monitored so far. The opportunity to dispose of a business unit such as (1) operating the taxi, (2) holding the taxi or (3) holding the licence needs to be monitored separately by looking at their individual realizable incomes. Assuming a market rental of £500 per annum can be established for use of the licence, and £1,000 per annum for use of the taxi, realizable incomes before considering the effects of interest are as follows:

	Operating the taxi £	Holding the taxi £	Holding the licence £	Whole business £
199X	1,500	760	300	2,560
199X + 1	1,500	760	1,100	3,360

The calculation of these results can be illustrated by reference to 199X. Operating profit of £1,500 is the operating cash flow of £3,000 less rental for the taxi (£1,000) and for the licence (£500). The holding gain for the taxi is rental income (£1,000) less depreciation on a realizable income basis (£240). The holding gain for the licence is rental income (£500) less fall in value (£200).

The treatment of interest

It is now necessary to consider the position of interest charges with regard to holding and operating activities. It is known that the bank overdraft was created by the purchase of the taxi (£2,000) and the licence (£1,500) and is reduced each year by operating cash flows.

Let us suppose that the cash history of the two holding activities is as shown in Exhibit 7.3.

The interest apportioned to operating activities during 199X and 199X +1 is then the difference between the interest on taxi and licence holding activities taken together, and the actual interest charges for Mark Tips's business as a whole. In 199X this is £420 − (74 + 136) = £210 and in 199X + 1 it is £33 − (81 − 64) = £16. This allocation assumes that dividends have been paid in past years out of operating cash flows and do not therefore affect the bank balances attributable to taxi holding and licence holding activities.

	Taxi holding £	Licence holding £
199X – 2		
Original investment	(2,000)	(1,500)
Interest on original investment	(300)	(225)
Rental	1,000	500
	(1,300)	(1,225)
199X – 1		
Interest	(195)	(184)
Rental	1,000	500
	(495)	(909)
199X		
Interest	(74)	(136)
Rental	1,000	500
	431	(545)
199X + 1		
Interest	64	(81)
Rental	1,000	500
	1,495	(126)

Exhibit 7.3 Cash histories of holding activities

The realizable incomes net of interest are as follows:

	Operating the taxi £	Holding the taxi £	Holding the licence £	Total £
199X				
Realizable income				
before interest	1,500	760	300	2,560
Interest	210	74	136	420
Realizable income	1,290	686	164	2,140
199X + 1				
Realizable income				
before interest	1,500	760	1,100	3,360
Interest	16	(64)	81	33
Realizable income	1,484	824	1,019	3,327

There is no change in the efficiency with which operations have been conducted as between 199X and 199X + 1. This is reflected by the constant realizable income (£1,500) before the interest effects of operating the taxi. However, once the effect of interest earned on 199X's retained operating cash flows is taken into consideration, total realizable income from operations in 199X + 1 is higher than in 199X (£1,484 against £1,290). These total realizable incomes from operations include financing effects. This is because the main thrust of the presentation (separate columns) is designed to distinguish operating activities from holding activities whilst a secondary distinction (separate rows) highlights the difference between financing and non-financing activities.

The columns for holding activities show that although before interest effects there is no change in the performance of taxi holding, holding the licence has improved in 199X +1 as against 199X. The interest charged in the above calculations for the realizable incomes of holding activities is based upon the original funds invested when the assets were purchased, adjusted for subsequent rentals and accumulated interest. The realizable incomes therefore relate back to the original investment decision. They measure the *incremental* effect of 199X and 199X + 1 holding activity upon the total realizable income earned since the purchase of the assets.

A different insight is achieved by basing the interest charge for holding activities upon the funds invested in the taxi and licence at the beginning of the year in question rather than on the basis of the cash history from the time of purchase. For example, 199X interest charged in respect of holding the taxi would be 15% of £480, being the realizable value of the taxi at 1.1.9X. With interest calculated on this basis, realizable incomes only relate back as far as the decision to hold the assets during the year. They measure the gain or loss from the decision to hold the taxi and licence during the year. In this calculation of gain or loss the interest on the funds invested in the assets at the beginning of the year is treated as an opportunity cost. It is what could have been earned if the assets had not been held but had been liquidated at the start of the year. Presentation of the realizable incomes might be as in Exhibit 7.4.

The treatment of interest in Exhibit 7.4 can be explained by reference to 199X and the taxi holding activity. The total interest charge attributable to taxi holding during 199X is £74 (Exhibit 7.3). This is split into (1) £72 (15% of £480) attributable to the decision to hold the taxi during 199X, and (2) £2 (£74 − 72) which is presumed to relate to the initial decision taken at the beginning of 199X − 2 to invest in the taxi.

Thus, the difference between interest charged on funds invested in the taxi and licence at the beginning of the year and the actual interest charge attributed to the holding activity is treated as a prior year adjustment since it relates back to holding decisions taken in previous years. Line 3 shows

199X	Operating the taxi £	Holding the taxi £	Holding the licence £	Total £
1 Realizable income before interest	1,500	760	300	2,560
2 Interest	(210)	(72)	(210)	(492)
3 Realizable income	1,290	688	90	2,068
4 Prior year adjustment		(2)	74	72
5 All inclusive RI	1,290	686	164	2,140
199X + 1				
1 Realizable income before interest	1,500	760	1,100	3,360
2 Interest	(16)	(36)	(180)	(232)
3 Realizable income	1,484	724	920	3,128
4 Prior year adjustment		100	99	199
5 All inclusive RI	1,484	824	1,019	3,327

Exhibit 7.4 **Interest effects of current year versus initial decisions**

the realizable income for 199X in respect of holding decisions taken during the year. Line 5 – the 'all-inclusive' realizable income – shows the incremental effect of the year on total realizable income in respect of the original purchase decision.

CONCLUDING DISCUSSION

In essence holding activities are closely associated with capital in the sense that they could not be achieved without the provision of initial capital either from shareholders or from the bank. Gains or losses from holding activities reflect on management's speculative skills. Operating activity, however, is achievable without significant financial capital in any environment where fixed asset services can be obtained by rental. Operating activities reflect on managerial skills in terms of (1) productive efficiency and (2) allocative efficiency by way of creating products of the type and in the volumes required by the market-place. Operating and holding returns are interconnected. Higher operating returns will lead to higher rentals and higher rentals will lead to higher market values for the assets in question. Even though both operations and holding activities may be showing healthy realizable incomes, there may be a case for disposal of one or other business activities on the grounds of risk spreading, as discussed previously. The reason for showing separately the performance of operating and holding activities is that it allows decisions about the disposal or development of individual operating or holding activities to be made with a better appreciation of their respective contributions. Senior management of an organization should continually challenge the organization's existing mix of activities. The selection of the mix of activities is itself a management activity – an important aspect of strategic management. Accounting information should attempt to both support and provide feedback on the different management skills, be they strategic, allocative, productive or speculative.

The Mark Tips case study has examined the distinction between holding and operating activities in circumstances where *holding activities* are carried out in a *highly market orientated environment*. This environment is characterized by the existence of (1) a second-hand market for Mark Tips's tangible assets (the car), (2) a market for Mark Tips's intangible assets (the licence), and (3) a rent or buy option for each of Mark Tips's assets. In such an environment it is possible to distinguish the performance of operating and holding activities and the performance of holding activities is best described through a realizable value framework. Many businesses and most public sector holding activities operate in an environment which is in one or several respects less market oriented than that experienced by Mark Tips. The separation of holding and operating activities where there is a less market orientated environment for holding activities is covered in subsequent chapters. The relevant case studies are Sidney Widget, Age and Beauty, and Bonnie and Clyde. In Sidney Widget there is no second-hand market for the tangible assets, no market for intangible assets and no rental option. In Age and Beauty there is the added complication of technological change. Bonnie and Clyde operate in the public sector. As a consequence there is lower market orientation than for Mark Tips in operating as well as holding activities. It is seen that the existence of markets facilitates the measurement of performance in both holding and operating activities. As the capitalist economies become more sophisticated the number of markets increases and so do the opportunities for distinguishing the results of holding and operating activities.

SELF-STUDY EXERCISE 7.1

CentroCitta Cabs

CentroCitta Cabs Limited is a taxi business operating a single taxi which is licensed by the local authority. The licence runs indefinitely and is a marketable asset since it may be transferred to a new entrant, subject to council approval.

At the beginning and end of 19X2 the market values of the taxi licence and taxi are as follows:

	Market value 1.1.X2	Market value 31.12.X2
Taxi licence	£5,700	£4,900
Taxi	£1,200	£600

The market values shown above in respect of the taxi are the realizable (sale) values when selling to a dealer. The dealer normally adds 20% to his purchase price when selling a second-hand taxi. There are no transaction costs associated with the transfer of a licence.

The taxi was purchased new on 1 January 19X0 for £4,000 and has an expected life of four years. CentroCitta anticipates purchasing another new replacement cab on 1 January 19X4 for £8,000. The present cab is not expected to have any trade-in value by that time.

The taxi licence was purchased on 1 January 19X0 for £3,300.

During 19X2 the company's net cash inflow was £7,000 from the taxi operation. CentroCitta is a cash business and does not have any debtors or creditors. For convenience assume that the £7,000 cash inflow was received on the last day of 19X2.

CentroCitta has share capital of £100 which was used to pay for the formation of the company on 1 January 19X0. Since formation, CentroCitta's business has been entirely financed by bank overdraft on which interest is paid at 10% per annum. At the beginning of 19X0 the overdraft was £7,300, being created by the purchase of the licence and taxi. During 19X0 and 19X1 net operating cash after payment of both interest and dividends has amounted to £2,000, reducing the overdraft at 1 January 19X2 to £5,300. No dividends are paid in respect of 19X2's profit.

Required:

1 Prepare CentroCitta's balance sheet at 1 January 19X2 on a historical cost basis, assuming straight line depreciation for the taxi.

2 Prepare CentroCitta's profit statement for 19X2 on a historical cost basis.

3 Prepare CentroCitta's profit statement for 19X2 with depreciation based on the future replacement cost of the taxi.

4 Prepare CentroCitta's profit statement for 19X2 on a deprival value basis.

5 Prepare CentroCitta's statement of realizable income for 19X2.

6 Suppose a taxi operative can rent a taxi complete with licence for £2,200 per annum. Hence CentroCitta is in effect in two businesses, namely (a) operating the taxi and (b) holding the taxi and taxi licence. Analyse the realizable income for 19X2 to show separately the performance of (a) operations and (b) holding activities.

7 At the beginning of 19X2 CentroCitta could have (a) sold its taxi and its licence and then (b) rented a taxi for 19X2 in order to allow operations to continue. Prepare a statement to indicate whether CentroCitta was correct in its decision to hold on to its taxi and licence during 19X2 as opposed to renting. Assume that any proceeds of sale could have been invested at 10% per annum.

8 Briefly discuss the significance of the various profit figures calculated in parts 1 to 7.

CHAPTER 8

A 'non-market' environment for capital assets

THE SIDNEY WIDGET CASE STUDY

Sidney Widget Limited is a manufacturing company which makes the well-known 'widget', named after Sidney Widget the company's founder and only significant shareholder. It purchases its production machinery at time T_0 for £100 using funds from the issue of shares. At T_0 the purchase price index for the machinery is 100. The production facility has a life of two years. At the end of the first year (time = T_1), the machinery price index is 120 and at T_2 it is 150. The company generates operating cash flow of £150 for each of the two years. Although there is a specific price rise for Widget's machinery there is no general inflation. Widget's working capital requirements are insignificant. Widget pays a dividend of £90 in year 1 and £75 in year 2.

INTRODUCING CURRENT REPLACEMENT COST

There are two ways in which Widget's operational depreciation charge for year 1 can be calculated on a replacement cost basis. These alternatives are current replacement cost (CRC) and prospective (future) replacement cost (FRC). Future replacement cost takes the expected cost of replacement of the asset at the time of replacement and allocates that future cost over the expected life of the asset. Whilst FRC is looking forward to replacement, CRC is concerned with attributing a current value to the amount of the asset's total lifetime service potential or productive capacity which is consumed by operations during the year. This chapter is about the use of CRC in a typical manufacturing environment.

The discussion of CRC is in the context of the separation of holding and operating activities, thus continuing the theme of the Mark Tips chapter. However, Sidney Widget differs from Mark Tips in the extent to which its holding activity takes place in a market environment. First of all there is no second-hand market for widget-making machinery and secondly there is no rental alternative to purchase of the machinery. In these circumstances the approach taken in this chapter is to treat depreciation calculated on a CRC basis as a substitute for the 'rental' paid by the operating activity to the holding activity. Similarly the value of the asset on a CRC basis is taken as a substitute for the market value of the asset.

Sidney Widget's first year

At the end of year 1 the replacement cost of a new widget-maker is £120. Since the first year has exhausted 50% of the widget-maker's lifetime productive capacity the first year can be charged with 50% of £120 = £60 depreciation. This represents the current value at the end of year 1 (i.e. based on year end prices) of the consumption of the machine during the year. This depreciation is treated as a (rental) charge against the operating activity and as (rental) income for the holding activity. The assumption is that if it were possible to rent the machine, then the rental would need to cover the CRC depreciation. The profit statement for operating and holding activity and year end balance sheet for year 1 on this (CRC) basis are shown below with the historical cost (HC) equivalent shown for comparison:

Year 1 profit statement

	CRC operating £	CRC holding £	HC £
Income	150	60	150
Rental/depreciation	(60)	(40)	50
	90		100
Dividends	90		90
Retained operating profit/holding gain	Nil	20	10

For operations the income is operating cash flow against which is charged the depreciation of £60. This depreciation is treated as 'rental' income for the holding activity against which is charged the drop in value of the widget-making capability from two years' service capacity valued at £100 at the beginning of the year to one year's remaining capacity valued at £60 at the end of the year. Because of the absence of relevant markets it has been necessary to regard the CRC as a surrogate for the year end value of the machine. The presentation assumes that dividends are paid out of operations. It also assumes that there are no interest costs or earnings. There are no interest costs since the company has no loans or overdraft. The question of interest earnings on cash balances is discussed later. Any interest costs would be borne in the first instance by the holding activity but recharged to operations, along with CRC depreciation, as part of the 'rental'. The year end balance sheets on a CRC and HC basis are as follows:

Year 1 balance sheet

	CRC £	HC £
Machinery	120	100
Depreciation	60	50
	60	50
Cash	60	60
	120	110
Share capital	100	100
Holding gains	20	
Retained operating profit	Nil	10
Shareholders' funds	120	110

Sidney Widget's second year

At the end of year 2 the current replacement cost of a new widget-maker is £150. Since the second year has exhausted the remaining 50% of the widget-maker's lifetime capacity, the second year can be charged with a 'rental' equivalent to 50% of £150 = £75 depreciation. This represents the current value at the end of year 2 of the consumption of the machine during year 2. The profit statement and balance sheet for year 2 on a CRC basis are shown below with the HC comparatives:

Year 2 profit statement

	CRC operating £	CRC holding £	HC £
Income	150	75	150
Rental/depreciation	75	60	50
	75		100
Dividends	75		75
Retained profit	Nil	15	25

Year 2 balance sheet

	CRC	HC
	£	£
Machinery	150	100
Depreciation	150	100
	Nil	Nil
Cash	135	135
	135	135
Share capital	100	100
Accumulated holding gain	35	
Retained profit	Nil	35
Shareholders' funds	135	135

The £15 gain from the holding activity is taken to be a 'rental' of £75, equivalent to the CRC depreciation less a loss in value of the machine from £60 at the beginning of the year to zero at the end of the year when the service capacity of the machine is exhausted. The second year's holding gain of £15 is added to the first year's gain of £20 to give an accumulated holding gain of £35 in the second year balance sheet.

The replacement issue

It can be seen from the year 2 balance sheet that Sidney Widget has £135 cash. This is £15 short of the amount needed to purchase the replacement widget-maker. Sidney Widget's activities do not therefore generate sufficient funds to maintain operating capacity. In order to generate sufficient funds to replace the widget-maker it is necessary for Sidney Widget to invest the first year's cash balance of £60 at a rate of interest (25%) which will generate the £15 shortfall at the end of year 2. Thus the operating activity is dependent on this financing activity if operating capacity is to be maintained without recourse to further borrowing. The financing activity has to earn interest at the same rate as the price rise for the widget-making machine.

It is seen from the Sidney Widget example that if CRC operating profits (£90 in year 1 and £75 in year 2) are paid out as dividends, then the company does not necessarily have enough cash at the end of year 2 to pay for the replacement machine. Widget's year 2 balance sheet shows a cash balance of £135 whereas £150 is needed at the end of year 2 to fund a new widget-making machine. Hence CRC accounting does *not* necessarily provide for machine replacement. Its relevance as an accounting system depends upon the depreciation charge being the *current* value of the machine consumption at the time of consumption. It is, therefore, more appropriately thought of as a current value accounting system rather than a (future) replacement cost accounting system.

ANALYSING THE RESULTS

CRC matches the current value of resources created from operations with the current value of resources consumed by operations. The main thrust of operating activity is concerned with matching, and hence with the (operating) profit statement rather than the balance sheet. It should be noted that as far as the balance sheets are concerned all resources and sources of resources relate to holding activities. Hence holding activities start with a machine of £100 (T_0) going to a machine of £60 and cash of £60 (T_1) and ultimately to cash of £135 (T_2). Holding gains are £20 for year 1 and £15 for year 2. Hence, as a percentage of opening assets, year 1 generates $20/100 = 20\%$ whilst year 2 only manages $15/120 = 12.5\%$. However, this return is artificially low since it does not include any return from the potential investment of the end of the first year's cash balance of £60. In any event both years' holding gains reflect on the decision taken at T_0 to invest in the widget-making machinery since Sidney Widget does not have the opportunity to sell the widget-making machine at T_1.

Trend analysis shows the level of CRC operating profit (before dividends) falling from £90 in year 1 to £75 in year 2. This reflects the fact that the (machine) resource consumed is more highly valued by the market in year 2 than it was in year 1. Widget has been unable to match the rise in the value of the resources consumed with a compensating rise in the value of its sales. This is the aspect of economic 'reality' which is reflected by CRC as indicated below:

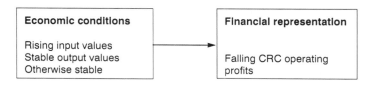

Of course it is the value to the *economy* of the machine resource consumed which has risen. Presumably this is either because there is a valuable alternative use for the widget-making machine or, more likely, because the resources required to make widget-making machines are increasing in value. The cost to Sidney Widget of two years' capacity of the machine, however, remains £100 looking backwards (historical cost) and £150 looking forwards (FRC). Neither of these costs changes during years 1 and 2. Hence CRC provides an economy-wide perspective on Widget's performance rather than a firm or shareholder perspective. Its primary use therefore is for a profitability analysis designed to judge the contribution of Sidney Widget's operations to the economy as a whole. It should be noted that in Sidney Widget's case, this declining contribution reflects on the decision made at time T_0 to invest in the widget-making machine. It is not a reflection of any subsequent decisions or on day-to-day operating performance. Any decline in operating performance would have an additional effect on CRC operating profits.

Comparison with historical cost

Shareholders benefit from both operational and holding gains. Over the two years these aggregate (net of dividends) to £35 and this aggregate total is shown by both the CRC and the HC balance sheet. However, the HC figures give a quite different impression of operating trends. HC profits (before dividends) remain constant for the two years reflecting the fact that day-to-day operating costs and sales have remained at a static level. CRC operating profits (before dividends), however, fall in relation to sales from £90/150 to £75/150, reflecting the unrecovered increasing value to the 'economy' of widget-making machines. Hence the HC and CRC figures show different perspectives on Sidney Widget's performance over the two years.

CONCLUDING COMMENTS

The Sidney Widget case is used to demonstrate how separate results for operating and holding activities can be imputed in a manufacturing environment where there is no active market for second-hand machines and no rental alternative to purchase. In this chapter current replacement costs have been used to impute market values for second-hand machines (based on current replacement costs) and for rentals (based on current replacement depreciation). It is seen that from a shareholder perspective both CRC and HC show the same shareholders' funds albeit that in the Sidney Widget example under CRC those shareholders' funds are shown as holding gains rather than retained operating profits. The principal advantage of CRC is to provide an economy-wide perspective on operating activity since under CRC the value of revenues is matched with the current value *to the economy* of the machine resources consumed. In the case of Sidney Widget there is little value in treating the operating and holding activities as separate business units since the absence of a second-hand market and a rental alternative means that the two activities must be carried out jointly.

SELF-STUDY EXERCISE 8.1

Long, Short and Maybe

The Long, Short and Maybe Company (LSM) has three divisions, each of which purchases fixed assets of £150 on 1 January 19X1. The fixed assets purchased by the Long and Short divisions each have a life of two years. The Maybe division's fixed asset has a life of three years. The Long division has a four-year non-transferable contract to supply its only customer. The contract generates an annual operating cash flow of £150. The Short division has a two-year non-transferable contract to supply its only customer. This contract also generates an annual cash flow of £150.

The Maybe division does not supply against a contract but sells in the open market at the prevailing market price. Maybe's annual sales volumes vary so as to maintain an annual operating cash flow of £150. There is an open market for each division's product but in the case of the Long and Short divisions their respective contracts account for 100% of productive capacity. The contracts assume a market price of £5 for each product. During years 1 and 2 the market price of each division's product moves as follows:

	L	S	M
	£	£	£
T_0	5	5	5
T_1	3	6	3
T_2	1	8	7

The fixed assets for the Long and Short contracts are not marketable. The replacement cost index for the fixed assets moves as follows:

	L	S	M
	£	£	£
T_0	100	100	100
T_1	120	120	110
T_2	150	150	120
T_3			120

The fixed asset of the Maybe division is saleable and its realizable value is as follows:

	£
T_0	150
T_1	70
T_2	50

Required:

1 For each division calculate profits for years 1 and 2 on a historical cost basis, a current replacement cost basis and a future replacement cost basis.

2 For the Maybe division calculate profits for years 1 and 2 on a realizable value basis.

3 Provide the current replacement cost balance sheets at T_1 and T_2 for each division.

4 Discuss the relevance of the various alternatives to historical cost profits to the circumstances of each division.

Assume for parts 1, 2 and 3:

(a) that the purchase of fixed assets at T_0 is funded by the issue of shares;

(b) that operating cash flows are received on the last day of each year and are invested at the bank for the following year at an interest rate of 10%; and

(c) no dividends are paid.

CHAPTER 9

Technological change

INTRODUCTION

Many organizations, public and private, carry out their activities in an environment susceptible to technological change. Technological change is one of the dynamics of today's economy. Those industries which make large-scale, long-term capital investments are amongst the most susceptible. As seen in the Quickneasy example (Chapter 4), technological change accentuates the speculative nature of investment and it provides openings for new competitors (such as Suretype) to enter the market. The company (or economy) which is unencumbered by yesterday's plant and yesterday's skills has a great opportunity to move in on established companies (economies) *provided* it has the funds to invest in the new plant and the new skills. Each new wave of technological advance generates a new economic impetus. To protect their position, established companies must continually monitor technological developments and their likely impact on the existing plant and the existing methods. Management may have to look forward to the replacement of equipment rather than backwards to the purchase of the existing equipment and considerations of how to squeeze more years of service from the existing assets.

Another aspect of the problem is the relationship between production methods and product. The search for new methods of production or service delivery almost always provides opportunities for the product service to be redesigned or redeveloped. Similarly the drive to develop new products or services generates ideas for revising methods of production or service delivery. A different production process or delivery system often implies a different product or service. This is as true for the public service as it is for private business. For example, as universities change their mode of operation to cope with increased student numbers and a lower per student unit of resource, the nature of the service provided to the student and the degree product itself change significantly.

The drive for cost reduction interacts with the technological dynamic in various ways. Sometimes the desire for cost reduction provides the impetus for developing new technology which causes the product to be re-evaluated or redesigned rather than costs reduced. In some cases the cost of technologically advanced production equipment puts such a strain on finances that the organization itself has to be reorganized and refinanced. Again these considerations can be as relevant for the public service as for private business. The National Health Service (NHS) is a classic case and is discussed in the next chapter.

This chapter and the one after revolve around two case studies, in each of which technological advance is a significant consideration. In the first case study Age plc has held a monopoly position in its particular niche market for ten years. Its product is high-class and upmarket. After ten years, technologically advanced production methods allow Beauty to enter the market and compete with Age. Beauty's equipment is expensive to buy but cheap to operate compared to Age's older plant. This illustrates a common experience with the 'latest' equipment – there is a trade-off between purchase (fixed) cost and operating (variable) cost. However, the market for the high-class product is limited and there is now acute overcapacity. A price war is avoided since neither Age nor Beauty wish the product to lose its high-class image. However, market share is sensitive to promotional activity.

The second case study concerns the NHS. Bonnie and Clyde are two NHS hospitals providing treatment for condition 'X'. Bonnie uses old-fashioned equipment whereas Clyde has invested in the latest hi-tech laser. The Bonnie and Clyde case is used to explore the suitability of different performance measures in the public sector. The Age vs. Beauty case introduces the distinction between performance from the point of view of shareholders and performance from the point of view of efficiency in the economy as a whole.

The figures used in both case studies are unrealistic and chosen to enable ease of computation. The main thing is to concentrate on the principles at stake. It is important to note that both case studies assume zero inflation – the focus of both studies is not inflation but *technological change*, which can and does impact on the price of replacement equipment, but which must be distinguished from the problem of inflation in the economy at large.

THE AGE AND BEAUTY CASE STUDY

Age plc purchased its brand-new production facilities on 1 January 198X for £10,000. Ten years later on 1 January 199X a competitor, Beauty plc, entered the same market with brand-new production facilities at a cost of £30,000. Both plants have a productive capability of 1,000 units per annum and both plants have a physical life of 20 years with no residual value. Thus Age's plant has ten years to run. The product sells for £7 per unit and this price has been unaffected by Beauty's entrance to the market which is price insensitive. However, market share is sensitive to promotional activity. Beauty's modern plant is more efficient than Age's with variable unit costs of £1.50 per unit as opposed to £3 for Age.

In the year ended 31 December 199X, Beauty's production was 600 units and Age's 600 units. All production was sold. Before Beauty entered the market Age had always produced and sold its entire productive capacity of 1,000 units. In order to capture its share of the market Beauty has spent £200 on promotion during the year ended 31 December 199X.

Assume:

1 Production of 1,000 units represents the only possible size of plant.

2 The technological development is a 'one-off' and no further technological changes are expected.

3 There are no price changes other than for the productive plant.

4 There are no year end stocks.

Age's profits for 199X can be simply calculated as follows:

	£
Sales	4,200
Variable expenses (600 @ £3)	(1,800)
Depreciation (£10,000/20)	(500)
	1,900

It is assumed that during the first ten years of the plant's life it was expected that the plant would produce 1,000 units per annum for 20 years. Per unit depreciation would therefore be £10,000/20 × 1,000 = 50p, and annual depreciation in cost of sales would be 1,000 units at 50p = £500. At the end of the first ten years, therefore, the net book value of the plant is £10,000 − 10 × 500 = £5,000. For the second ten years of the plant's life, following the introduction of Beauty, the per unit depreciation is expected to be 5,000/600 × 10 = 83.3p per unit and the annual depreciation in cost of sales is 600 units at 83.3p = £500. Hence the depreciation for 199X is £500. This is equivalent, in the circumstances of the question, to taking the cost of the plant (£10,000) and allocating it equally over its expected useful life of 20 years.

Assuming that share capital is minimal and the original purchase of the plant has been funded by a £10,000 loan at 5% interest then net profit is:

	£
Operating profit	1,900
Loan interest	500
	1,400

Age's *opening* cash position for 199X, after ten years of operations, is assumed to be:

		£
Sales	10 × 7 × 1,000	70,000
Variable expenses	10 × 3 × 1,000	(30,000)
Loan interest	10 × 500	(5,000)
		35,000

This ignores dividends paid and interest earned on cash balances.
  Age's opening retained profit for 199X is assumed to be:

		£
Sales	10 × 7 × 1,000	70,000
Variable expenses	10 × 3 × 1,000	(30,000)
Depreciation	10 × 500	(5,000)
Loan interest	10 × 500	(5,000)
		30,000

Age's opening balance sheet for 199X is assumed to be:

Resources		Sources of resources	
	£		£
Fixed asset at cost	10,000	Loan	10,000
Depreciation	5,000	Retained profits	30,000
	5,000		
Cash	35,000		
	40,000		40,000

INTRODUCING (FUTURE) REPLACEMENT COST ACCOUNTING

Age's £1,900 profit for 199X is calculated on a historical cost basis. This basis looks back historically to the amount actually paid by Age for its

F

plant at the beginning of 198X. This amount of £10,000 is then allocated across the 20 years for which Age's plant is expected to be in service to give an annual 'historical' depreciation charge of £500. Future replacement cost (FRC) accounting provides an alternative to historical cost (HC). FRC accounting looks forward to the expected cost of replacing the plant at the end of the existing plant's life and allocates this future replacement cost over the expected life of the existing plant to give an annual 'replacement' depreciation.

In the Age and Beauty case, if it is assumed that the technological change is a 'one-off', then Age may expect to replace its existing plant in ten years' time with a plant similar to Beauty's and costing £30,000. Annual FRC depreciation can be calculated by allocating this expected replacement cost of £30,000 over the 20 years' expected life of the existing plant. In this case annual FRC depreciation is £30,000/20 = £1,500. If the technological change is a 'one-off' then from the date of this change onwards, future replacement cost equals current replacement cost, i.e. the cost of replacing the plant in the future is, assuming zero inflation, going to be the same as the cost of replacing the plant today. Since the Age and Beauty case assumes that the technological change is a 'one-off', the rest of this chapter does not distinguish 'future' from 'current' replacement cost and merely refers to the generic term 'replacement cost' (RC). Some companies operate in environments where technological change is not 'one-off' in character but frequent or continuous. In these circumstances future replacement cost and current replacement cost are no longer equivalent and future replacement cost can become difficult to predict and therefore problematic.

RC profits for Age for 199X are as follows:

	£
Sales	4,200
Variable expenses	(1,800)
Depreciation (30,000/20)	(1,500)
Operating profit	900
Interest	(500)
Net profit	400

It should be noted that although RC profits are after charging depreciation on the basis of future replacement of the machine, variable expenses are on the basis of the actual machine currently in use and interest is on the basis of the actual loan currently outstanding.

If it is assumed that during the first ten years from 198X, Age could not have been expected to anticipate the technological development which enabled Beauty to enter the market, then Age's replacement cost profit for the first ten years would be the same as its historical cost profits. The closing RC balance sheet at 31 December 199X − 1 would, therefore, be:

Resources	£	Sources of resources	£
Fixed asset at RC	10,000	Loan	10,000
Depreciation	5,000	Retained profits	30,000
	5,000		
Cash	35,000		
	40,000		40,000

However, as soon as knowledge of the new plant becomes available at the beginning of 199X, this balance sheet should be changed to reflect the new replacement costs as follows:

Resources	£	Sources of resources	£
Fixed assets at RC	30,000	Loan	10,000
Depreciation	15,000	Retained profits	20,000
	15,000	Revaluation reserve	20,000
Cash	35,000		
	50,000		50,000

In this balance sheet fixed assets have been revalued from a replacement cost of £10,000 to one of £30,000. This leads to a revaluation reserve of £20,000 (£30,000 − £10,000). Retained profits are reduced from £30,000 to £20,000 to absorb backlog depreciation of £10,000. This backlog represents the RC depreciation which would have been charged in the first ten years if there had been full knowledge of the future technological development (i.e. $10 \times 1,500 = £15,000$) less the depreciation actually charged ($10 \times 500 = £5,000$). The amount of Age's retained RC profits (£20,000) is the maximum amount which at the beginning of 199X can prudently be distributed as dividends to those who own the company, bearing in mind the need to replace the plant at the end of its 20-year life.

The behavioural dimension

One of the key attractions of replacement cost accounting is behavioural. Instead of thinking about the recovery of historical cost, management is encouraged to think about replacement of assets since replacement cost becomes the basis of accounting profits and hence performance.

Compared to RC accounting, HC accounting may induce a greater reluctance on the part of management to invest in new technology. For example, if management feel they are judged by HC profits they will be reluctant to invest in new plant with higher depreciation charges. The nature of the problem can be indicated by a study of the impact which investment in the new modern plant would have on Age's HC and RC profits. For Age (without Beauty's arrival on the scene) investment in the new plant would change the HC profits as follows:

	Old plant £	New plant £
Sales	7,000	7,000
Variable expenses	(3,000)	(1,500)
Depreciation	(500)	(1,500)
Operating profit	3,500	4,000
Interest	(500)	(2,000)
Net profit	3,000	2,000

It is seen that replacing the plant results in a rise in the HC operating profits but a fall in HC net profits due to interest. (The interest charge assumes that an additional loan of £30,000 is taken out for the new plant.) The HC net profits for the new plant would be further reduced by the need, under existing accounting standards, to write off the net book value of the old plant in the year of its replacement. The HC net profit figures provide a strong disincentive against investing in the new plant. However, this neglects the strategic importance of keeping potential contestants such as Beauty out of the market!

Similarly Age's investment in new plant would change the RC profits as follows (ignoring Beauty's arrival):

	Old plant £	New plant £
Sales	7,000	7,000
Variable expenses	(3,000)	(1,500)
Depreciation	(1,500)	(1,500)
Operating profit	2,500	4,000
Interest	500	2,000
Net profit	2,000	2,000

In this example RC operating profits generated by the new plant benefit from the new plant's considerably lower variable costs thus providing operational management with an incentive to replace. However, the additional interest cost associated with the loan necessary to purchase the new plant (or reduced interest earnings if the plant is internally financed) reduces net profits down to £2,000. Hence net profit is the same before and after the replacement and there is, at least in this example, no in-built disincentive to replace.

Of course decisions to invest in more technologically advanced equipment should be based on strategic considerations – the need to keep out contestants – and upon discounted cash flow analysis as much as the effect upon profits, whether those profits be HC or RC. However, managers are influenced by the effect upon their perceived performance measures. If managers perceive that their performance is judged on the basis of profits, then HC accounting (as opposed to RC accounting) may induce a greater reluctance on the part of managers to replace equipment.

ANALYSING THE RESULTS

Beauty's results

Beauty's HC and RC results for 199X are identical as follows:

	HC £	RC £
Sales	4,200	4,200
Variable expenses		
600 @ £1.5	(900)	(900)
Depreciation	(1,500)	(1,500)
Promotion	(200)	(200)
Operating profit	1,600	1,600
Interest	(1,500)	(1,500)
Net profit	100	100

These figures assume that Beauty has no knowledge of any further likely technological advances and therefore expects to replace its new plant in 20 years' time with an identical plant for, in the absence of inflation, an identical price of £30,000. HC and RC depreciation are therefore both £1,500. It is also assumed that Beauty's share capital is minimal and that it has a £30,000 loan to pay for its new equipment, giving interest charges of £1,500.

Age vs. Beauty

Age and Beauty's profits for 199X are summarized as follows:

| | Age | | Beauty | |
	HC	RC	HC	RC
	£	£	£	£
Sales	4,200	4,200	4,200	4,200
Variable expenses	(1,800)	(1,800)	(900)	(900)
Depreciation	(500)	(1,500)	(1,500)	(1,500)
Promotion			(200)	(200)
Operating profit	1,900	900	1,600	1,600
Interest	500	500	1,500	1,500
Net profit	1,400	400	100	100

Has Age or Beauty performed best during the year? This is probably a meaningless question since Beauty is trying to establish itself against an established incumbent. Hence it is difficult to compare the two companies. Both HC and RC profit figures suggest that Age is more profitable than Beauty during 199X. At the operating profit level Beauty has higher RC profits than Age, but this advantage is lost due to Beauty's far higher interest charges. However, the key question is not how profitable have the two companies been during 199X, but rather which of the two has positioned itself so as to have the better prospects for the future?

The key constraint is sales and the key to sales is promotional expenditure. Beauty only has one course of action open to it. It is to increase promotional expenditure and secure a larger market share. However, Age must anticipate this and increase its promotional expenditure if it is to maintain its market share. In fact Age has a number of strategic options open to it:

1 it could abandon its old plant and invest in the new modern plant;
2 it could stay in the market with its old plant and compete for market share with Beauty;
3 it could adopt an aggressive promotional policy designed to force Beauty out of the market;
4 it could pull out of the market.

The first of the above is not an attractive option. It involves investing £30,000 in a market which, assuming the market demand expands no further, now has acute overcapacity. The relevant net present value analysis is given in Exhibit 9.1. To invest now in new plant would be

An NPV analysis, if carried out at the beginning of 199X, would also suggest that it was not worthwhile for Age to invest in new plant once Beauty had entered the market. Assuming that Age holds on to its market of 600 units for the ten years from 1 January 199X, then a new plant for Age at 1 January 199X would generate annual savings of £600 × (£3 − £1.5) = £900, being the savings of variable expenses. At an interest rate of 5%, £1 every year for ten years is worth £7.722 today and £900 every year for ten years is therefore worth £6,950. Investing in a new plant today costs £30,000 compared with investing in the new plant in ten years' time (when the existing plant is exhausted) which would cost £30,000 × 0.614 = £18,420 at net present value. Hence the additional *outlay* of investing in new plant is £30,000 − £18,420 = £11,580 compared to a *benefit* in cost savings of £6,950, with both costs and benefits expressed in terms of their NPV.

Exhibit 9.1

shutting the stable door after the horse has bolted. Age should have invested in the new plant before Beauty did and then Beauty would have been unlikely to contest the market. The fourth option is also unlikely to be popular with management unless Age is well placed to develop alternative activities. The second option is possible but Beauty can justify spending larger sums on promotion than Age. In order to push its sales up to 1,000 units Beauty can justify spending 400 × £5.50 (contribution) = £2,200 as opposed to Age's 400 × £4 = £1,600.

Such a policy is likely to enable Beauty to get even more established. Let us assume that Age opts for the bold strategy of attempting to force Beauty out of the market. During its ten years of monopolistic activity Age has built up cash resources of £35,000. It is therefore in a strong position to spend on promotional activity. Much depends upon the financial muscle behind Beauty and how quickly its financial backers become disenchanted with low profits. If Beauty's backers lose their nerve then it may be possible for Age to purchase Beauty's new plant for a 'knock-down' price.

Having decided upon its strategy Age must not lose its nerve, and its management must ensure that its strategic objectives permeate all departments, and especially marketing. Strategic objectives must not become an excuse for financial indiscipline. However, it will be necessary to accept marketing proposals which do not appear worthwhile in conventional profitability terms. For example, in profitability terms it is worth Age spending no more than £400 (100 × £4) on promotion in order to achieve an extra 100 units of sales. However, in order to fulfil the strategy much greater sums may have to be expended in order to achieve successive 100 unit inroads into Beauty's market share. This example serves to highlight the friction which can exist between strategic objectives and shorter-term profitability considerations.

SHAREHOLDER VS. ECONOMY-WIDE PERSPECTIVES

This section discusses whether Beauty's entrance into the market is likely to be of benefit to the economy as a whole assuming that before Beauty's entrance, Age was the only producer. From an economy wide perspective there are two separate considerations:

1 Now that Beauty has entered the market what would be the best outcome in the battle for market share?
2 Would it have been better if Beauty had stayed out of the market?

Question 1

The market has expanded from 1,000 units to 1,200 units as a result of Beauty's entrance and promotional activity. The expansion may be due to the promotional activity or there may previously have been unsatisfied demand of 200 units as a result of the 1,000 unit limit on production. In either case it cannot be assumed that demand will continue to grow. If there is no further growth in demand then the market of 1,200 units is likely in future to be divided between Age and Beauty in proportion to their promotional activity. From the point of view of the economy as a whole, once Beauty has decided to invest, then it makes sense for as much production as possible to flow from the more productively efficient plant. Hence the best (most allocatively efficient) outcome is that annual sales of 1,200 units will be split 1,000 to Beauty (equivalent to Beauty's production limit) and 200 to Age. Whether this happens or not depends upon the relative cash resources which Beauty and Age commit to promotion. As mentioned previously, Age may already have the resources as a result of ten years of unchallenged monopolistic activity. It seems unlikely that Age will accept the losses associated with a sales level of 200 units.

Question 2

In answering this question much depends upon whether or not the market size has grown from 1,000 to 1,200 units in response to Beauty's promotional activity or as a result of unsatisfied demand due to the previous ceiling of 1,000 units caused by Age's production capacity. If the total market size can be expanded beyond 1,200 units through promotional activity then the entrance of Beauty with its active promotional policy will be more advantageous than it is otherwise. The following discussion, however, examines the situation where the market cannot be expanded beyond 1,200 units and hence further promotional activity influences market share but not market size.

The analysis compares industry performance in the ten years from 1 January 199X assuming Age to be the only industry producer, with industry performance assuming both Age and Beauty as producers. It is assumed that Age and Beauty have 600 units each for 199X and that thereafter they share the market 200 : 1,000 units respectively, i.e. the most efficient possible allocation.

Contribution during the year ended 31 December 199X is:

			£
from Beauty	600 @ £5.50		3,300
from Age	600 @ £4		2,400
			5,700

For the 1,000 : 200 split between Beauty and Age, the annual contribution generated by all sales towards the industry's fixed costs is likely in future to be:

			Contribution
			£
from Beauty	1,000	units @ £5.50	5,500
from Age	200	units @ £4	800
			6,300

Over the next nine years up to the point when Age's plant is time expired, the total contribution is £56,700.

It follows that during the ten-year period from the date of Beauty's entrance to the time expiry of Age's plant, the industry's contribution to its total fixed costs is:

		£
9 years	at £6,300	56,700
1 year	at £5,700	5,700
		62,400

If Age had continued to have the market to itself, contribution to its fixed costs over the same ten-year period would have been:

$$10 \times 1,000 \times 4 = \pounds40,000$$

It is seen that the contribution to the industry's fixed costs is enhanced by £22,400 (62,400 − 40,000) through Beauty contesting the market. However, the industry's total fixed costs also rise as a result of Beauty's investment in plant of £30,000. Assuming that half of this sum needs to be covered by sales in its first ten years of operation, then the additional contribution of £22,400 has to cover additional fixed costs of £15,000 leaving a net surplus of £7,400. This net surplus of £7,400 is insufficient to cover the additional interest costs generated by Beauty's investment. Such interest costs are £10 × 1,500 = £15,000. In addition, this net surplus of £7,400 over the ten-year period from Beauty's entrance to the market *assumes* that:

1 as much production as possible (1,000 units) shifts to Beauty, the low cost producer, and

2 Age neither withdraws nor modernizes but stays in business to provide the 200 units making up the rest of the market, and

3 no resources are spent on promotion.

In the new competitive environment the third of these assumptions is unrealistic. Indeed it is likely that Beauty will have to increase promotional expenditure beyond the present £200 per annum already spent during the year ended 31 December 199X if it is to succeed in pushing up its sales to the allocatively efficient target of 1,000 units.

It is possible to construct a situation in which Beauty's variable costs, although lower than Age's, are sufficiently high that Beauty's entrance to the market could never be beneficial to the economy as a whole irrespective of interest charges or the amounts spent on promotion. For this to be the case Beauty's variable costs would need to be roughly £2.27 per unit. Check this as follows:

For year ended 31 December 199X:		£
Contribution by Beauty 600 × 4.73	=	2,838
by Age 600 × 4	=	2,400
		5,238

For the next nine years:

Contribution by Beauty $9 \times 1,000 \times 4.73 = 42,570$

        by Age $9 \times 200 \times 4$ $= \underline{7,200}$

                                            55,008

Less industry's additional fixed cost created

by Beauty's investment $\underline{15,000}$

                                            $\underline{40,008}$

This net contribution of £40,008 is virtually identical to the £40,000 contribution which would have been made if Age had continued without Beauty's arrival in the market. It follows that if Beauty's variable costs were higher than £2.27 per unit, there would for certain be a smaller contribution than if Age had continued alone.

CONCLUDING COMMENTS

The Age and Beauty case study raises important questions as it draws out the relationship between financial results (both HC and RC) and the economic variables of market size, market share, price, elasticity of demand, investment longevity, cost structures and level of competition/ contestability. Age and Beauty have investments which are large scale and long term providing a market which is relatively static in terms of both size and price. Age is an established producer with ageing productive facilities. New production technology opens up an attractive investment opportunity for Beauty to contest the market. From Beauty's point of view the invest- ment is well worthwhile and should in time earn a healthy (proprietorial) return. Beauty is more productively efficient than Age and once Beauty has invested, allocative efficiency requires that as much of the market as possible is captured by Beauty.

The analysis shows that there can be circumstances in which Beauty contesting the market is not advantageous from the point of view of the economy as a whole. Much depends upon the level of Beauty's variable costs, the level of promotional expenditure which the new competitive environment requires, and the degree of success which Beauty has in capturing the lion's share of the market. It follows that there can be circumstances in which Beauty's entrance is proprietorially successful but not economically helpful. Of course there are also cases of companies in uncontested markets failing to innovate or bring in new productive techniques when to do so would be beneficial to the economy. In such circumstances the entry of a contestant into the market is both proprietorially advantageous and helpful to the economy as a whole. In many cases, however, the ideal is not for a contestant to enter the market but for the incumbent to keep abreast of developments and modernize in line with technological change. To encourage such behaviour it could be argued that the use of RC accounting rather than HC accounting would be beneficial. RC accounting may not contain the disincentive to new investment which can be induced by the use of HC accounting as the primary performance measure for management.

SELF-STUDY EXERCISE 9.1

Aged Airways and Beautiful Airways

1 Aged Airways have held the only licence for the Edinburgh to Luton route for ten years, from 1 January 1980. On 1 January 1980 they purchased new a 100-seater plane for £20 million. The plane has an expected life of 20 years, at the end of which it has no value. It is depreciated on a straight line basis. Aged Airways use the plane solely on the Edinburgh to Luton route on which it operates for 250 days in the year making two return journeys per day. From 1 January 1980 to 31 December 1989 the plane operated at 100% capacity (i.e. the flights were always full). Excluding depreciation and other overheads the additional cost of each return flight is £1,000 and the additional cost of each passenger carried is £10 per return journey. The fare for the journey is £50 single (£100 return).

Required:

Calculate the historical cost profit of the Edinburgh to Luton route for the year ended 31 December 1989, charging depreciation of the plane but excluding other overheads. It is not currently company policy to charge interest costs when calculating the profitability of individual routes.

2 On 1 January 1990 the UK government decided to license a second operator on the Edinburgh to Luton route. The second operator – Beautiful Airways – purchased new a 60-seater plane for £15 million on 1 January 1990. The plane has an expected life of 20 years, no scrap value, and is depreciated on a straight line basis. Beautiful Airways use the plane solely on the Edinburgh to Luton route on which it operates in direct competition to Aged Airways for 250 days in the year, making two return flights per day. Excluding overheads and depreciation, the additional cost of each return flight is £600 and the additional cost of each passenger carried is £10 per return journey. The fare for the journey remains at £50 single (£100 return) for both operators. Beautiful Airways' flights operate at 100% capacity (i.e. each flight is full) but the introduction of the second operator causes Aged Airways' loading to drop from 100% to 60% (i.e. each flight carries 60 passengers).

Required:

Calculate the historical cost profit of the Edinburgh to Luton route for the year ended 31 December 1990, charging depreciation of the plane but excluding other overheads, for (1) Aged Airways and (2) Beautiful Airways. Assume that Aged Airways continues to operate two return flights per day with the 100-seater plane and that its total depreciation and unit variable costs are unchanged from the previous year. Ignore interest.

3 Aged Airways have a director responsible for each route and the director's performance is judged by his ability to improve the route's profitability. Aged Airways have no alternative use for the 100-seater plane used on the Edinburgh–Luton route and the board of directors decide that the plane must continue to be used on that route. The director responsible for Edinburgh to Luton feels that he is being required to compete with what now, in the new circumstances, is an unsuitable plane. He has asked that from 1 January 1990 onwards the profit of the route be calculated on a replacement cost basis whereby depreciation charged is based on the hypothetical assumption that the 100-seater plane were replaced by a new 60-seater plane as used by Beautiful Airways. The board of Aged Airways has asked for your advice in respect of the director's request.

Required:

Indicate what advice you would give to the board and calculate Aged Airways' results for the year ended 31 December 1990 on the Edinburgh–Luton route on a replacement cost basis.

4 Discuss briefly whether the government's decision to issue a second licence on the Edinburgh–Luton route has been a success based on the evidence of 1990's results.

CHAPTER 10

Public sector activities

INTRODUCTION

This chapter provides a brief introduction to the issues surrounding the use of financially derived cost statistics in order to understand the performance of activities where there are no easily obtained market prices for outputs. These activities have traditionally been funded by the public purse.

The discussion proceeds by reference to two hospitals – Bonnie and Clyde – which both provide treatment for the same medical condition. The case is as follows.

BONNIE AND CLYDE: AN NHS CASE STUDY

Bonnie and Clyde are two hospitals within the same health authority each providing treatment for condition 'X'. Each uses identical equipment (an alpha laser) having a historical cost of £1,000.

At each hospital during the year ended 31 December 199X – 1, 20 treatments are administered with a variable cost per treatment of £30. In the original capital appraisal each alpha laser was expected to provide for 200 treatments at a variable cost of £30 per treatment. By the beginning of 199X each had been used for 100 treatments and was therefore halfway through its useful life. At 1 January 199X, a new piece of equipment (the beta laser) becomes available at a price of £2,000, an expected life of 200 treatments and associated variable cost of £30 per treatment. It gives twice the success rate of the alpha laser. The alpha lasers have no realizable value. Bonnie stays with the old alpha laser for the year ended 31 December 199X, whereas Clyde purchases the new beta laser at 1 January 199X and gives its alpha laser away for scrap. Both hospitals administer 20 treatments during the year in line with anticipated variable costs.

Cost per treatment

The first statistic to be discussed is the cost per treatment at Bonnie and at Clyde during 199X.

The costs per treatment at both Bonnie and Clyde hospitals are calculated in Exhibit 10.1. Both the third column and the bottom line of Exhibit 10.1 can be ignored for the moment.

Costs per treatment are lower at Bonnie (£35 against £42.5) since the overhead recovery is lower at £5 rather than £12.5 per treatment, and £2.5 of the £12.5 represents recovery of the outstanding unrecovered costs of £500 on Clyde's unwanted alpha machine. In Exhibit 10.1, these costs are being recovered against the anticipated 200 treatments to be carried out by the new beta machine. Alternatives to this procedure are discussed later.

Cost per successful treatment

Exhibit 10.1 (bottom line) shows the costs per successful treatment at Bonnie and at Clyde during 199X, based on a success rate of 25% for the alpha machine and 50% for the beta machine.

The cost per successful treatment is £85 at Clyde as opposed to £140 at Bonnie, the main influence being the higher success rate of Clyde's beta machine.

Comparison of cost per treatment with cost per successful treatment makes an important point. Bonnie is cheaper in terms of inputs alone since its costs per treatment are lower. However, when the inputs are related to outputs it is seen that Clyde gives a better deal since its costs per successful treatment are lower. For public sector activities the notion of 'success' can be difficult to define and measure. In our case a successful treatment may

	Bonnie staying with old machine £	Clyde using the new opportunity £	Clyde assuming beta at £20,000 £
Fixed costs			
per treatment	5	10	100
Variable	30	30	30
	35	40	130
Backlog on previous			
machine 500/200	—	2.5	2.5
Cost per treatment	35	42.5	132.5
Cost per successful treatment	140	85	265

Exhibit 10.1 Cost per treatment and per successful treatment (year ended 31 December 199X)

be one that causes a complete recovery or it may be a more limited notion of success such as relief from pain or an extension to life expectancy. Although 'success' may be a matter on which a consensus is hard to find, one thing is clear from our example. Performance measures which focus only on inputs will be misleading.

INTERPRETING PERFORMANCE

The performance ladder

The above discussion leads nicely into a consideration of which hospital has performed 'better' during the year. As previously suggested, performance is a matter of relating inputs and outputs, i.e. of relating cost and benefits. Moreover, the benefits are hard to measure objectively. Efficiency questions arise at a number of levels, as follows:

1 Is there an optimum allocation of resources between health care and other competing activities? That is, as a community how much should we invest in health care?

2 Given that the resources for health care have been fixed, is there an optimum allocation of resources between treatment for condition 'X' and other conditions competing for resources?

3 Given that the resources available for condition 'X' have been determined is the investment in equipment for treating X optimal?

4 Given that the choice of equipment has been made, is it operated economically and effectively?

This 'hierarchy' of levels at which performance may be assessed can be called a 'performance ladder'.

Starting at the bottom of the ladder, both Bonnie and Clyde have operated their equipment in accordance with expectations, both in respect of variable costs (economy) and success rates (effectiveness). There is therefore nothing to choose between Bonnie and Clyde in terms of operating performance at level 4. In our example cost differences are attributable to level 3 and the choice of equipment. First impressions, based on the comparative statistics, are that Clyde has performed better at level 3 as a result of investing in the new beta laser.

However, interpretation of these comparative statistics is tricky whenever the two hospitals have different objectives or emphases. This can happen, for instance, if:

1 level 2 decision-taking is *devolved* to the unit of comparison (i.e. to each hospital); or

2 the relevant health authority employs a policy of *specialization*.

Devolution

Suppose the health authority gives a block grant to each hospital, allowing each hospital the discretion to allocate resources between treatments for different conditions. In effect, level 2 decisions are being taken by the hospital and it may be quite in order for Clyde to give priority to treatment of condition 'X' whereas Bonnie elects to give priority to condition 'Y'. Clyde therefore invests in the latest beta laser whereas Bonnie continues with the alpha. In this case the difference in the cost per treatment of condition 'X' reflects the different policy objectives of the two hospitals.

Specialization

Suppose that the decision has been taken by the relevant health authority responsible for both hospitals to limit the authority's total capital expenditure on treatment of 'X' to £2,000. It makes little sense to allocate £1,000 to each hospital since that sum is inadequate for the new beta machine. Instead it makes sense to establish the new facility at one of the two hospitals. Clyde has done well to convince the authority that it should receive the investment rather than Bonnie. However, Bonnie may be receiving funds to develop specialist facilities for conditions other than 'X'. In these circumstances the difference in the cost per treatment of 'X' reflects the health authority's policy of specialization. Clyde's lower costs indicate its success in acquiring the specialized facility. This may indicate political acumen and/or the ability to impress in an open tender. A hospital's past record in using resources and its existing concentration of skills are likely to be relevant in the choice by the health authority.

It follows that comparative statistics should be used with extreme care whenever different institutions strive to do different things or to specialize in different things, whether that be due to their own choice or by imposition from the relevant authority. However, where two institutions do strive to serve the same needs and they both have access to the necessary resources then inter-institutional comparisons are valuable. If the health authority had a limit of £4,000 for condition 'X' – sufficient to fund beta machines at Bonnie *and* Clyde − then the comparative statistics would show a much better performance by Clyde. In these circumstances Clyde has kept in touch with new developments and moved swiftly to make the latest technology available to its patients. Bonnie has not. Clyde's better performance reflects its ability to invest promptly and wisely.

Resource allocation arrangements

The above discussion makes a crucial point. Comparative performance indicators mean different things depending upon the arrangements for allocating resources, and upon the availability of resources. A proper understanding of this background provides the key to sensible interpretation of the statistics. In a period when resources are reasonably plentiful comparative indicators are less problematic and more useful than in a period where the increasing cost of health care coupled with resource constraints creates a need for specialization. However, at the same time as the NHS moves from the former to the latter environment, health authorities are paying greater attention to comparative indicators. These will need to be interpreted carefully.

The premature retirement problem

The problem caused by the premature retirement of the alpha machine can be looked at from either a cost recovery (backlog depreciation) or a loan repayment (funding) perspective. The depreciation perspective regards the unrecovered cost of the alpha laser (£500) as part of the cost of going for the new beta laser. Total cost of the new beta laser is therefore £2,500 which is depreciated over beta's 200 treatments to give an annual depreciation recovery of £12.5 per treatment (£10 for the beta laser and £2.5 backlog for the alpha laser). The funding perspective uses a different argument to arrive at a recovery figure of £12.5 per treatment. During the period when Clyde was using the alpha machine the 'price' paid for each treatment would have covered, amongst other things, depreciation of £5 per treatment. Since alpha was used for 100 treatments this would have generated £500 available for investment in a replacement laser or for repayment of the original loan of £1,000 which had enabled the alpha laser to be purchased by Clyde. Assume that a new loan of £2,000 is used to purchase the new beta laser, that the £500 is used to pay off part of the original £1,000 loan which now reduces to £500, and that repayment of this £500 is rescheduled to coincide with the end of the ten-year expected lifespan for the beta machine. The remaining outstanding loan of £500 is repaid by recovering £2.5 per treatment in the price of the next 200 treatments over the life of the beta machine. This is added to the £10 per treatment necessary to repay the beta loan over 200 treatments.

It follows that at 1 January 199X Clyde has a capital fund of £2,500 representing £2,000 for the new beta laser and £500 in respect of the backlog on the old alpha laser. In order to provide the interest (assumed to be 10%) on this fund it is necessary to 'charge' £250 per annum or a further £12.5 per treatment on the basis of 20 treatments per annum. In the public sector there is much emphasis on fund accounting whereby the fund represents amounts paid for a particular purpose less amounts returned. As in our example a capital fund is not necessarily matched by assets. For example, the fund includes £500 in respect of the now unused alpha laser. In the private sector this £500 would be written off capital employed in order that capital employed was matched by assets in use.

Total costs per (successful) treatment at Clyde can be recalculated as follows to include interest:

	Perspective	
	Depreciation	Funding
	£	£
Beta laser:		
Historical cost depreciation	10	
to repay beta loan		10
Alpha laser:		
Backlog depreciation	2.5	
to repay alpha loan		2.5
Interest:		
On beta loan	10	10
On alpha loan	2.5	2.5
Variable costs	30	30
Cost per treatment	55	55
Cost per successful treatment	110	110

THE HEALTH AUTHORITY AS CUSTOMER AND AS INVESTOR

It is useful to distinguish the role of the health authority as customer from that of investor. As a customer the authority pays for treatment on behalf of the patient. As an investor the authority makes available the funds necessary for investment in equipment and facilities, and in the case of Clyde the outstanding funds are £2,500. Interest on this needs to be added to Clyde's treatment costings. In our example it increases costs by £12.50 per treatment.

As a customer, therefore, the health authority should expect to pay £110 per successful treatment. If capital resources have been made available to both hospitals to purchase the beta laser, then this 'price' should be offered to both hospitals, being that based on the latest technology. If capital shortage enables only Clyde to purchase the beta machine then different prices will have to be paid to the two hospitals. The price per successful treatment of £110 provides sufficient funds to cover variable costs of £30 per treatment, a replacement beta laser at the end of 200 treatments (assuming no price rise) and a return of £250 per annum on the capital investment of £2,500.

It should be noted, however, that this price calculation of £110 per successful treatment – in common with much accounting – does not recognize that interest can be earned on the amount set aside to provide for the loan repayment. It follows that costs will reduce after the first year as a result of this interest factor. A better approach is to keep costs constant during the use of the beta laser by charging a constant annual amount in respect of capital repayment/interest sufficient to repay the loans in the required timescale. Under such an arrangement, as used in an ordinary repayment mortgage, each payment is mostly interest in the early years whereas in later years it is mostly capital repayment. However, the annual charge remains the same throughout the period of the loan. Mortgage redemption tables show that at a 10% per annum interest rate compounded annually, a payment of approximately £406 at the end of each year would clear the £2,500 mortgage in ten years. Cost per treatment would therefore be better calculated as follows:

		£
Repayment/interest	£406/20 =	20.3
Variable costs		30.0
Cost per treatment		50.3

The charge per treatment of £20.3 approximates to the per treatment rental cost of the beta machine assuming that the owner requires a 10% return on his finance.

Alternative treatments of the premature retirement problem

There are various possible alternatives to the particular treatment of the premature retirement problem espoused in the preceding paragraphs. First the outstanding alpha loan of £500 could be written off and no attempt made to charge the £500 unrecovered cost of the alpha laser. The effect of this is that the health authority in its capacity as investor suffers a £500 loss since its loan is not repaid and no interest is earned. However, the health authority as a consumer benefits since the price per treatment does not have to cover any backlog depreciation. A second alternative is to continue to depreciate the £500 unrecovered cost of the alpha laser over its original schedule. In this case the cost (and price) of the first 100 beta treatments would include a £5 depreciation charge in respect of the now unused alpha machine. The first 100 treatments would generate £500, sufficient to repay the outstanding alpha loan. The health authority as investor recovers its loan more quickly at the expense of the health authority as consumer of the first 100 beta treatments. Yet another possibility is to charge sufficient for the beta treatments to cover interest on the £500 alpha loan but not sufficient to allow the loan to ever be repaid. Each alternative treatment corresponds to a different arrangement with respect to the repayment of the alpha loan.

Funding versus depreciation perspectives

Traditionally the public sector has adopted a funding perspective with the primary focus being the funding and refinancing of assets rather than depreciation. If funds for capital investment are provided to a public body without any requirement for repayment or interest – as has been the case in the past with the NHS – then the result is very little effective management of assets. Where capital finance is provided by loans and those loans are identified with specific assets (as in the Bonnie and Clyde case), then management of the assets and the management of the loans can be kept in tandem. Where specific loans are not identified with specific assets then fund management and asset management become separate issues. The different ways of charging for prematurely retired assets are, however, still identifiable with different *notional* financing alternatives. The Bonnie and Clyde case shows that the funding and refinancing of assets can be done on different (notional) bases (e.g. different loan repayment terms), and each basis carries implications for unit costing and prices.

In the private sector the focus is on depreciation rather than the funding and refinancing of assets. Nevertheless, in the private sector, different methods of calculating depreciation can be identified with different notional funding arrangements. For example, *future replacement* cost depreciation can be identified with the presumption that funds for the replacement of assets will be provided by current revenues. This presumption is not identifiable with historical cost depreciation which assumes that any additional funds necessary to replace assets will be obtained by new borrowing.

Customers consume and investors invest. On the face of it consumption and investment activities are quite distinct and this distinction is at the heart of accounting in both the public and private sectors. However, the distinction between the performance of investment and consumption activities may not be completely straightforward due to the dependence of costing (which measures consumption) on funding assumptions.

PRODUCT COMPLEXITIES

The third column of Exhibit 10.1 shows treatment costings on the assumption that the new beta laser costs not £2,000 but £20,000. The cost per successful treatment is now £265 and well in excess of the equivalent statistic (£140) for the alpha machine. If interest costs are included the gap between the alpha and beta laser is even greater. Prima facie there is no case for investing in the beta laser and if Clyde went ahead with this investment its performance would rightly be seen to be worse than that of Bonnie.

And yet it does not always follow that you should not invest in a machine which gives higher successful treatment costings. The machine's effect on waiting lists and upon the number of people requiring repeated treatments should also be considered. Both of these are important product considerations which the cost per successful treatment statistic fails to embrace. Further statistics are required to provide information on these matters. It seems likely that the greater success rate of the beta machine will lead to shorter waiting lists and fewer people suffering the distress of a failed treatment.

In a complex product like health care, it is unlikely that a single statistic such as cost per successful treatment will capture all cost/benefit considerations. A carefully constructed 'set' of performance indicators is likely to be needed. Investment decisions should bear in mind the consequences of the investment for all of the indicators.

CONCLUDING REMARKS

Bonnie and Clyde is designed to emphasize a few basic points relating to public sector activities:

1 'Success' in a public sector activity may be difficult to define. However, to focus only on input comparisons without reference to the success of the output will be misleading.

2 To measure performance by reference to a single input–output statistic may be misleading especially if the product is complex. A set of indicators is required for a proper understanding of public sector activity.

3 Comparative statistics should be interpreted in the light of the resource allocation arrangements and the degree of autonomy given. Where organizations are free to follow different internal resource allocation policies or have different resource allocation policies imposed upon them, then any comparison has to allow for such policy differences.

4 Accounting for assets has traditionally been weak in the public sector. The primary focus has been on the management of funds rather than the management of assets. However, the way in which depreciation/loan repayments and financing (interest) costs are treated has a significant effect on any unit costings.

SELF-STUDY EXERCISE 10.1

Consider the following information regarding three health authorities (HA1, HA2 and HA3) for 19X1:

	HA1	HA2	HA3
Expenses	£	£	£
Labour	100	120	120
Materials	100	120	100
Depreciation (historical cost)	150	150	80
Balance sheet			
Fixed assets cost	600	600	320
Cumulative depreciation	150	150	240
Capital fund	450	450	80
Population (000s)	1,500	1,000	1,000
Percentage of elderly	33.3	20	50
Waiting lists	medium	short	long

HA1 and HA2 have modern hospitals and equipment but HA3 does not. In past years the health authorities have been funded on the basis of expenses. For 19X1 funding is as follows:

	£
HA1	350
HA2	390
HA3	300
	1,040

Required:

For 19X2 it is proposed to be more discriminating in the funding allocations. What funding would you suggest for HA1, HA2 and HA3? Assume that elderly people use the health service twice as much as others. Assume a funding 'envelope' of £1,040 and no inflation.

CHAPTER 11

Stock: costs and values

INTRODUCTION

The key to an understanding of the accounting treatment of stocks is to separate the activities of a business into production and other (non-production) activities. Other activities include selling, distribution, administration and financing. A company which does not engage in production and whose activities are limited to 'buying and selling' normally values its stocks held for resale at the purchase cost. This chapter discusses accounting for stocks with particular attention to the performance of production activities. It centres on a company, Booze Limited, which deals in fine wines and 'plonk'. Whilst the fine wines are held for the long term and mature (a production process), plonk is a fast turnover, high volume, buying and selling business. The two businesses are thus very different and lend themselves to differing treatments of stock. Some introductory discussion is necessary before introducing the Booze case study.

PRODUCT VS. PERIOD COSTS

The expenses of a company are treated in one of two ways. Some expenses are 'collected' for inclusion in the cost of stock and are termed *product* costs. Such costs are identified with units of production and are charged against profit when those units of production are sold. The amount of the product costs charged against sales in any period is termed the cost of sales. If units of production remain unsold at the year end, then the product costs of those units form the stock figure in the balance sheet. Expenses which are not identified as product costs are charged against profit in the year in which they are incurred and are not collected for inclusion in stocks. Such expenses are termed *period* costs. Under SSAP 9 (the accounting standard on stock) those expenses which are collected for inclusion in stocks are those connected with *production* as opposed to selling, distribution, administration or financing charges. Thus the key distinction on which the conventional treatment of stocks is based is the split between production and non-production activities. Production provides a narrower focus than operations since the latter term is normally taken to include activities such as selling, distribution and administration (but not interest charges). The result of charging the production costs of the units sold against sales revenue is termed the gross profit. In a historical cost framework gross profit is only recognized in respect of the units sold and no gross profit is taken on units produced but not sold. Such a gross profit does not therefore provide a complete picture of *production* performance and this will become clear later in respect of the fine wines division. Once gross profit is calculated it is reduced by selling, distribution and administration costs in order to calculate operating profit.

The basic schema

In a conventional manufacturing environment the cost collected for stocks usually consists of three elements: (production) materials, labour and overheads. Let us suppose that each unit of production takes £1 of materials, £1 of labour and £1 of overhead giving a total unit cost of £3. Further, let us suppose that we start the year with 2 units of stock, we sell 4 units during the year and produce 5 units. The movements in stock during the year are shown as follows:

	Units of opening stock 2	Units produced 5	Units sold (4)	Units of closing stock 3
	Opening stocks (cost) £	Collected costs £	Cost of sales £	Closing stock (cost) £
Materials	2	5	(4)	3
Labour	2	5	(4)	3
Overheads	2	5	(4)	3
Total	6	15	(12)	9
	OS	CC	COS	CS

The closing stock of units (3) equals opening stock (2) *plus* production (5) *less* units sold (4). Similarly the historic cost of closing stock (£9) equals the opening stock (£6) *plus* the costs collected during the year for inclusion in stock (£15) *less* the costs attributed to the units sold (£12). The basic formula is:

$$OS + CC - COS = CS$$

It is frequently the case that the accountant knows the cost of closing stock but does not know cost of sales. In this case the formula may be rewritten:

$$COS = OS + CC - CS$$

There is a quick way of calculating closing stock or cost of sales provided the information is available. Closing stock equals the number of units in closing stock times the unit cost (3 × 3 = £9) and cost of sales equals the number of units sold times the unit cost (4 × 3 = £12).

Typically the accountant might count the number of units in stock at the year end and use the quick formula (no. of units × unit cost) to establish the closing stock. If the number of units sold is unknown then the formula $COS = OS + CC - CS$ can be used to calculate the cost of sales.

THE BOOZE LTD CASE STUDY

Booze Ltd imports two products – plonk which it sells rapidly and fine wines which it buys speculatively and 'puts down' for the future. A small percentage of the fine wines are sold each year. During the year ended 31 December 199X the company's stocks and trading transactions are as follows:

	As at 1.1.9X		During year ended 31.12.9X		As at 31.1.9X	
	Original cost (for fine wines this includes storage) £	Realizable value £	Wine purchases £	Sales £	Original cost (for fine wines this includes storage) £	Realizable value £
Plonk	100	90	230	360	70	95
Fine wines	200	310	25	75	270	340

During the year other expenses, allocated between plonk and fine wines, are as follows:

	Plonk £	Fine wines £
Storage	20	60
Distribution	70	5
Administration	18	7
Interest	5	25

Storage costs are included in stock where appropriate but interest cost is not. It is considered by the directors to be appropriate to include storage costs in the cost of fine wines but not of plonk. Assume that cash is zero at 1 January 199X and there are no debtors or creditors.

The schema for Booze

Booze collects two cost elements for inclusion in stock. They are wine purchases and storage costs. The schema for Booze is shown below. The schema includes figures to the extent that they are available from the question.

	Opening stock £	Collected costs £	Cost of sales £	Closing stock £
Wine purchases		255		
Storage		60		
	300	315		340

Figures are for Booze as a whole. No details are given for the opening and closing stocks but cost of sales can be calculated using the formula COS = OS + CC − CS (COS = £300 + 315 − 340 = £275).

Lower of cost and net realizable value

SSAP 9 requires accountants to work with a 'lower of cost and net realizable value' rule. This rule is enshrined in the accounting standards (SSAP 9) and represents a departure from the historical cost framework in the interests of prudence. In the case of Booze the effect is to reduce the opening stock on 1 January 199X by £10 and to reduce the closing stock on 31 December 199X − 1 by the same amount. This write-down reduces the stock of plonk from its historical cost of £100 to its net realizable value of £90. The effect on profits for 199X − 1 and 199X is as follows:

	199X − 1	199X
Opening stock	Unchanged	↓£10
plus		
Collected costs	Unchanged	Unchanged
less		
Closing stock	↓£10	Unchanged
equals		
Cost of sales	↑£10	↓£10
Effect on profit	↓£10	↑£10

The effect on profit is the reverse of the effect on cost of sales. It is seen that writing the stock down by £10 at the end 199X − 1/beginning 199X has, all other things being equal, the effect of transferring £10 of profit from 199X − 1 to 199X.

It should be noted that the 'lower of cost or net realizable value' rule as currently practised does not permit offsets. For example, the write-down of £10 on stock of plonk at 1 January 199X cannot be offset against the £110 surplus of net realizable value over historical cost in respect of fine wines. Thus the opening stock figure in 199X for Booze as a whole is £290, being:

	NRV	HC	Total
	£	£	£
Plonk	90		90
Fine wines		200	200
	90	200	290

BOOZE LTD
Profit for the year ended 31 December 199X

		Note
Turnover	435	1
Cost of sales	265	
Gross profit	170	
Distribution and storage	95	
	75	
Administration	25	
	50	
Interest	30	
Profit before tax	20	

Note 1
Turnover represents invoiced sales of plonk and fine wines. The contributions of these two activities to profit and turnover are as follows:

	Turnover	Profit before tax
	£	£
Plonk	360	(3)
Fine wines	75	23

Exhibit 11.1

	Plonk	Fine wines	Both
	£	£	£
Sales	360	75	435
Opening stock	90	200	290
Purchases	230	25	255
Storage		60	60
	320	285	605
Closing stock	70	270	340
Cost of sales	250	15	265
Gross profit	110	60	170
Distribution and storage	90	5	95
Administration	18	7	25
Interest	5	25	30
	113	37	150
Profit	(3)	23	20

Exhibit 11.2 Calculation of profit by product line

The formula for Booze's 199X cost of sales now gives:

$$COS = £290 + 315 - 340 = £265$$

Booze's results

Exhibit 11.1 gives a statement of the profit for the year calculated on a historical cost basis in a format which analyses expenses by function. A note to the statement gives information about how the various product lines have contributed to profit.

The calculation of the profit figure by product line is given in Exhibit 11.2. Product line information is crucial to management in managing the launch, promotion, life expectancy and retirement of products. Prima facie such information is also valuable to investors.

THE GOSPEL ACCORDING TO SSAP 9

Accounting standard number 9 defines the 'cost' of stock as being 'that expenditure which has been incurred in the normal course of business in bringing the product or service to its present location and condition.' This expenditure should include in addition to cost of purchase such costs of conversion as are appropriate to the location and condition of the stock. Cost of conversion comprises:

1 costs which are specifically attributable to units of production, i.e. direct labour, direct expenses and subcontracted work;

2 production overheads;

3 other overheads, if any, attributable in the particular circumstances of the business to bringing the product or service to its present location and condition.

Production overheads comprise overheads incurred in respect of materials, labour or services for production, based on the normal level of activity, taking one year with another. For this purpose each overhead should be classified according to function (e.g. production, selling or administration) so as to ensure the inclusion in the cost of conversion of those overheads (including depreciation) which relate to production, notwithstanding that these may accrue wholly or partly on a time basis.

For purposes of applying SSAP 9 it is necessary to consider separately the storage costs of plonk and fine wines. Storage of fine wines is part of the maturing or production process. Such storage costs can therefore be regarded as necessary for bringing the stock to its present condition and, following SSAP 9, would be regarded as 'other overheads' to be included in the cost of conversion. The same argument does not apply to plonk where storage does not enhance the quality of the product. In a manufacturing environment storage of materials necessary to production processes is to allow production to take place and such storage costs can therefore be regarded as production costs. In a buying and selling type of operation such as 'plonk' there is no obvious production and hence the only collected costs are the costs of purchases for resale. Following SSAP 9 storage costs of plonk are likely to be excluded from stock.

Marginal costing

SSAP 9 opts for a version of full costing whereby all 'production' costs are included in stock irrespective of whether they be fixed or variable. There are many who believe that marginal costing, in which only variable costs are included in stock, is preferable to full costing. With marginal costing, costs are subdivided into variable costs and fixed costs. Variable costs are those which increase whenever the volume or the quality of stock is increased. Fixed costs remain constant whatever the stock volume or quality, provided the stock volume or quality is within the capability of the production unit concerned. The issue of marginal versus full costing is examined in the next chapter.

THE REALIZABLE INCOME ALTERNATIVE

A company earns realizable income whenever the realizable value of its assets increases. Thus if a company holds fine wines and the saleable value of those fine wines goes up, then realizable income has been earned, irrespective of the fact that no actual sale has taken place.

The realizable value of the assets at the beginning of the year are:

	Plonk	*Fine wines*	*Total*
Stocks	£90	£310	£400

During the year money items (cash plus debtors less creditors) move from zero to minus £30 as follows:

	Plonk		*Fine wines*		*Total*
	£	£	£	£	£
Sales		360		75	
Purchases	230		25		
Storage	20		60		
Distribution	70		5		
Administration	18		7		
Interest	5	343	25	122	
		17		(47)	(30)

Thus the realizable value of the assets at the end of the year are:

	Plonk	*Fine wines*	*Total*
	£	£	£
Stocks	95	340	435
Money items	17	(47)	(30)
	112	293	405

Realizable income is the difference between the opening and closing realizable values (RV) of the assets and is calculated as follows:

	Plonk	*Fine wines*	*Total*
	£	£	£
Closing RV	112	293	405
Opening RV	90	310	400
	22	(17)	5

These realizable incomes may be reconciled with historical trading profits by adjusting the historical profit for the difference between the opening and closing unrealized gains in stock, an unrealized gain being the difference between the stock's net realizable value and its cost. The calculation is as follows:

	Plonk £	Fine wines £
Unrealized gain/loss – opening	0	110
Unrealized gain/loss – closing	25	70
	25	(40)
Trading profit/loss	(3)	23
Realizable income	22	(17)

The realizable incomes can also be calculated by using the formula COS = OS + CC − CS but substituting in the formula not the historical cost of opening stock and closing stock but their realizable values. Hence:

	Plonk £	Fine wines £
Opening stock	90	310
Collection costs	230	85
Closing stock	(95)	(340)
Cost of sales	225	55

Realizable income is then calculated as:

	Plonk £	Fine wines £
Sales	360	75
Cost of sales	(225)	(55)
Gross profit	135	20
Storage	(20)	
Distribution	(70)	(5)
Administration	(18)	(7)
	27	8
Interest	(5)	(25)
	22	(17)

G

Interpreting the cash flows

During the year plonk has generated £17 of cash whilst fine wines has absorbed £47 of cash. In general it is natural for a business which generates cash to be matched with a business which absorbs that cash and converts it into longer-term capital growth. In principle therefore the cash generating plonk business and the cash absorbing fine wines businesses are a good fit. However, fine wines has absorbed more cash than plonk has generated causing a £30 negative cash flow for Booze as a whole. In addition it should be noted that the cash which plonk has produced has been through a run-down of its stocks. Thus plonk's stocks in its historical, 'lower of cost and net realizable value' accounts have been liquidated to the extent of £20 (being £90 − 70) of which £3 has been absorbed by losses (cash expenditure in excess of income), leaving a cash surplus of £17. Clearly plonk cannot, other than in the short term, continue to run down its stocks.

Fine wines shows in its historical cost accounts a profit of £23 and yet it has a negative cash flow of £47. In effect its cash flow and profit have combined to generate a £70 increased investment in stock (£270 − £200).

HISTORICAL COST PROFIT VS. REALIZABLE INCOME

Fine wines is a long-term production business whereas plonk is essentially a shorter-term trading operation. For fine wines it is important to use a profit/income measure which recognizes the performance of production in the right time period. For plonk it is important to recognize the performance of its trading operations (purchasing and selling) in the right time periods. The following paragraphs discuss the timing of income recognition under historical cost profit and realizable income in respect of purchasing, production and selling. Replacement cost profit is also discussed.

Historical cost profit has the following key features:

1 revenue is recognized at the time of sale (the realization concept);

2 expenses are matched with that revenue (the matching concept); and

3 expenses are charged at their purchase cost (the historical cost concept).

The last feature is specific to historical cost accounting but the first two features are shared with replacement cost accounting. Although replacement cost accounting uses the matching principle, it is current replacement costs at the time of sale which are matched with sales revenue in order to calculate 'operating' profit. The difference between the historical purchase cost and the replacement cost at the time of sale is called a 'holding' gain. If at the end of the accounting period the stock has not been sold, then that period's holding gain is the difference between purchase cost and year end replacement cost.

The historical cost system identifies profit (HC profit) with selling. It is the period in which the sale is made which makes the entire difference between historical purchase cost and sales revenue. No profit is attributed to the period in which purchasing takes place or to the period in which production takes place unless these coincide with the period of sale. And yet certain types of business rely upon either purchasing skills or productive efficiency as a key source of profit.

These problems do not apply in such large measure to replacement cost accounting since purchasing skills will be reflected in holding gains rather than operating profit. In a manufacturing environment replacement cost still suffers from the fact that productive efficiency is recognized in operating profit for the period in which the product is sold rather than the period in which it is produced.

Realizable income abandons the realization principle. As a result:

1 purchasing skills are recognized in the period in which the purchase takes place;

2 productive performance is reflected in profit (realizable profit) for the period of production; and

3 selling performance is reflected in the profit (realizable profit) for the period of sale.

The problem with realizable income is, for most businesses, the practical one of knowing the realizable value of an asset when it has not yet been sold.

Purchasing skills

Suppose the normal purchasing price of 'X' is £30 but the purchasing officer identifies an opportunity to buy at £25, giving a favourable variance of £5. In historical cost accounting this £5 which has been earned through purchasing is recognized when 'X' is sold. With realizable income the £5 is recognized in the period in which the purchase takes place. For example, if the selling price of 'X' is stable at £40, realizable income of £15 (40 − 25) is recognized as soon as the purchase takes place. This £15 includes £5 in respect of the purchasing activity. In replacement cost accounting the £5 immediately generates a £5 holding gain as against the 'normal' purchase price. This holding gain is included in the performance of holding activities in the period of the purchase. Hence, like realizable income accounting, replacement cost accounting recognizes purchasing skills in the appropriate time period.

Productive performance

Suppose that production at factory A transforms materials and labour with a combined realizable value of £25 into stock with a stable selling value of £40, whilst factory B transforms the same inputs into stock with a stable selling value of £35. In historical cost accounting this difference in performance between the two factories is not recognized until their respective stocks are sold. The same is true of replacement cost accounting since replacement cost accounting includes gains from production as part of the operating profit only when the products are sold. With realizable income the difference in productivity between the two plants is recognized as soon as production takes place since factory A immediately records realizable income of £15 whilst factory B records realizable income of £10.

It should be noted that although the benefits of purchasing and production are impounded in the realizable income for the year in which those skills are exhibited, the effects of those skills are not separately identified within the realizable income figure. Nevertheless realizable income is the only system which recognizes gains from production in the appropriate time period.

The period recognition problems associated with historical cost accounting, and to a lesser extent replacement cost accounting, are avoided by realizable income. However, for many businesses, realizable income is not practical due to the absence of active markets for its second-hand machinery or partially complete products. In other cases the adoption of realizable income is unnecessary because purchasing, production and selling take place in a short timescale and only a small minority of these activities are affected by the period recognition problem, i.e. the problem is immaterial.

Plonk and fine wines

The discussion now addresses the question of whether it is practical/desirable to adopt an alternative to historical cost accounting in the circumstances of the question. Readers with a knowledge of the fine wines market will know that a well developed market exists, with quoted prices, for fine wines at various stages of maturity. The fine wines business therefore passes the practicality test as regards realizable income. Furthermore, the maturing (production) period for fine wines is a lengthy one and so the adoption of realizable income passes the materiality test. In our example fine wine has made a historical profit and a realizable loss. The historical profit reflects performance over the long period since purchase in respect of the small volume of fine wine actually sold during the year. Realizable income reflects performance during the year in respect of the whole 'portfolio' of fine wine under management's control.

Fine wines is in a long-term production business. However, in the particular circumstances of this business, production is essentially a maturing activity, and as such is virtually indistinguishable from a holding activity. If it is important to recognize the performance of this production/ holding activity in the period in which the holding takes place then realizable income is the most appropriate accounting basis. The realizable loss of the fine wines business during the year suggests that the production/ holding activity has not been successful during the year. Booze would have been advised to sell its stock of fine wines at the beginning of the year and buy it back at the end.

Readers with knowledge of the plonk business will appreciate that purchasing skill plays a key role. Spotting the undiscovered vineyard with a good crop of grapes and striking a good bargain is an important element of success. If a season's production is purchased in one year but sold in the next, then the period recognition problems associated with historical cost accounting *can* be significant. Plonk has made a historical loss and a realizable profit. The historical loss could be caused by poor sales performance this year and/or poor purchasing performance last year. If the latter then the historical loss is not a fair reflection of this year's activity.

Plonk is not a production business but a 'buying and selling' business. As previously explained, historical cost accounting is deficient if buying and selling takes place in different accounting periods. However, either realizable income or replacement cost accounting will recognize sales and purchasing skills in the period in which those skills are employed. Hence, Plonk's current realizable profit could have come from a good sales performance and/or a good purchasing performance but in either case it would be the performance in the *current* year.

BALANCE SHEET RECOGNITION PROBLEMS

The previous discussion has concerned income recognition, following the principle that performance in purchasing, production or selling should be recognized in the period in which the respective activity takes place. There is a separate issue relating to the recognition of assets and liabilities in the balance sheet. Suppose that Booze's historical cost balance sheet at the end of 199X is as follows:

	Resources		Sources of finance	
	£			£
Stocks	340	Share capital		160
Cash	(30)	Loan		150
	310			310

Now suppose that an agreement is reached with a finance house for the finance house to buy 70% of the stocks of fine wines (£270) for £189. This cash is used to pay off the overdraft and the loan and hence the balance sheet becomes:

	Resources		Sources of finance	
	£			£
Stocks	151	Share capital		160
Cash	9			
	160			160

This balance sheet now looks much healthier than before. The company now has no borrowings, a positive cash position and appears to be making its £20 historical cost profit from a much smaller capital employed (£160 against £310).

However, suppose the agreement with the finance house contained an option allowing the finance house to sell the fine wine back to Booze in five years' time at a price of £189 plus interest. The agreement is now revealed as a 'contrivance' to improve the appearance of Booze's balance sheet. Even though the terms of the agreement may be given in the notes to the financial statements, the balance sheet itself no longer 'recognizes' the commitment to buy back the stock. This type of agreement is not uncommon and it raises serious issues as to when and on what criteria assets and liabilities should be included (recognized) by the balance sheet. Such balance sheet recognition problems are not discussed in detail at this stage but the user of published financial statements is well advised to read the notes carefully!

CONCLUDING COMMENTS

Booze requires a three-way analysis in order to understand its business clearly. First it is necessary to do a product performance analysis where plonk and fine wines are treated as separate products. To do this analysis it is necessary, as far as possible, to identify the costs attributable to each product. In our example administration costs are higher for plonk than for fine wines. This reflects the fact that administration of the many transactions of plonk is more expensive since the level of such activity for fine wines is far lower. It may be desirable for Booze to institute an activity-based costing system in which the administrative costs associated with each product are related to cost 'drivers' such as the number of transactions for each product. In our example the 18 : 7 split in administrative costs would then reflect an 18 : 7 split in the number of transactions involving plonk and fine wines. Distribution costs for plonk are far higher than for fine wines, whereas in the case of storage the reverse holds. The important point is that overall costs are attributed to the two products on a basis which properly reflects each product's influence on those costs. In this way the cost structures of each business activity are properly understood and it becomes possible to devise measures to contain the costs. For example, distribution expenses for plonk might reflect the number of journeys made by the delivery vehicle and any attempt to reduce distribution costs must start by addressing the number of journeys. Finally it is important to attribute interest costs. Since much more money is tied up in the stocks of fine wines, the interest cost attributed to this product is far higher. Cost attribution to products should not be restricted to product costs or even to operational costs otherwise a misleading picture may emerge as to the overall relative performance of each product.

Even when the performance of each product has been identified, care needs to be taken in deciding upon a course of action. For example, pulling out of fine wines might lose customers who require a single purchasing source for both plonk and fine wines. On the costs side interdependence might also be a problem. For example, both the plonk and fine wines business volumes might be required to negotiate a discount on the storage rates. Interdependence provides a brake on the ability to assess separately the performance of related products.

The second analysis for Booze is by function. Under the Companies Acts most companies show separately sales, cost of sales, gross profit, selling and distribution expenses, administration expenses, operating profit, interest and net profit. However, it is difficult from this format to identify separately the respective performances of the selling, production and purchasing functions. High sales and high margins (gross profit to sales) can reflect good performance in all or any of these functions. It becomes necessary to seek further information, including non-financial information, to assess fully the performance of each function. For example, production performance may be judged on the basis of unit costs, unit volumes, target volumes, wastage rates and a quality index.

The third analytical dimension is time. It is necessary to choose an accounting system which for a production-led business recognizes (good) production performance in the period in which that performance takes place. Similarly it is important that for a trading company (good) purchasing performance is recognized when that purchasing activity takes place. The discussion on Booze has highlighted that the historical cost framework may be inappropriate or by itself inadequate for long-term production processes or where buying and selling take place in different time periods. It follows that the choice of accounting framework should be influenced by the nature and timescales of the business activity. A suitable accounting framework will attribute costs and benefits to the key functions of the business in the appropriate time periods. The costs and benefits of each function should, as far as possible, be attributed to each product to show product performance.

SELF-STUDY EXERCISE 11.1

Firewater Limited

Firewater Limited deals in two products – blended whisky which it sells rapidly and malt whisky which it allows to mature over several years. A small percentage of the malt whisky is sold each year. During the year ended 31 December 199X the company's stocks and trading transactions were as follows:

	As at 1.1.9X		During year ended 31.12.9X		As at 31.12.9X	
	Original cost (for malt this is including storage)	Realizable value	Wine purchases	Sales	Original cost (for malt this is including storage)	Realizable value
	£	£	£	£	£	£
Blend	200	180	460	720	140	190
Malt	400	620	50	150	540	680

During the year other expenses, allocated between blend and malt whiskies, are as follows:

	Blend	Malt
	£	£
Storage	40	120
Distribution	140	10
Administration	36	14
Interest	10	50

Storage costs are included in malt whisky stock but not in blended whisky stock. Interest is not included in stock.

Required:

1 Prepare separate profit statements for the blended whisky and malt whisky businesses for the year ended 31 December 199X with stocks being treated at the lower of cost and net realizable value. Assume that the treatment of storage costs indicated in the question is acceptable.

2 Prepare separate profit statements for the blended whisky and malt whisky businesses for the year ended 31 December 199X with opening and closing stocks being valued at net realizable value.

3 Prepare separate cash flow statements for the blended whisky and malt whisky businesses for the year ended 31 December 199X, on the assumption that all sales and purchases are for cash.

4 Interpret briefly the performance of the blended and malt whisky businesses and indicate the major tasks facing Firewater's management.

CHAPTER 12

Accounting for production

INTRODUCTION

This chapter focuses on production. Production involves costs which vary in proportion to the number of units produced (variable costs) and costs which do not vary with production volumes provided production is within the normal range of output (fixed costs). The most obvious variable costs are the materials which go into the product. The appropriate categorization for the wages of those who work on the product depends on the nature of the production process. If labour works directly on the product then the amount of labour required is likely to vary directly with the number of units produced. It is this treatment of labour as a variable cost which is adopted in this chapter. Increasingly, however, labour is necessary to supervise the robotic machinery and must be paid whenever the production facility is in use irrespective of the number of units produced. In this case labour is closely identified with the equipment, and could be treated in the same way as the cost of the equipment. Equipment may expire as a result of the number of units produced (expiry through use) or it may expire through the passage of time irrespective of the number of units produced (expiry through time). The latter is more common in a high technology environment where machines become obsolete before they wear out through use. In the discussion contained in this chapter it is assumed that the equipment expires through time. This chapter discusses two similar companies – High Hopes and High Anticipation – for both of which variable costs and the equipment used are identical. Only the firms' production volumes and stockholding activities are different. The discussion assumes an historical cost framework as opposed to a value framework. However, within the historical cost framework, two different treatments of depreciation are considered. In one case the cost of the machine is allocated equally to the accounting periods during the lifetime of the machine. In the second case the lifetime production of the machine, before it expires through time, is estimated, and the cost of the machine allocated equally to the units of production.

THE HIGH HOPES AND HIGH ANTICIPATION CASE STUDY

High Hopes (HH) and High Anticipation (HA) both start in business at the same time making an identical product. During the first three periods the market is expanding rapidly and both companies experience rapid growth. The two companies perform as follows:

	Period 1		Period 2		Period 3	
	HH	HA	HH	HA	HH	HA
Units of production	200	250	400	450	800	900
Opening stock (units)	Nil	Nil	Nil	50	Nil	100
Closing stock (units)	Nil	50	Nil	100	Nil	200
Sales units	200	200	400	400	800	800
Sales price	£5	£5	£5	£5	£5	£5
Material/labour cost (per unit)	£2	£2	£2	£2	£2	£2

It is seen that the difference between the two companies is in their respective stockholding policies. Whilst HA is building up stocks, HH has a policy of keeping zero stocks and exactly matches production with demand for each period. Both companies purchase, at the beginning of period 1, a machine costing £1,200 and having a life of three periods. The machine has a productive capacity of 1,000 units per period. It is technically obsolete at the end of the third period, has no scrap value, and requires replacement if the market dominance of the two companies is to be protected from incoming competition. To replace the 1,000 units capacity with new technology machines once again costs £1,200 at the end of period 3.

HH and HA results

The operating profits of the two companies over the first three years can be calculated by valuing stock and cost of sales on either a full costing basis or a marginal costing basis. On a marginal costing basis the results of both HH and HA are as in Exhibit 12.1.

	Period		
	1	2	3
	£	£	£
Sales	1,000	2,000	4,000
Cost of sales			
Fixed cost overhead	(400)	(400)	(400)
Variable costs	(400)	(800)	(1,600)
Operating profit	200	800	2,000

Exhibit 12.1 Marginal cost operating profits

			Period			
		1		2		3
	HH	HA	HH	HA	HH	HA
	£	£	£	£	£	£
Sales	1,000	1,000	2,000	2,000	4,000	4,000
Variable costs	400	500	800	900	1,600	1,800
Cash from operations	600	500	1,200	1,100	2,400	2,200
Opening balance	(1,200)	(1,200)	(720)	(820)	408	198
Interest	(120)	(120)	(72)	(82)	41	20
Closing balance	(720)	(820)	408	198	2,849	2,418

Exhibit 12.2 Cash flows and interest

In this treatment the expiry of the fixed asset costing £1,200 is clearly treated as a time-driven activity, and each time period suffers an equal £400 depreciation charge as a fixed cost overhead. Only marginal costs, i.e. those which vary with the volume of sales, are treated as variable costs. The operating profits of HH and HA are identical and hence they are unaffected by the difference in the companies' production and stock-holding activities. At the net profit level, however, the two companies will show different profits since HA has money tied up in stocks and hence suffers a higher interest charge. The cash flows and interest charges, assuming a 10% interest rate on the opening cash balance, for the two companies is given in Exhibit 12.2. There is an assumption that the machine is purchased by overdraft.

Hence HA suffers an additional interest charge of £10 in period 2 and a smaller interest receipt of £21 in period 3 consequent to its policy of holding stocks.

FULL COST PROFITS

Following SSAP 9, fixed production costs or overheads should be included in stock and cost of sales on the basis of a 'normal' level of activity taking one year with another. The concept of a normal level of activity implies that basically a company is experiencing equilibrium conditions. Clearly this is not so in our case study where both companies are in a start-up situation. Over the three years of the machine's life HH produces 1,400 units and HA produces 1,600 units. It follows that *on average* HH must charge each unit of production with £0.857 (1,200/1,400) and HA must charge £0.75 per unit (1,200/1,600) if sufficient funds are to be generated for replacement of the machine. Using these per unit production overhead costs, the operating profit statements on a full cost basis are shown in Exhibit 12.3.

Under full costing the production overhead charged in cost of sales varies in proportion to the volume of sales. Hence the expiry of the fixed asset appears to be volume driven (i.e. to vary with volume) even though ·the life of the fixed asset is determined by the passing of three periods rather than the number of units produced.

It is seen from Exhibit 12.3 that there are differences between HH's and HA's operating profits on a full costing basis caused by HA's higher production levels and consequent lower unit cost. Hence HA's operating profit is £31 higher in period 1, £43 higher in period 2 and £86 higher in period 3.

Exhibit 12.2 shows that cash flows and interest are unaffected by whether stock and cost of sales employ marginal or full costing. The accounting treatment of stock does not affect cash flow or interest cost. Hence HA's higher operating profits under full costing are reduced by HA's higher interest charges. The net effect is a £31 higher net profit for HA in period 1, a £33 higher net profit in period 2 and £65 higher net profit in period 3.

Periods 1–3: operating profit

Exhibit 12.4 displays the operating profits of HH and HA for periods 1 to 3.

A cross-sectional analysis of Exhibit 12.4 comparing HH with HA shows that marginal cost operating profits are unaffected by the different stockholding policies of the two companies. Full cost operating profits are,

	Period					
	1		2		3	
	HH	HA	HH	HA	HH	HA
	£	£	£	£	£	£
Sales	1,000	1,000	2,000	2,000	4,000	4,000
Cost of sales						
Variable cost	(400)	(400)	(800)	(800)	(1,600)	(1,600)
Production overhead	(171)	(150)	(343)	(300)	(686)	(600)
Operating profit	429	450	857	900	1,714	1,800

Exhibit 12.3 Full cost operating profits

		Marginal cost		Full cost	
		HH	HA	HH	HA
Period		£	£	£	£
1		200	200	429	450
2		800	800	857	900
3		2,000	2,000	1,714	1,800
		3,000	3,000	3,000	3,150

Exhibit 12.4 Periods 1–3: operating profit

however, affected by the different stockholding policies during a period of growth. HA's cumulative operating profits are £150 higher, reflecting the fact that production overhead of £150 (200 units @ £0.75) has not been charged against profit but has been included in stock at the end of period 3.

A time series analysis of Exhibit 12.4 comparing period 1, 2 and 3 operating profits shows marginal cost profit growth which is higher than full cost profit growth. Full cost profits double each period, reflecting the growth in sales volumes. Marginal cost profits more than double each period as a result of the fixed cost element in cost of sales. The ratio of sales growth to profit growth is not 1 : 1 and hence there is 'gearing' (a ratio other than 1 : 1) which makes marginal cost profits more volatile to changes in business volumes.

A PERIOD OF EQUILIBRIUM

During periods 3, 4, 5 and 6 both HH and HA experience level demand with sales at 800 units per period. HH continues its policy of not holding stocks whilst HA maintains its stocks at 200 units. For each company, production in periods 4 to 6 is provided by a 'new technology' machine purchased at the beginning of period 4. This new machine also costs £1,200 and has a life of three years. There is no alteration in the selling price which remains at £5, but material/labour costs increase to £3 per unit for periods 4 to 6.

HH's operating profits on a marginal cost basis in periods 4 to 6 are identical, and in each period are as in Exhibit 12.5.

The fall as against the equivalent period 3 profit of £2,000 (Exhibit 12.1) is caused by the increase in unit labour/material cost.

Turning now to HA, HA's operating profits on a marginal cost basis benefit in period 4 from its stockholding policy since period 4's sales

	Period 4 £	Period 5 £	Period 6 £
Sales	4,000	4,000	4,000
Cost of sales			
Fixed cost overhead	(400)	(400)	(400)
Variable costs	(2,400)	(2,400)	(2,400)
Operating profit	1,200	1,200	1,200

Exhibit 12.5 HH marginal cost operating profit

include 200 units manufactured in period 3 at the lower unit labour/ material cost of £2. HA's results are given in Exhibit 12.6.

Full costing in periods 4 to 6

Assuming that sales demand and production remains at 800 units for periods 4 to 6, then the per unit production cost throughout periods 4, 5 and 6 for both HH and HA is £0.50 (1,200/2,400). During period 4 HA sells 200 units produced in period 3, assuming that stock is dealt with on a first in first out (FIFO) basis. These 200 units provide a bonus to HA's period 4 profit since their labour/material costs are £2 rather than £3 per unit. However, this bonus is reduced to the extent that their unit overhead production costs are £0.75 rather than £0.50. The full cost operating profits of period 4 are given in Exhibit 12.7.

	Period 4 £	Period 5 £	Period 6 £
Sales	4,000	4,000	4,000
Cost of sales			
Fixed cost overhead	(400)	(400)	(400)
Variable costs			
200 @ £2	(400)		
600 @ £3	(1,800)		
800 @ £3		(2,400)	(2,400)
Operating profit	1,400	1,200	1,200

Exhibit 12.6 HA marginal cost operating profits

	HH	HA
	£	£
Sales	4,000	4,000
Cost of sales		
Labour/material	(2,400)	
Production overhead	(400)	
For 200 units:		
labour/material		(400)
production overhead		(150)
For 600 units:		
labour/material		(1,800)
production overhead		(300)
Operating profit	1,200	1,350

Exhibit 12.7 Period 4 full cost operating profits

The period 5 and period 6 full cost operating profits for both HH and HA are £1,200 being:

	£
Sales	4,000
Cost of sales	
Labour/material	(2,400)
Production overhead	(400)
	1,200

Profits during a period of equilibrium

The time series of operating profits during periods 4, 5 and 6 is given in Exhibit 12.8.

	4	5	6	Exhibit
	£	£	£	
HH marginal cost basis	1,200	1,200	1,200	12.5
HA marginal cost basis	1,400	1,200	1,200	12.6
HH full cost basis	1,200	1,200	1,200	12.7
HA full cost basis	1,350	1,200	1,200	12.7

Exhibit 12.8 Times series for periods 4 to 6

Exhibit 12.8 shows HH's profits, whether given on a marginal or full cost basis, to be static during periods 4 to 6. This reflects the underlying business reality of static demand, production and (zero) stock levels. During periods 4 to 6 HA also experiences a static operating environment in the form of stationary demand, production and (200 unit) stock levels. However, between periods 4 and 5 this stationary state is not reflected by the operating profits which fall by £200 on a marginal cost basis and £150 on a full cost basis.

This apparent lack of correspondence with underlying reality can be corrected by separating in period 4 the results of HA's operating and (stock) holding activities. The holding of 200 units of stock between periods 3 and 4 enabled HA to make a gain or saving of £200 on a marginal cost basis, attributable to a lower labour/material unit cost in period 3, or £150 on a full cost basis. The latter is attributable to a £200 saving on labour/material costs offset by a £50 loss (25p per unit) on production overheads. Separating out these holding gains reduces HA's operating profits in period 4, on both marginal and full cost bases, to £1,200, and hence HA's operating profit is shown as constant throughout periods 4 to 6.

HA's stockholding policy

The benefits of HA's stockholding policy can now be assessed. The holding gains realized in period 4 need to be set alongside the higher interest costs incurred by building up stocks in periods 1 to 3. Hence the benefits of the policy during periods 1 to 3 have been:

	Marginal cost £	Full cost £
Holding gain	200	150
Interest cost of stockholding		
Period 2	(10)	(10)
Period 3	(21)	(21)
Cumulative gain	169	119

In the case study the price rise for labour/material at the end of period 3 is so substantial that the stockholding policy shows a tangible financial benefit. However, in practice more modest price rises will often lead to stockholding activity being a (tangible) financial loser. In such circumstances the cost of the policy must be set against other, possibly less tangible items such as the ability to meet unexpected demand and less volatile production schedules.

Period	Marginal cost HH £	Marginal cost HA £	Full cost HH £	Full cost HA £
1	200	200	429	450
2	800	800	857	900
3	2,000	2,000	1,714	1,800
Cumulative	3,000	3,000	3,000	3,150
4	1,200	1,400[1]	1,200	1,350[2]
5	1,200	1,200	1,200	1,200
6	1,200	1,200	1,200	1,200
Cumulative	6,600	6,800	6,600	6,900

(1) being operating gain of £1,200 and a holding gain of £200.
(2) being operating gain of £1,200 and a holding gain of £150.

Exhibit 12.9 Periods 1–6 operating profit

Six-year profit summary

Exhibit 12.9 displays the operating profits of HH and HA for periods 1 to 6 showing cumulative totals at the end of periods 3 and 6. From Exhibit 12.9 it is seen that HA's cumulative operating profits at the end of period 6 on a marginal cost basis are £200 higher than those of HH (£6,800 as against £6,600), reflecting HA's gain (before interest) from its stockholding policy. On a full cost basis HA's cumulative profits are a further £100 higher at £6,900. This reflects the £100 of production overhead (200 units @ 50p) which on a full costing basis is not charged against profit but is included in stock at the end of period 6.

The production overhead element included in HA's stock valued on a full costing basis moves as follows:

	£
Included in stock at the end of period 3	150
Charged against the holding gain in period 4	(50)
Included in stock at the end of period 6	100

AN OVERVIEW OF THE PRODUCTION PROCESS

Exhibit 12.10 demonstrates production as the process of converting labour, material and production facilities into stocks to satisfy sales and stockholding requirements.

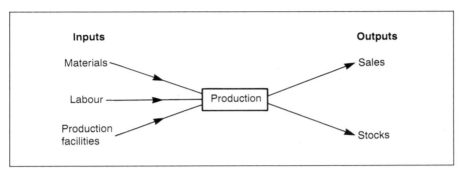

Exhibit 12.10 The production process

At the accounting level, accounting for production is the process of taking the costs of materials, labour and production facilities and converting these into the cost of sales during the accounting period and the cost of stocks held at the end of that period. This chapter to date has concentrated at the output end of Exhibit 12.10 upon the impact of different methods of accounting for production (marginal and full costing) upon both the profits generated by sales and upon the cost of stock in the balance sheet. It is now time to concentrate at the input end of Exhibit 12.10 upon the different methods of accounting for production and their relationship with the consumption of labour/materials and the provision of production facilities. In this analysis insight into the significance of marginal and full costing is obtained by treating the holding and supply of production facilities as a separate business activity from other operations.

The two-business perspective

Let us regard HA as being involved in two businesses:

1 a service by way of the provision of production facilities;

2 a manufacturing and selling operation.

Furthermore let us assume the objective of the first business is to break even in the medium/long term. It then follows that in the first three years the production facilities would be offered by business 1 to business 2 at a per unit price of £0.75 on the basis that business 1 expects to recover its initial outlay of £1,200 in three years, i.e. it makes a business judgement that total custom in the three years will be 1,600 units. If any possible interest and other costs associated with the provision of the production facilities are, for convenience of exposition, ignored, then the first year gross profits of the two businesses are as follows:

	Business 1		Business 2	
	£		£	
Sales	187.50	(250 @ £0.75)	1,000	(200 @ £5)
Fixed costs	(400.00)		(150)	(200 @ £0.75)
Variable costs			(400)	(200 @ £2)
Gross profit/(loss)	(212.50)		450	Full cost profit
Combined profit from both businesses			237.50	
Adjustment			(37.50)	(£187.50 − £150)
Marginal cost profit			200.00	

Business 1 sales to business 2 are on the basis of the number of units (250) which have used the production facility at the price of £0.75 per unit. Business 1's expense is the time-driven depreciation charge of £400. Business 2's sales are 200 units at £5 each against which are matched the unit driven costs of 200 units. From the perspective of business 2 both the original variable costs of £2 per unit and the use of the production facility at £0.75 per unit are unit driven.

Business 1 makes a gross loss of £212.50 whereas business 2 shows a gross profit of £450. The combined profit for both businesses is £237.50 (£450 − £212.50). However, suppose that when preparing the profit statement for HA as a whole, income and expenses which are entirely internal between the two businesses are excluded. This requires the exclusion of business 1's sales to business 2 (£187.50) and the exclusion of business 2's variable expenses (£150) relating to use of business 1's production facility. The effect of these exclusions is to reduce the combined profit by £37.50 (£187.50 reduction in sales less a £150 reduction in expenses). The combined profit, net of this adjustment of £37.50, is £200.

It is seen that in year 1, the profit of HA on a full costing basis equals the profit (£450) of business 2 alone. However, the profit of HA on a marginal cost basis equals the combined profits (£200) of businesses 1 and 2, after elimination of internal revenues and expenses. By eliminating internal revenues and expenses, HA's profit on a marginal basis ignores any internal distinction between the two business activities. However, HA's full cost profit recognizes the distinction between the two activities but only reports the performance of one of those activities (business 2). Thus the 'two-business perspective' provides an insight into the significance of full cost profits. Full cost profit reflects the results of its manufacturing/selling activity but ignores the results of supplying the production facility. Full costing might be supportable on the basis that business 1 is designed to break even in the long term and hence its results can be ignored for periodic reporting. However, the fact that a business attempts to break even in the long run does not normally remove the need for reporting its annual performance.

It may therefore be preferable to show the results of the two business activities separately rather than adopt an approach which is exclusively based on either marginal costing or full costing. HA's results for the first five years are:

Year	Business 1 (service) Supplying production facilities £	Business 2 (manufacturing) Production operations £	Adjustment £	Combined profits £
1	(212.5)	450	(37.5)	200
2	(62.5)	900	(37.5)	800
3	275.0	1,800	(75)	2,000
4	Nil	1,350	50	1,400
5	Nil	1,200	Nil	1,200
		= full cost profits		= marginal cost profits

The reader should check the figures for business 1 and business 2 in years 2–5 by reperforming the calculations done in year 1.

CASH RECONCILIATION EFFECTS OF FULL VS. MARGINAL COSTING

The remaining paragraphs of this chapter explore the consequences of full vs. marginal costing for stocks and subsequently for the reconciliation of cash flow from production with accounting profit. Since HH does not hold stocks, the exposition is by reference to HA.

HA's stock figures under marginal and full costing are as in Exhibit 12.11. Since period 6 does not introduce any new problems not covered by period 5, it is ignored.

The fully costed stock figures are higher because they include a proportion of fixed costs or production overheads.

HA's cash flows, assuming no debtors or creditors, are as in Exhibit 12.12. The period 1 figures assume that the original purchase of the machine was paid for by the issue of shares.

	Marginal		Full	
Period	Opening	Closing	Opening	Closing
	£	£	£	£
1	0	100	0	137.5
2	100	200	137.5	275
3	200	400	275	550
4	400	600	550	700
5	600	600	700	700

Exhibit 12.11 HA's stocks

	Period				
	1	2	3	4	5
	£	£	£	£	£
Sales	1,000	2,000	4,000	4,000	4,000
Variable costs	500	900	1,800	2,400	2,400
Cash from operations	500	1,100	2,200	1,600	1,600

Exhibit 12.12 HA's cash flows from operations

It is important to notice that cash expenditure on variable cost items is based on units of production and not sales units. Cash expenditure is driven by production whereas cash income is driven by sales.

The reconciliations between accounting profits and operating cash flows are as in Exhibit 12.13.

Alternatively the reconciliation for full costing can be done using the depreciation figure credited to the fixed asset account and the total movement in the stock figure as follows:

	£	£	£	£	£
Profits	450	900	1,800	1,350	1,200
Depreciation					
(based on production)	187.5	337.5	675	400	400
	637.5	1,237.5	2,475	1,750	1,600
Stock movements	137.5	137.5	275	150	0
	500.0	1,100.0	2,200	1,600	1,600

It is seen from the above that increasing the level of stocks is a drain on HA's cash flows in each of the first four periods. During the first three periods the stock movement is caused by the increasing quantity of stock,

	Period				
	1	2	3	4	5
	£	£	£	£	£
For marginal costing					
Profits	200	800	2,000	1,400	1,200
Depreciation (fixed cost)	400	400	400	400	400
	600	1,200	2,400	1,800	1,600
Stock movements	100	100	200	200	0
Operating cash flow	500	1,100	2,200	1,600	1,600
For full costing					
Profits	450	900	1,800	1,350	1,200
Depreciation (charged in cost of sales)	150	300	600	450	400
	600	1,200	2,400	1,800	1,600
Stock movements (excluding overhead)	100	100	200	200	0
	500	1,100	2,200	1,600	1,600

Exhibit 12.13 Reconciling profits and cash flow

whereas during period 4 it is due to the price rise for labour/materials. Holding stocks might have been an extravagant policy, since interest would be lost in respect of the reduced cash flows and there would likely be storage costs incurred in respect of the stocks. However, in our case study HA's stockholding policy pays off when there is a large labour/material cost increase at the end of period 3.

CONCLUDING COMMENTS

This chapter has investigated the differences between marginal and full cost operating profits during periods of sustained growth and during periods of stationary demand and production for two companies which apply different stockholding policies. High Hopes (HH) is the company which does not hold stocks. High Anticipation (HA) is the company which does. Periods 1 to 3 are periods of sustained growth. Periods 4 to 6 experience stationary demand and production. It is found that differences between the profits of HH and HA arise as a consequence of their different stockholding policies. With marginal costing the differences are restricted to HA's holding gains on stock. With full costing there are further differences during the growth phase as a result of the (increases in) production overhead included in HA's period end stocks.

Differences between the full and marginal cost profits of the stock holding company arise during the growth phase. These differences can be investigated by consideration of the holding and supply of production facilities as a business activity distinct from other operations. The implication of this chapter's analysis is that a better overall understanding of the business is obtained by showing the results of the provision of production facilities separately from the results of other manufacturing/ selling operations. This may be preferable to an arbitrary selection of the marginal or full costing option.

SELF-STUDY EXERCISE 12.1

Abracadabra

Abracadabra plc invested in £120 of machinery at the beginning of 19X1. The machinery has a two-year life and is financed through a share issue. The machine is used to manufacture magic roundabouts and each magic roundabout takes £5 of labour and £4 of materials to make in 19X1. At the beginning of 19X2 these costs rise to £6 for labour and £5 for materials. During 19X1, 20 magic roundabouts are produced and 10 are sold. During 19X2, 10 magic roundabouts are produced and 20 are sold. The selling price is £30 per roundabout throughout 19X1 and 19X2.

Required:

1 Calculate the full cost profit for 19X1 and for 19X2 assuming that the directors foresee the pattern of production from the start and therefore wish to charge depreciation into stock by allocating the machine cost equally between its expected 30 units of production.

2 Calculate the profit for 19X1 and for 19X2 on the assumption the directors are uncertain as to the pattern of production and wish to charge depreciation into stock each year by taking the annual straight line depreciation of £60 and allocating this cost equally between the year's units of production.

3 Calculate the profit for 19X1 and for 19X2 on a marginal cost basis.

4 Assume that Abracadabra regard their business as (a) the provision of production facilities and (b) a manufacturing and selling operation. Furthermore, assume that the provision of production facilities is to be non-profit-making over the two years 19X1 and 19X2 taken as a whole. Calculate the profits/losses for each of the two business activities for 19X1 and for 19X2.

5 Reconcile the profits obtained in 4 above with the full cost profits obtained in 1 above and the marginal cost profits in 3 above.

6 Ten units of stock are manufactured in 19X1 for sale in 19X2. Calculate the effect of this on business (a) and business (b)'s profits for 19X1 and 19X2 as against the alternative of producing in the year of sale.

7 Calculate the full cost profit for 19X1 and 19X2 on the assumption that profits are recognized upon production rather than upon sale.

8 Provide a brief commentary on the significance of results 1 to 7 above.

CHAPTER 13

Stock controlling activity

INTRODUCTION

This chapter contains two case studies of companies which change over to a just in time (JIT) stock policy. The first case (abcd makes ZY) looks at the intricacies of a database information system necessary to control stock. The second case (Stock Maintains Delivery) looks at the financial impact of a change in stockholding policy and its potential interaction with other strategic objectives of the company.

THE ABCD MAKES ZY CASE STUDY

The 'abcd Makes ZY' company assembles two products, Z and Y. The two products each have common parts (a, b, c and d) and are assembled in two stages. The first stage is performed by department 1 and the second by department 2. At the beginning of week 12 (a 35-hour week) the company has the following stocks:

	Z	Y
Finished stock	12 units	2 units
Work in progress (completed dept 1)	4 units	2 units
Raw materials stocks		
Part a	5 units	
b	10 units	
c	7 units	
d	4 units	

Gross profit per unit sold is £10 for Z and £5 per unit for Y.

Stock parts (abcd) take 1 week from order to delivery. Production in the two departments involves the following:

Department		Parts (units) Z	Parts (units) Y	Labour (hours) Z	Labour (hours) Y
1	a	3	1	1	3
	b	2	4		
2	c	1	3	5	1
	d	3	1		

Thus, for example, to assemble one complete unit of product Z, department 1 requires three units of component a and two units of component b, whilst department 2 requires one unit of c and three units of d.

One person is employed in each department. In addition to the two departments there are raw material stores, production scheduling and marketing departments. The marketing department forecasts sales of 15 units for product Z and 4 units of product Y during each of weeks 12 and 13.

Required:

1 What production schedule is optimum for week 12 and for week 13 assuming that at the beginning of week 12 the company decides to change to JIT (a just in time system)?

2 What materials (parts) should we be ordering now (beginning of week 12) to satisfy the production schedules for week 13 assuming JIT?

3 What are the major information components of a materials scheduling system and how can the system go wrong?

Simplifying assumptions

A just in time stock policy involves minimizing finished good stocks by a matching of production with demand, minimizing work in progress through reduction of production times, and minimizing stocks of raw materials by matching deliveries from suppliers with production needs. In the case study a number of assumptions are made to simplify the analysis. First, in the case of abcd Makes ZY the assumed objective of the JIT system is to finish each week with zero finished goods stock, zero raw materials stocks (parts) and minimum work in progress. It is assumed that the production process is essentially one of assembly and that there are no constraints of machine capacity. It is further assumed that the labour in each department is specialized and non-transferable. Hence labour provides a potential constraint which must be considered separately for each department. Finally it is assumed that assembly production can be carried out sufficiently quickly in each department that demand can be met instantaneously subject to the constraints of parts, which take one week (and a bit) to arrive, and labour.

ANALYSING THE CONSTRAINTS

The case study considers *short-term* constraints, being either the availability of parts, labour or demand. *For week 12* each constraint is examined in turn, starting with department 2.

Demand

Department 2 – week 12

Demand for completed products during week 12 is forecast as 15 units of Z and 4 units of Y. In stock at the beginning of week 12 are 12 units of Z and 2 units of Y. Assuming the just in time stock policy, this places a demand driven limit on week 12's production of completed units of 3Z and 2Y. Such production would allow week 12's demand to be met and, consistent with the just in time policy, give no stock left over at the end of week 12.

Labour

A requirement of 3Z and 2Y completed units can be met during week 12 by taking 3Z and 2Y from the opening work in progress which has completed department 1 (4Z and 2Y) and applying 17 hours of labour in department 2, being 3×5 hr (for Z) plus 2×1 hr (for Y). Seventeen hours is significantly less than the 35 hours of labour available in department 2 and hence labour is less of a constraint than demand.

Parts

To complete 3Z and 2Y in department 2 during week 12 requires the following parts:

	3Z	2Y	Total
c	3	6	9
d	9	2	11

This requirement is more than the available parts for both c (availability $= 7$)

and d (availability = 4) given that it takes a full week from order to delivery of parts. Hence the availability of parts during week 12 is limited to the stock in hand at the beginning of the week.

It follows that of the three possible constraints (demand, labour and parts) the availability of parts is the most severe constraint of all. In terms of the available parts it is possible to produce the following alternatives during week 12:

	Production		Parts required		Gross profit
	Z	Y	c	d	contribution
First option	1	1	4	4	£15
Second option		2	6	2	£10
Third option	1		1	3	£10

On the basis of gross profit contribution the most beneficial week 12 production schedule for department 2, operating within the parts constraint, is 1Z and 1Y, giving a contribution of £15.

Continuing with department 2, each constraint is now considered in turn *for week 13*.

Department 2 – week 13

Demand

Demand for completed products during week 13 is forecast to continue at 15 units of Z and 4 units of Y. Following the new just in time stock policy, opening stock of completed units is zero and hence this demand has to be met as far as possible from week 13 production. Therefore the demand driven limit on week 13 production in order to avoid closing stocks is 15Z and 4Y.

Labour

A production of 15 completed Z and 4 completed Y during week 13 would require 79 hours of labour being 15 × 5 hr (for Z) plus 4 × 1 hr (for Y). This is in excess of the available 35 hours and hence for week 13, labour is a more severe restraint than demand. In terms of labour it is possible to produce, for example, the following alternatives during week 13, within the demand constraints of 15Z and 4Y:

	Production		Labour hours		Gross profit
	Z	Y	required		contribution
First option	7		35	£70	
Second option		4	4	£20	(demand constrained)
Third option	6	4	34	£80	

On the basis of gross profit contribution the most beneficial production schedule for department 2 during week 13 is 6Z and 4Y, giving a contribution of £80.

Parts

Parts do not provide a constraint on week 13's production since whatever parts are required for week 13 can be ordered at the beginning of week 12 and will arrive at the beginning of week 13 given a one week lag between order and delivery.

The production schedules of department 2 for weeks 12 and 13 have been established as follows:

	Weeks	
	12	*13*
Z	1	6
Y	1	4

It is now necessary to consider the production schedules for department 1. This consideration begins by examining each constraint in turn starting with *week 12*.

Department 1 – week 12

Demand

For department 1 the demand depends upon the week 12 requirements of department 2. As it happens department 2's week 12 production requirements (1Z and 1Y) can be met from the opening work in progress (4Z and 2Y) which has already completed department 1 by the beginning of week 12. There is therefore no need for department 1 to produce anything during week 12 in order to satisfy the requirements of department 2. Any production would simply add to work in progress and would be contrary to the just in time policy.

Hence department 1's production schedule during week 12 is, following the demand driven constraint, for zero production. Continuing with week 13 the constraints are as follows:

Department 1 – week 13

Demand

Demand is a function of the week 13 requirements of department 2. These requirements are calculated as follows:

	Z	Y
Work in progress at the beginning of week 12 which has completed department 1	4	2
Department 2's week 12 production	(1)	(1)
Work in progress at end of week 12	3	1
Department 2 production schedule for week 13	6	4
Shortfall to be met by department 1	3	3

This calculation shows that, in order for department 2 to meet demand for the completed product during week 13, it is necessary for department 1 to produce 3Z and 3Y for department 2.

Labour

A production of 3Z and 3Y through department 1 during week 13 requires 12 hours of labour being 3×1 hr (for Z) and 3×3 hr (for Y). Thus the demand (from department 2) constraint is more severe than that provided by the availability of labour which is a constraint of 35 hours.

Parts

Once again parts cannot be a constraint on week 13 since it is possible to order all that is necessary at the beginning of week 12.

The production schedules of department 1 for weeks 12 and 13 have been established as follows:

	Weeks	
	12	13
Z	0	3
Y	0	3

Ordering of parts

Production can be translated into parts requirements using the product-to-part breakdowns (or product 'explosions' as they are sometimes called). Hence the parts required during week 12 are as follows:

		Parts required			
Production		*a*	*b*	*c*	*d*
Dept 2	1Z			1	3
	1Y			3	1
		—	—	4	4

Parts required during week 13 are:

		Parts required			
Production		*a*	*b*	*c*	*d*
Dept 1	3Z	9	6		
	3Y	3	12		
Dept 2	6Z			6	18
	4Y			12	4
		12	18	18	22

The parts which need ordering can be calculated by taking into account the opening stock:

	Parts to be ordered			
	a	*b*	*c*	*d*
Required for production:				
week 12			4	4
week 13	12	18	18	22
	12	18	22	26
Opening stock week 12	5	10	7	4
Order requirement	7	8	15	22

In accordance with just in time the parts ordered, together with the opening stock, are sufficient to meet production but do not provide for any closing stocks.

THE MATERIALS SCHEDULING SYSTEM

The case serves to highlight that even for a very simple assembly process and without the constraint of machine capacity, a two-product, two-department business activity requires a complex 'solution' for production and materials scheduling. In a large-scale sophisticated business the complexities are that much greater.

In the *abcd Makes ZY* case the inputs to the scheduling are:

1 a sales forecast;

2 suppliers' lead times;

3 labour availability;

4 opening stock levels;

5 product explosions (into parts);

6 gross profit contributions.

An error in any of these inputs can lead to inadequate or over-ordering of stock. The analysis is essentially a short-term one. In the longer term it may be possible to:

1 improve sales through product development and/or marketing;

2 reduce suppliers' lead times by working with key suppliers;

3 improve labour flexibility through training and new work practices (or reduce labour if it is in over-supply);

4 change the composition of the product explosions by redesigning the product; or

5 improve gross profit contribution through product redesign, marketing or pricing policy.

THE STOCK MAINTAINS DELIVERY CASE STUDY

Whilst the first case emphasizes the importance to stock control of an effective production and materials scheduling system, the second case focuses on the relationship between stock reduction and financial performance. The case is as follows.

Stock Maintains Delivery (SMD) Limited runs a warehousing facility for the building trade. It carries a wide range of stocks and its proud boast has been that it can always deliver any item of stock which the trade needs. However, the directors feel that stock levels have become excessive and

H

19X2 is to be a year when a stock reduction programme is to be introduced as part of a strategic move to concentrate on high volume stock lines.

The results of SMD Limited for the year ended 31.12.X1 are as follows:

Profit statement for 19X1

		£000
Turnover		928
Cost of sales		725
Gross profit		203
Administration expenses		155
Operating profit		48
Interest receivable (bank)	2	
Interest payable (loan)	3	
		(1)
Net profit		47
Retained profit brought forward		36
Retained profit carried forward		83

Balance sheet as at 31.12.X1

		£000
Fixed assets		36
Current assets		
Stocks	445	
Debtors	117	
Bank balance	26	
	588	
Creditors	506	
Net current assets		82
Total assets less current liabilities		118
Capital and reserves		
Share capital		5
Retained profit		83
		88
Long-term loan (10%)		30
		118

The directors of SMD have asked you to prepare a forecast profit statement for 19X2 and balance sheet as at 31.12.X2 in line with the stock reduction programme and on the following basis:

1 Turnover is expected to increase 10% in terms of number of units sold but unit prices are expected to drop by 3%. (High volume and low volume stock lines sell for similar unit prices and gross margins.)

2 Cost of sales is expected to increase in line with the number of units sold.

3 Administrative expenses are expected to vary in line with the value of sales turnover.

4 Fixed assets are expected to be £34,000 at the end of 19X2.

5 The long-term loan remains at £30,000 at the end of 19X2. Interest on the loan is paid on the last day of the year.

6 The cash surplus generated during 19X2 is to remain at the bank where it earns interest for 19X2 of 10% on the balance at the end of 19X2.

7 Stock turnover is expected to reduce by 100 days, debtors to fall by 10 days and creditors to fall by 60 days.

8 Creditors are for items chargeable to both cost of sales and administrative expenses.

Required:

1 Prepare (to the nearest £000) the forecast profit statement for 19X2 and the forecast balance sheet as at 31.12.X2.

2 Comment briefly upon the directors' intentions in the light of the forecast.

Discussion

The 19X2 budget is constructed by making the suggested amendments to the 19X1 results. For turnover, cost of sales and administrative expenses these are straightforward proportionate changes to the 19X1 figures:

	19X1 actual £000	Conversion	19X2 £000
Turnover	928	$\frac{110}{100} \times \frac{97}{100}$	990
Cost of sales	725	$\frac{110}{100}$	797.5
Administrative expenses	155	$\frac{110}{100} \times \frac{97}{100}$	165

The factor 110/100 represents the anticipated 10% volume increase and 97/100 the anticipated price drop. The question specifies that both factors affect forecast turnover and administrative expenses, whereas cost of sales is only affected by the volume increase.

The forecast operating profit can now be calculated as follows:

	£000
Turnover	990
Cost of sales	797.5
	192.5
Administrative expenses	165
Operating profit	27.5

Interest receivable is the next line in the profit statement, but this cannot be calculated until the cash flow forecast is finalized so that the bank balance, on which interest is calculated, is known. The cash flow forecast requires a forecast of cash flows from customers and to suppliers, which in turn requires figures for closing stocks, debtors and creditors at the end of 19X2. It follows that the next task is to forecast stocks, debtors and creditors. These figures are determined using the intended movements in stock, debtors and creditors turnover, as shown in Exhibit 13.1.

The calculation of forecast creditors is not straightforward. First, it is assumed that stock levels do not move during 19X1 in which case 19X1 purchases equal the cost of sales of £725. This figure is added to the

19X1 turnover (days)	Adjustment (days)	19X2 turnover (days)
$\dfrac{\text{Closing stock}}{\text{Daily cost of sales}} = \dfrac{445}{725/365} = 224$	100	$124 = \dfrac{\text{Closing stock}}{797.5/365}$
		(Closing stock = £271)
$\dfrac{\text{Closing debtors}}{\text{Daily sales}} = \dfrac{117}{928/365} = 46$	10	$36 = \dfrac{\text{Closing debtors}}{990/365}$
		(Closing debtors = £98)
$\dfrac{\text{Closing creditors}}{\text{Daily purchases}} = \dfrac{506}{880/365} = 210$	60	$150 = \dfrac{\text{Closing creditors}}{788.5/365}$
		(Closing creditors = £324)

Exhibit 13.1 Calculation of forecast stock, debtors, creditors

administration expenses of £155 to give total purchases of both stock and non-stock items of £880 and a creditors turnover for 19X1 of 210 days. Hence the target creditors turnover for 19X2 is 150 days. However, it has been established that during 19X2 stock is forecast to fall from £445 to £271. Using the formula:

$$\text{Opening stock} + \text{Stock purchases} - \text{Cost of sales} = \text{Closing stock}$$

$$\text{gives } £445 + \text{Stock purchases} - £797.5 = £271$$

$$\text{and} \qquad \text{Stock purchases} = £623.5$$

Hence total forecast stock and non-stock purchases is £623.5 + £165 = £788.5. This figure is used to calculate the forecast creditors for 19X2.

From Exhibit 13.1 and the information given in the question it is possible to complete the balance sheet *except for* (1) retained profit and (2) the bank balance. It is as follows:

Balance sheet as at 31.12.X2

		£000
Fixed assets		34
Current assets		
Stocks	271	
Debtors	98	
Bank	B	
	(B + 369)	
Creditors	324	
Net current assets		(B + 45)
Total assets less current liabilities		(B + 79)
Capital and reserves		
Share capital		5
Retained profit		R
		(R + 5)
Long-term loan (10%)		30
		(R + 35)

Similarly the profit statement can be completed subject to bank interest receivable which is 10% of the closing bank balance presumably before crediting the interest. Hence interest (I) is given by:

$$I = 0.1 \ (B - I)$$
$$= B/11$$

But the retained profit (R) is:

Operating profit $+$ I $-$ Interest payable $+$ Retained profit brought forward

So R $= 27.5 + I - 3 + 83$
$= I + 107.5$

Substituting for I gives:

$$R = B/11 + 107.5 \qquad (13.1)$$

and from the balance sheet:

$$R + 35 = B + 79 \qquad (13.2)$$

Subtracting $(13.2) - (13.1)$ gives:

$$35 = 10B/11 - 28.5$$

So $\qquad \dfrac{10B}{11} = 63.5$

Therefore $\qquad B = 70$
$R = 114$
$I = 6.5$

The profit statement and balance sheet are now completed:

Forecast profit statement for 19X2

	£000
Turnover	990
Cost of sales	797.5
	192.5
Administration expenses	165
Operating profit	27.5
Interest receivable	6.5
payable	3
	3.5
Net profit	31
Retained profit brought forward	83
	114

Forecast balance sheet as at 31.12.19X2

		£000
Fixed assets		34
Current assets		
Stocks	271	
Debtors	98	
Bank	70	
	439	
Creditors	324	
Net current assets		115
Total assets less current liabilities		149
Capital and reserves		
Share capital		5
Retained profit		114
		119
Long-term loan		30
		149

Assessing the forecast

Traditionally SMD has followed a policy of keeping a very wide range of stock lines. The directors wish to change this by ceasing to maintain the low turnover lines, whilst promoting the high turnover lines through competitive pricing. Stocks of the high turnover lines are not to be increased and so more frequent deliveries will be required from suppliers. The cooperation of suppliers will be encouraged through a significant improvement in the speed of payment by SMD.

The forecast demonstrates that if the directors' intentions are fulfilled, operating profit will fall from £48,000 in 19X1 to £27,500 in 19X2. The fall in net profit, from £47,000 to £31,000, is not so marked as the fall in operating profit. This is because lower stockholdings in 19X2 result in an improved bank balance allowing a small increase in earnings from financial activity. Nevertheless, the directors' new strategy is forecast to affect adversely both operating and net profit. Of course the forecast only looks one year ahead and the strategic change might be a response to a longer-term trend. Even so it would appear desirable to revisit both the logic for, and the implementation of, the new strategy. Some of the key questions are:

1 Is it necessary to increase administrative expenses in line with sales turnover? This costs 165 − 155 = £10,000.

2 Is it necessary to reduce prices by 3% in order to increase sales volumes by 10%? Each per cent drop costs approximately £9,000 based on the 19X1 turnover.

3 Will a drop in prices be sufficient to achieve the turnover increase without a marketing budget to attract new customers?

4 Is it possible that the decline in stock coverage and any 'stock-outs' due to any failure of the frequent deliveries policy will lead to a fall in customer confidence and loyalty?

5 Have alternative strategies been fully explored? For example, would it be better to keep all existing stock lines but to increase prices (and margins) on the low volume lines, whilst maintaining prices and margins on the high volume lines?

To summarize, SMD's goodwill and market position has been based on a reputation for specialist and reliable supply. The proposed strategic change appears to put this reputation in jeopardy ... and without leading to increased profitability unless delivery can be reorganized to reduce administrative expenses.

CONCLUDING COMMENTS

This chapter has covered two case studies concerned with a change of strategy towards reduced stockholding. The first case study (abcd Makes ZY) emphasizes the point that if this strategic change is to be implemented successfully then a sophisticated stock control, ordering and production system is required. The case study serves to highlight the important point that the strategic change cannot be implemented at the operational level without appropriate control and information systems. These must be in place and tested before the change in strategy. It is one thing to change the strategy. It is another to make sure that the personnel and systems required by the new strategy are in place and committed. The implementation of strategy in a complex organization is a subject in its own right.

The second case study (SMD) demonstrates the importance of testing proposals for strategic change in terms of forecast profitability. In the case study forecast profitability for 19X2 in terms of return (net profit) on total net assets is 20.8% ($31/149 \times 100$) compared to an equivalent 19X1 figure of 39.8% ($47/118 \times 100$). The proposed strategy sounds good in terms of reduced capital tied up in stocks and a concentration on high turnover lines. However, if the information provided by the directors is correct then the strategy will result in reduced profitability and should be re-examined. It is important not to be carried away by 'fashion'. Strategic changes being made by competitors should be monitored and considered for adoption. However, strategic advantage should not be abandoned. SMD's strategic change would change its position in the market from a broadly based reliable supplier for all parts into a keen competitor on the high volume lines. It appears that the move *may* be giving away its strategic advantage, having built up a reputation for its mode of operation. Nevertheless, if its competitors are taking away SMD's business regarding the high turnover products through a policy of concentration and keen pricing, then SMD may have no choice but to rethink its position.

SELF-STUDY EXERCISE 13.1

R. U. Greene Ltd

You are the financial consultant to 'R. U. Greene Ltd', a medium sized manufacturer of environmentally friendly lead-free pencils. The ambitious managing director has asked you to predict what the company's position will be at the end of the current financial year if turnover was to be increased by 10% in value over the figure for the year just ended (31 January 19X0). You start by discussing the potential consequences of this action with the company's senior management and gather the following fragments of information.

1 The production director tells you that all fixed assets were already being fully utilized at the end of the previous year and that additional sales would therefore require a proportionate increase in the manufacturing capacity of the company. You are also informed that the problems associated with bringing new plant on stream are likely to result in an overall decrease in operational efficiency with a consequent 2.5% increase in operational expenditure above the previous year. This is in addition to the expected proportionate increase in all operational expenditure which comes as a result of expanding operations by 10%. He also mentions that on one or two occasions production has come very close to stopping due to a lack of raw materials. This must not be allowed to happen in the future.

2 The director of sales is of the opinion that the market in lead-free pencils is stagnant and that to obtain a 10% sales increase would require a 2% decrease in the unit sales price plus a 20 day extension in the average period of credit given to customers. She also points out that the problems of holding low buffer stocks of finished goods have resulted in lost sales in the past and that in order to achieve any increase in sales no stock-outs can be tolerated.

3 The purchasing director is (now) aware of the dangers of low stock levels and suggests that a ten day increase in the stock turnover period would suffice to cure these problems. However, he is aware that in order to ensure adequate and regular supplies of stock the suppliers will have to be sweetened by a 15 day decrease in the (currently long) creditors turnover period.

4 The company secretary informs you that under the memorandum and articles of the company the level of gearing (measured on the basis of total creditors plus loans to total funding) is not to exceed 75% and also that the overdraft limit agreed with the bank of £1,250,000 will not be extended any further.

5 The finance director advises you that the annual interest charge for a long-term loan is 12.5% and for an overdraft is 15% and that he would not like to see R. U. Greene Ltd paying any more interest than it has to.

6 The managing director is the majority shareholder and does not want to see his control of the company diluted by a sale of additional shares, nor does he want the dividend reduced.

From the above information and from the following profit and loss account and balance sheet for R. U. Greene Ltd, construct the predicted profit and loss account for the year to 31 January 19X1 and balance sheet as at 31 January 19X1 based on a 10% increase of turnover and its consequences.

Note: The tax charge has been ignored in order to simplify the calculations.

Profit and loss account for the year to 31 January 19X0		Balance sheet as at 31 January 19X0		
	£000		£000	£000
Turnover	2,500	Fixed assets		3,000
Cost of sales	1,250			
	1,250	Current assets		
Other operating expenses	825	Stock	25	
	425	Debtors	35	
Interest	225	Bank	–	
	200		60	
		Current liabilities		
Dividend	100	Creditors	350	
Retained profit	100	Overdraft	1,000	
			1,350	
				(1.290)
				1,710
		Long-term loan		(600)
				1,110
		Ordinary share capital		500
		Retained profit/reserves		610
				1,110

CHAPTER 14

Accounting for financial products

INTRODUCTION

This chapter looks at the accounting implications of different financial products for both the provider and customers of those products. The discussion centres on a financial services company – Easymoney – which offers three different financial products.

The first part of the chapter illustrates the accounting treatment of each product in a customer's financial statements. In each case the treatment follows existing accounting practice – notably SSAP 21 on leases. It is shown how, following accounting standards, the choice of financial product affects the customer's capital employed and hence the return on capital employed. It is a further example of how return on capital employed is a measure of the financial efficiency of capital rather than productive or allocative efficiency.

The second part of the chapter illustrates the accounting treatment of each product in the financial statements of the provider (Easymoney). Once again current accounting practice is followed. It is assumed that Easymoney would wish to record separately the performance of each product. Thus financial statements are presented and interpreted for each product. The discussion illustrates how the performance of each product in terms of profit must be interpreted in the context of that product's design characteristics particularly with respect to the repayment schedule and contractual arrangements for both repairs and the right to return equipment.

The third section of the chapter looks at the performance of each product from a macroeconomic viewpoint in terms of its impact on the cash balances held within the economy. Thus the case study demonstrates that the activities of the financial services sector impact on the macro-economy, particularly in helping to determine the rate of inflation. The final section of the chapter reverses this and looks at the impact of the rate of inflation on the performance of companies holding cash balances.

The chapter is more computational than most, providing ample revision of the preparation of basic profit statements, cash flow statements and balance sheets. However, the chapter also includes a discussion of conceptual issues surrounding SSAP 21. This discussion helps to explain the difficulties experienced in a comparison of the financial statements of companies employing different financial products. The problems are caused by the concentration of the accounting standard on the distinction between operating and financing activities at the expense of the distinction between operating and holding activities.

THE EASYMONEY CASE STUDY

Let us suppose that Easymoney plc is a financial services company which looks to earn 10% on whatever it lends. For Quickneasy, which needs to use equipment costing £4,000, it offers three services:

1 A £4,000 loan with interest at 10% payable annually in arrears. The loan is repayable in full at the end of four years.

2 A finance leasing arrangement under which legal ownership of the equipment stays with Easymoney but Quickneasy has constructive ownership for four years. Constructive ownership means that the terms of the lease provide for Quickneasy to have sole use of the asset for its four-year useful life. Quickneasy has responsibility for repairs and maintenance and is committed to a four-year schedule of payments of £1,262 per annum payable in arrears. This schedule of repayments provides Easymoney with its required 10% return.

3 An operating lease under which Quickneasy rents the equipment for £1,462 per annum payable in arrears. Under the terms of the operating lease Quickneasy can return the equipment to Easymoney at the end of the first, second or third years without penalty. Repairs and maintenance are the responsibility of Easymoney. The £1,492 per annum rental covers the £1,262 per annum necessary to provide Easymoney with its 10% return *plus* a £200 per annum premium to cover repairs and the possibility that Easymoney may have the equipment returned and be unable to find another operating lessee.

Consider the fate of three companies, QB Limited, QFL Limited and QOL Limited, which are identical in every respect except that QB buys its equipment with a £4,000 loan from Easymoney, QFL finance leases its equipment and QOL rents its equipment from Easymoney under an operating lease. As did Quickneasy in the original Quickneasy case study (Chapter 3), all three companies have annual operating cash flows of £3,000.

QB Limited

For QB Limited's equipment, the total purchase cost of £4,000 would be allocated over the four-year life to give an annual depreciation charge of £1,000. QB's reported results would be as in Exhibit 14.1, assuming that it were able to achieve a 10% return at the bank on its surplus operating cash.

Reported profit/cash flows

Year	Operating profit £	Interest charge £	Interest income £	Total profit £	Operating Cash flow £	Cash flow £	Cum. cash £
1	2,000	(400)	Nil	1,600	3,000	2,600	2,600
2	2,000	(400)	260	1,860	3,000	2,860	5,460
3	2,000	(400)	546	2,146	3,000	3,146	8,606
4	2,000	(400)	861	2,461	3,000	3,461	12,067
	8,000	(1,600)	1,667	8,067	12,000	12,067	

Loan repayment	4,000
	8,067

Reported balance sheets

	Years			
	1 £	2 £	3 £	4 £
Resources				
Equipment at cost	4,000	4,000	4,000	4,000
Depreciation	(1,000)	(2,000)	(3,000)	(4,000)
	3,000	2,000	1,000	Nil
Formation costs	100	100	100	100
Bank	2,600	5,460	8,606	12,067
	5,700	7,560	9,706	12,167
Sources of finance				
Share capital	100	100	100	100
Retained profit	1,600	3,460	5,606	8,067
Shareholders' funds	1,700	3,560	5,706	8,167
Loan	4,000	4,000	4,000	4,000
	5,700	7,560	9,706	12,167

Exhibit 14.1 QB's reported results

QFL Limited

QFL has elected to obtain its equipment by a finance lease. The accounting standard which deals with both finance and operating leases is SSAP 21.

Under SSAP 21 the finance lease is treated as a loan of £4,000 to purchase the equipment, with interest and capital repayments calculated as shown in Exhibit 14.2.

Interest is charged at 10% on the opening balance and the remainder of the annual repayment of £1,262 is treated as a part repayment of the original capital sum of £4,000.

In addition to interest paid on the lease, there would be interest earned on the bank balance as in Exhibit 14.3.

The reported profits of QFL for the four years would be as in Exhibit 14.4.

Under SSAP 21 QFL is deemed to have bought the equipment – even though legal ownership stays with the finance company – for £4,000 at the

	Year				
	1	2	3	4	Total
	£	£	£	£	£
Opening balance	4,000	3,138	2,190	1,147	4,000
Interest charged (10%)	400	314	219	115	1,048
Interest paid	400	314	219	115	1,048
Capital repayment	862	948	1,043	1,147	4,000
Total repayment	(1,262)	(1,262)	(1,262)	(1,262)	(5,048)
Closing balance	3,138	2,190	1,147	Nil	Nil

Exhibit 14.2 Capital repayments and interest

	Year				
	1	2	3	4	Total
	£	£	£	£	£
Opening balance (OB)	Nil	1,738	3,650	5,753	Nil
Operating cash flow	3,000	3,000	3,000	3,000	12,000
Interest (10% on OB)	Nil	174	365	575	1,114
Repayment under lease	(1,262)	(1,262)	(1,262)	(1,262)	(5,048)
Closing balance	1,738	3,650	5,753	8,066	8,066
Cash flow	1,738	1,912	2,103	2,313	8,066

Exhibit 14.3 Bank balance and interest

			Year		
	1	2	3	4	Total
	£	£	£	£	£
Operating cash flow	3,000	3,000	3,000	3,000	12,000
Depreciation	1,000	1,000	1,000	1,000	4,000
Operating profit	2,000	2,000	2,000	2,000	8,000
Interest charge (on lease)	(400)	(314)	(219)	(115)	(1,048)
Interest earned (at bank)	Nil	174	365	575	1,114
Financing results	(400)	(140)	146	460	66
	1,600	1,860	2,146	2,460	8,066

Exhibit 14.4 QFL's results

beginning of year 1 with a 10% loan, repayable in instalments. The interest element in these repayments is calculated and treated as a financing cost. In addition the equipment 'purchase' cost of £4,000 is treated as an asset purchase with a £1,000 annual depreciation charge against operations. It is seen that SSAP 21 separates the operating and financing activities present when a company finance leases equipment. The effect of SSAP 21 is that QFL's operating and financing results are (subject to £1 'rounding' difference in year 4) identical to those of QB, i.e. results are unaffected by whether the company buys equipment with a loan or leases it under a financing lease. Operating profits and financing results are identical in either case assuming that the rate of interest implicit in the lease is equivalent to the rate charged on the loan. If those rates of interest differ then the 'buy or finance lease' decision will result in different financing costs. Operating profits, however, will be unaffected.

Thus the operating and financing results of a company which finance leases, are consistent with those of a company which purchases its equipment.

QFL balance sheets

QFL's year end balance sheets are shown in Exhibit 14.5.

QFL's balance sheet includes the equipment of which QFL has 'constructive' but not legal ownership. Thus it is possible for a balance sheet to include assets which the company does not actually own. This is said to be an example of financial statements following economic substance (constructive ownership) rather than legal form, i.e. an example of substance over form. The leased equipment is separately identified in the balance sheet and described as 'leased' in order to make clear that it is not the legal property of QFL.

	Year ends				
	1	2	3	4	
	£	£	£	£	
Resources					
Leased equipment cost	4,000	4,000	4,000	4,000	
Depreciation	(1,000)	(2,000)	(3,000)	(4,000)	
Book value	3,000	2,000	1,000	Nil	
Formation costs	100	100	100	100	
Cash at bank	1,738	3,650	5,753	8,066	(Exhibit 14.3)
	4,838	5,750	6,853	8,166	
Sources of finance					
Share capital	100	100	100	100	
Opening retained profit	Nil	1,600	3,460	5,606	
Profit for year	1,600	1,860	2,146	2,460	(Exhibit 14.4)
Closing retained profit	1,600	3,460	5,606	8,066	
Shareholders' funds	1,700	3,560	5,706	8,166	
Loan outstanding	3,138	2,190	1,147	Nil	(Exhibit 14.2)
	4,838	5,750	6,853	8,166	

Exhibit 14.5 QFL's balance sheets

QOL Limited

Under SSAP 21 operating lease rentals are a charge against operating profit. Thus QOL's profits are as in Exhibit 14.6.

In Exhibit 14.6 the interest figures are calculated on the opening bank balance as in Exhibit 14.7.

The key point is that these interest figures relate only to the operating cash flows which are invested at the bank. Following SSAP 21 the whole of the rental payment is treated as an operating expense and no part of it is treated as interest. Hence, that part of the rental payment which in effect constitutes interest paid to Easymoney on the funds Easymoney has committed to purchase the equipment is *attributed* to operating expense in QOL's financial statements. This is compatible with an approach which, unlike that taken for finance leases, does not seek to separate financial and operational activities.

QOL balance sheets

QOL's balance sheet at the end of each year is given in Exhibit 14.8.

The balance sheet does not include the equipment which is leased under an operating lease.

	Years			
	1	2	3	4
	£	£	£	£
Sales	6,000	6,000	6,000	6,000
Typist	3,000	3,000	3,000	3,000
	3,000	3,000	3,000	3,000
Equipment rental	1,462	1,462	1,462	1,462
Operating profit	1,538	1,538	1,538	1,538
Interest	Nil	154	323	509
Total profit	1,538	1,692	1,861	2,047
Opening retained profit	Nil	1,538	3,230	5,091
Closing retained profit	1,538	3,230	5,091	7,138

Exhibit 14.6 QOL's profits

	Years				
	1	2	3	4	Total
	£	£	£	£	£
Opening balance	Nil	1,538	3,230	5,091	Nil
Operating cash flow	1,538	1,538	1,538	1,538	6,152
Interest	Nil	154	323	509	986
Closing balance	1,538	3,230	5,091	7,138	7,138
Cash flow	1,538	1,692	1,861	2,047	7,138

Exhibit 14.7 QOL's bank balance

	Year ends				
	1	2	3	4	
	£	£	£	£	
Resources					
Formation costs	100	100	100	100	
Cash at bank	1,538	3,230	5,091	7,138	(Exhibit 14.7)
	1,638	3,330	5,191	7,238	
Sources of finance					
Share capital	100	100	100	100	
Retained profit	1,538	3,230	5,091	7,138	(Exhibit 14.6)
	1,638	3,330	5,191	7,238	

Exhibit 14.8 QOL's balance sheets

ANALYSIS OF THE CASE STUDY

Conceptual problems with SSAP 21

The accounting standard for leases (SSAP 21) introduces the concept of constructive ownership. As previously stated, constructive ownership exists when the lease provides for the lessee to have sole control over the use and disposition of the asset for all or a substantial part of its expected useful life. Such a lease is called a finance lease and it is normal for a finance lease to give the lessee all the rights and responsibilities of ownership but without the lessee actually being the legal owner of the asset. Thus, typically, a lessee under a finance lease is responsible for repairs and insurance – responsibilities that normally follow ownership. SSAP 21 requires that the lessee under a finance lease should be treated in the financial statements as having purchased the asset with the help of a loan from the lease company. This is held to be the economic substance of the arrangements under the finance lease and SSAP 21 argues that the accounting treatment should follow economic substance rather than legal form.

It follows that QFL Limited – the company which goes for the finance lease – is regarded as engaging in an operating activity reflected by the depreciation of the asset and a financing activity reflected by the interest charge on the outstanding balance of the loan. This treatment is identical to that for QB Limited – the company which actually buys the asset with the help of a loan. On the other hand, QOL Limited – the company which goes for the operating lease – is regarded as engaging only in an operating activity reflected by the rental charge against operating profits. No attempt is made in QOL's financial statements to separate that part of the rental charge which covers depreciation of the asset, that part of the rental charge which covers the lessor's interest costs and that part which is a premium.

The SSAPs view of economic substance is, for QB and QFL though not for QOL, dictated by a perspective which divides business activity into operating and financing activities. It has been demonstrated in previous chapters that an equally valid perspective on economic substance divides business, not into operating and financing, but into operating and holding activities. From this perspective a company such as QB Limited, which both owns and operates the equipment, is engaging in both holding and operating activities. Depreciation of the equipment and interest on the loan are both treated as charges against the holding activity. Income for the holding activity is represented by an internal charge, equivalent to a lease rental, made against the operating activity. Moreover, from a holding vs. operating perspective, a company such as QFL Limited which does not have legal ownership of the equipment is only engaged in operating activity. This operating activity can be charged each year with the annual payment under the terms of the finance lease.

This division of business into operating and holding activities illustrates that there is more than one valid perspective on economic substance. The view of economic substance taken by SSAP 21 is partial. Under SSAP 21, QFL (but not QOL) is made to fit the ownership model of QB. This allows for a relatively easy comparison of the performance of QFL and QB but not for an easy comparison between either QFL or QB and QOL. Under a holding vs. operating approach both QB and QFL are made to fit the rental model of QOL. This would permit a comparison of all three companies.

Return on capital employed

The return on capital employed (ROCE) is a popular measure of the overall performance of a company. It can be calculated by dividing the total shown in the balance sheet as sources of finance into the operating profit for the year. Ideally it is the average sources of finance during the year which should be used in the calculation. This can be found by averaging the figures in the opening and closing balance sheets. However, for convenience we shall use the sources of finance figure in the opening balance sheet.

The following discussion uses the ROCE for year 3 as illustrative. The first problem is to decide what should be included in capital employed. For example, in the balance sheets, should a positive bank balance be treated as a resource or as a reduction in sources of finance (capital employed)? The approach adopted here is to identify physical resources with the operating activity and monetary resources with the financing activity. Following this approach a positive bank balance is treated not as a resource but as a reduction in capital employed. Whichever approach is taken, it is necessary to be consistent between the numerator (return) and denominator (capital employed) in calculating the ROCE. For example, in the case of QB, if the £4,000 loan is included in capital employed then the return must be that obtained before the £400 interest on the loan is charged against profit. If the £5,460 balance at the bank is subtracted from capital employed then the £546 interest earned on this balance must be excluded from the return.

The ROCE calculations for year 3 are as follows:

	QB		QFL		QOL	
	£	£	£	£	£	£
Operating profit		2,000		2,000		1,538
Sources of finance	7,560*		5,750*		3,330	
Positive bank balance	5,460		3,650		3,230	
Capital employed		2,100		2,100		100
ROCE (%)	$\frac{2,000}{2,100} \times 100 = 95\%$		$\frac{2,000}{2,100} \times 100 = 95\%$		$\frac{1,538}{100} \times 100 = 1,538\%$	

* Includes both loan finance and shareholders' funds.

It is seen that the ROCE for QOL is far higher than for QB and QFL, *even though* QOL is less profitable than QB or QFL. This provides a great deal of encouragement for management to lease equipment under an operating lease rather than a finance lease. QOL's return on capital employed adopts a narrow perspective since capital employed of £100 represents the formation costs originally contributed by shareholders. QB/QFL's return on capital employed adopts a wider economic perspective since capital employed of £2,100 represents all physical assets (equipment at £2,000 and formation costs at £100) used to generate the operating profit. ROCE is an inherently unreliable measure if comparing performance between companies which finance operations in different ways. As discussed in the previous section SSAP 21 adopts an operating versus financing perspective for QB and QFL but not for QOL. It follows that under SSAP 21 the ROCE for QB and QFL are comparable, but ROCE for QB and QFL are not comparable with the ROCE for QOL.

ROCE is also an inherently difficult measure of performance over time for companies with varying amounts invested in fixed assets. For example, the ROCEs for QB over the four years are as follows:

	Years			
	1	*2*	*3*	*4*
	£	£	£	£
Operating profit	2,000	2,000	2,000	2,000
Sources of finance/ assets employed	4,100	3,100	2,100	1,100
ROCE (%)	49%	65%	95%	182%

It is seen that QB's return on capital employed increases over the four years in response to the reducing capital employed which in turn reflects the falling net book value of the assets employed in operations. Economic reality, however, is that operations are unchanged over the four years since the same assets are used to create the same outputs in stable markets. The appearance of improvement given by the ROCE is potentially misleading, and does not represent the return earned from the operating activity. Indeed since ROCE is lower at the beginning of the project than at the end, concentration on ROCE as a performance measure could act as a discouragement to expansion or replacement.

In order to get a proper appreciation of the return on capital employed it is necessary to reorganize the balance sheet to show how the resources have been funded. This is done by changing the treatment of depreciation in the balance sheet. Instead of being subtracted from equipment at cost in the resources section of the balance sheet, it is added to the retained

profit in the sources section of the balance sheet. The reorganized balance
sheet for QB is shown below:

	Years			
	1	2	3	4
Resources	£	£	£	£
Formation expenses	100	100	100	100
Bank	2,600	5,460	8,606	12,067
Equipment at cost	4,000	4,000	4,000	4,000
	6,700	9,560	12,706	16,167
Sources of funds				
Share capital	100	100	100	100
Retained profit	1,600	3,460	5,606	8,067
Cumulative depreciation	1,000	2,000	3,000	4,000
Cash from activities	2,600	5,460	8,606	12,067
Loan	4,000	4,000	4,000	4,000
	6,700	9,560	12,706	16,167

This shows that, for instance, by the end of year 2 cash has been received
from share capital (£100), activities (£5,460) and the loan (£4,000). Cash
from activities has come from two years of operations (£6,000) *less* two
years' interest on the loan (£800) *plus* one year's interest on the bank
balance (£260). To date cash of £9,560 has been invested in formation
expenses (£100), a bank balance (£5,460) and equipment (£4,000).

From the reorganized balance sheet and QB's reported profits (Exhibit
14.1), the returns earned on QB's activities can be calculated as follows:

	Years			
	1	2	3	4
Return on operations	£	£	£	£
Operating profit	2,000	2,000	2,000	2,000
Operating assets	4,000	4,000	4,000	4,000
Return from operations	50%	50%	50%	50%
Return on financing				
Interest charge	400	400	400	400
Loan	4,000	4,000	4,000	4,000
Return	10%	10%	10%	10%
Interest earned	Nil	260	546	861
Bank balance	2,600	5,460	8,606	12,067
Return		10%	10%	10%

This shows a constant return on operations of 50% per annum on the funds committed to operating assets. It reflects the 'economic reality' of constant operating performance in stable markets.

EASYMONEY'S FINANCIAL STATEMENTS: A PRODUCT ANALYSIS

In this section Easymoney is used to illustrate that activities can be conceived not primarily in terms of operations and financing but in terms of the delivery of different products or services. For example, Easymoney delivers three distinct products to QB, QFL and QOL respectively. To understand Easymoney's performance it is helpful to consider the performance of each product. In this analysis each product is regarded as a separate activity. Interest costs are attributed to each product, and it is possible within each product analysis to retain a split between operations and financing.

Since Easymoney's operations involve the provision of finance, the distinction between operations and financing is more tenuous than for many other companies. The approach taken here, for products QB and QFL, is to treat interest earned by Easymoney on outstanding capital repayments from QB and QFL as operational (activity) profits and the interest paid/earned by Easymoney on its bank balance as financing (activity) costs. It is assumed that Easymoney is financed by a bank overdraft on which 5% interest is payable at the year end. Product QOL is more straightforward with rentals being treated as operational revenue and depreciation on the rented equipment as operational expenditure.

	Years				
	1	2	3	4	
	£	£	£	£	
QB					
Outstanding capital at beginning of year	4,000	4,000	4,000	4,000	
Interest earned (10%)	400	400	400	400	
QFL					
Outstanding capital at beginning of year	4,000	3,138	2,190	1,147	(Exhibit 14.2)
Interest earned (10%)	400	314	219	115	(Exhibit 14.4)

Exhibit 14.9 Operating revenue for the QB and QFL products

	Years			
	1	2	3	4
	£	£	£	£
Funds invested in rented equipment	4,000	4,000	4,000	4,000
Rental	1,462	1,462	1,462	1,462
Depreciation	1,000	1,000	1,000	1,000
	462	462	462	462
Operating return on funds invested	11.6%	11.6%	11.6%	11.6%

Exhibit 14.10 Operating profits for the QOL product

	Years				
	1	2	3	4	Total
	£	£	£	£	£
QB					
Opening overdraft	4,000	3,800	3,590	3,370	4,000
Interest paid (5%)	200	190	180	168	738
Cash received	(400)	(400)	(400)	(4,400)	(5,600)
Closing overdraft	3,800	3,590	3,370	(862)	(862)
Cash flow	200	210	220	4,232	4,862
QFL					
Opening overdraft	4,000	2,938	1,823	652	4,000
Interest paid (5%)	200	147	91	33	471
Cash received	(1,262)	(1,262)	(1,262)	(1,262)	(5,048)
Closing overdraft	2,938	1,823	652	(577)	(577)
Cash flow	1,062	1,115	1,171	1,229	4,577
QOL					
Opening overdraft	4,000	2,738	1,413	22	4,000
Interest paid (5%)	200	137	71	1	409
Cash received	(1,462)	(1,462)	(1,462)	(1,462)	(5,848)
Closing overdraft	2,738	1,413	22	(1,439)	(1,439)
Cash flow	1,262	1,325	1,391	1,461	5,439
Total overdraft	9,476	6,826	4,044	(2,878)	
Total cash flow	2,524	2,650	2,782	6,922	14,878

Exhibit 14.11 Interest costs by product

Exhibit 14.9 states the outstanding capital for products QB and QFL and the annual interest earned on these products by Easymoney. Exhibit 14.10 shows the operating profits for QOL.

Exhibit 14.11 gives the interest costs by product, and the product by product performance is given in Exhibit 14.12. Product balance sheets are given in Exhibit 14.13. In Exhibit 14.13 QFL's receivables are the capital repayments receivable (as in Exhibit 14.2) under the terms of the finance lease. At the end of each year QFL Limited is committed under the terms of the lease to make the following capital repayments:

		End of year		
		1	*2*	*3*
		£	£	£
Repayment	for year 2	948		
	for year 3	1,043	1,043	
	for year 4	1,147	1,147	1,147
		3,138	2,190	1,147

Interpreting the results

It is possible from a product based activity analysis for Easymoney to understand the performance of its respective products *provided* the analysis is conducted in the context of each product's characteristics. Each of its three products has required an initial capital injection of £4,000. Exhibit 14.12 shows that over the four years QOL has delivered the highest total profits. This is because, for this product, Easymoney has been able to charge an annual premium of £200 to cover repair costs and to allow for the fact that QOL Limited has the right to return the equipment at the end of each year. In the event this right has not been exercised and no repair costs have been incurred. The premium has therefore provided additional profits. Consequently the cumulative *operational* profits for the QOL product are £800 (4 × £200) higher than for QFL over the four years (£1,848 against £1,048). The *annual* profits of QOL and QFL are not comparable because of the different accounting treatments employed for the two products. For QOL, the whole of the annual payment received is operating income whereas for QFL part of the annual payment received is treated as a reduction of capital.

Exhibit 14.12 shows that QB is the second best performing product with total profits over the four years of £862. Although QB and QFL earn the same return (10%) on funds employed in operations (Exhibit 14.9), QB's operating profits are consistently higher than those of QFL. The reason for QFL's annual fall in operating profits (£400 → £115) is that each year

		Years			
	1	2	3	4	Total
	£	£	£	£	£
QB					
Operational (Exhibit 14.9)	400	400	400	400	1,600
Financial (Exhibit 14.11)	(200)	(190)	(180)	(168)	(738)
QB profits	200	210	220	232	862
Retained profit	200	410	630	862	
QFL					
Operational (Exhibit 14.9)	400	314	219	115	1,048
Financial (Exhibit 14.11)	(200)	(147)	(91)	(33)	(471)
QFL profits	200	167	128	82	577
Retained profit	200	367	495	577	
QOL					
Operational (Exhibit 14.10)	462	462	462	462	1,848
Financial (Exhibit 14.11)	(200)	(137)	(71)	(1)	(409)
	262	325	391	461	1,439
Retained profit	262	587	978	1,439	
Total profits					
Operational	1,262	1,176	1,081	977	4,496
Financial	(600)	(474)	(342)	(202)	(1,618)
	662	702	739	775	2,878
Retained profit	662	1,364	2,103	2,878	

Exhibit 14.12 Results by product

less capital is employed in operations (£4,000 → £1,147) as shown by Exhibit 14.13. Indeed, each year investment is switched from operating activity to financing activity. For instance, during the first year funds invested in operations are reduced from £4,000 to £3,138, a reduction of £862. These funds are switched to the financing activity and together with new funds of £200 generated by profits they reduce the bank overdraft by £1,062 (shown in Exhibit 14.11, from £4,000 to £2,938). Because QFL switches funds from operations where they earn a return of 10% to financing where they earn a return of only 5%, it is a less profitable product than QB where £4,000 remains invested in the more profitable operating activity throughout the life of the product.

For example, by the beginning of year 2, QFL has switched funds of £862 from earning 10% to earning 5%. This results in QFL earning £86 less than QB by way of operating profits (10% of £862) but saving £43 (5%

	Beginning of year				
	1	2	3	4	5
	£	£	£	£	£
QB					
Receivables	4,000	4,000	4,000	4,000	Nil
	4,000	4,000	4,000	4,000	Nil
Retained profit (Exhibit 14.12)	Nil	200	410	630	862
Bank overdraft (Exhibit 14.11)	4,000	3,800	3,590	3,370	(862)
	4,000	4,000	4,000	4,000	Nil
QFL					
Receivables (Exhibit 14.2)	4,000	3,138	2,190	1,147	Nil
	4,000	3,138	2,190	1,147	Nil
Retained profit (Exhibit 14.12)	Nil	200	367	495	577
Bank overdraft (Exhibit 14.11)	4,000	2,938	1,823	652	(577)
	4,000	3,138	2,190	1,147	Nil
QOL					
Funds invested in equipment	4,000	4,000	4,000	4,000	Nil
Depreciation	Nil	(1,000)	(2,000)	(3,000)	Nil
	4,000	3,000	2,000	1,000	Nil
Retained profit (Exhibit 14.12)	Nil	262	587	978	1,439
Bank overdraft (Exhibit 14.11)	4,000	2,738	1,413	22	(1,439)
	4,000	3,000	2,000	1,000	Nil
Total					
Equipment (QOL)	4,000	3,000	2,000	1,000	Nil
Receivables (QB + QFL)	8,000	7,138	6,190	5,147	Nil
	12,000	10,138	8,190	6,147	Nil
Retained profit (Exhibit 14.12)	Nil	662	1,364	2,103	2,878
Bank overdraft (Exhibit 14.11)	12,000	9,476	6,826	4,044	(2,878)
	12,000	10,138	8,190	6,147	Nil

Exhibit 14.13 A product balance sheet

of £862) against QB by way of financing costs. Overall QFL has lower profits than QB by £43. This deficit increases in years 3 and 4. The deficits are caused because the cash repayments made by QFL Limited under the finance lease are invested by Easymoney at the bank through a reduction in its overdraft. If the cash repayments were invested by Easymoney at 10% rather than 5% then the finance lease product would be as profitable as the loan product.

The above discussion has interpreted the performance of each of the three products — QB, QFL and QOB — through knowledge of each product's characteristics and how those design characteristics affect the accounting treatment. Understanding the characteristics of financial products is the key to any understanding of their financial performance through accounting.

Strategically Easymoney needs to move towards products which offer higher margins and/or higher volumes. This is likely to be achieved by having innovative products for borrowers. In the case study it is assumed that Easymoney is financed by bank overdraft. If Easymoney were financed by attracting savings then it would be necessary to promote volumes not only by attracting customers (borrowers) but also by attracting suppliers (savers). Consequently it would be necessary, as for banks and building societies, to design innovative products for suppliers as well as customers.

For Easymoney the cost of capital for each product is 5% and the rate of interest returned by each product is 10%. Hence margins are the same for each product. However, QOL has been the most successful product because it brings in additional and highly profitable business in the form of a premium to cover potential equipment return and repair costs. Arguably QOL is the most innovative of the three products. The least innovative is QB. Nevertheless QB is the second most successful product because it maintains a higher volume of lending during the four years than does QFL.

THE MACROECONOMIC PERSPECTIVE

The financial services industry, and particularly banking, plays a key role in determining the supply of money in the economy, and hence its activities have a direct impact on inflation. Let us suppose that the economy consists only of three non-financial companies (QB, QFL and QOL Limited), Easymoney and a bank. The cash flows of QB, QFL, QOL and Easymoney are deposited at the bank and hence become cash balance increases capable of being used by the bank to fuel demand in the economy. QB, QFL and QOL are providers of funds to the bank and the bank pays them 10% interest. Easymoney is a net borrower from the bank and the bank charges Easymoney 5% interest. Thus the bank incurs losses since its charges do not cover its costs.

The cash flows associated with each product during the four years are shown in Exhibit 14.14.

Total cash flows are similar for each product (£12,929 vs. £12,643 vs. £12,577). However, the QB product generates slightly more cash for the

			Year			
	1	*2*	*3*	*4*	*Total*	
	£	£	£	£	£	
QB product						
QB Limited	2,600	2,860	3,146	(539)	8,067	(Exhibit 14.1)
Easymoney (QB product)	200	210	220	4,232	4,862	(Exhibit 14.11)
	2,800	3,070	3,366	3,693	12,929	
QFL product						
QFL Limited	1,738	1,912	2,103	2,313	8,066	(Exhibit 14.3)
Easymoney (QFL)	1,062	1,115	1,171	1,229	4,577	(Exhibit 14.11)
	2,800	3,027	3,274	3,542	12,643	
QOL product						
QOL Limited	1,538	1,692	1,861	2,047	7,138	(Exhibit 14.7)
Easymoney (QOL)	1,262	1,325	1,391	1,461	5,439	(Exhibit 14.11)
	2,800	3,017	3,252	3,508	12,577	

Exhibit 14.14 Macro cash flows by product

economy (£12,929) and hence has slightly greater potential for promoting the demand side of the economy than do the other two products. The reason for the greater cash flow is that with the QB product most cash remains with QB Limited as long as possible before being transferred to Easymoney in year 4. This is beneficial because QB Limited earns 10% of interest on its cash whereas Easymoney only obtains 5%.

It is interesting to note that QOL is the most beneficial product from the point of view of Easymoney (a cash flow of £5,439) but has proved to be the least beneficial from the point of view of the company investing in the equipment (QOL Limited has a cash flow of £7,138). In one sense this is an example of an innovative financial product enabling the financial services company to prosper at the expense of the non-financial sector. In another sense it can be argued that QOL Limited has benefited from peace of mind ('psychic income') during the four years (1) by knowing that the right to return the equipment provides insurance against technological obsolescence and (2) because QOL is not responsible for repairs.

The cumulative macroeconomic statistics for the four-year period are as follows:

Supply side	£
Product of QB, QFL, QOL	
4 years × 3 companies × £6,000 annual sales	72,000

			£
Demand side			
4 years × 3 companies × £3,000 annual wages			36,000
Cash bank balances by product (Exhibit 14.14)		£	
	QB	12,929	
	QFL	12,643	
	QOL	12,577	38,149
			74,149

Loss incurred by bank			£	
Interest charged to Easymoney				
	(Exhibit 14.12)		1,618	
Interest paid to:				
	QB	(Exhibit 14.1)	(1,667)	
	QFL	(Exhibit 14.3)	(1,114)	
	QOL	(Exhibit 14.7)	(986)	
				(2,149)
				72,000

Inflation and money items

It is assumed that QB, QFL and QOL all have annual cash sales of £6,000 and wage expenses of £3,000. In this case the supply side of the economy produces each year services to the value of $3 \times £6,000$ and over four years services to the value of $12 \times £6,000 = £72,000$. On the demand side it is assumed that the annual wages of $3 \times £3,000$ are all spent, giving a total demand over the four years of $12 \times £3,000 = £36,000$. Moreover, it is assumed that the cash at bank generated by QB, QFL and QOL over the four years (£38,149) is relent by the bank for spending in the economy. If so, total demand over the four years is £74,149, being £36,000 plus £38,149. Thus demand exceeds supply by £74,149 − £72,000 = £2,149, equal to the loss incurred by the (central) bank.

The loss incurred by the (central) bank in our 'mini' economy has, potentially, an inflationary effect on the economy. Moreover, in the early years there is likely to be excess demand in the economy due to simultaneous investment by QB, QFL and QOL in capital equipment. Most economies experience a capital expenditure cycle and this is a further reason why it is difficult for the (central) bank to match supply and demand in the economy on a period-to-period basis. When supply exceeds demand there is inflation, and this macroeconomic phenomenon has a significant effect on companies and individuals who hold positive (or negative) balances of cash or other money items such as liquid investments, loans, debtors or creditors.

Let us suppose that in our economy the general price index moves as follows:

	Year	General price index
1 Jan	1	100
1 Jan	2	110
1 Jan	3	120
1 Jan	4	125
31 Dec	4	130

The holding of positive cash balances (or money items such as debtors, receivable in a fixed amount of money) during a period of inflation is a loss-making activity, whilst the holding of negative cash balances generates a holding gain. For example, if a company starts the year with £50,000 cash and prices on average rise by 10%, it needs to hold £55,000 at the end of the year just to be in the same position in purchasing power terms. Hence the cash holding activity has generated a £5,000 loss. The loss is calculated as £50,000 × (110/100 − 1). The performance of Easymoney's cash holding activities is, calculated from the totals in Exhibit 14.13, shown in Exhibit 14.15.

In addition to its cash holding activities, Easymoney holds equipment in connection with the operating lease. It is possible to calculate an additional

			Year		
		1	2	3	4
		£	£	£	£
Bank overdraft		12,000	9,476	6,826	4,044
	×	(110/100)	× (120/110)	× (125/120)	× (130/125)
	=	13,200	10,337	7,110	4,206
	gain	1,200	861	284	162
Receivables		8,000	7,138	6,190	5,147
	×	(110/100)	× (120/110)	× (125/120)	× (130/125)
	=	8,800	7,787	6,448	5,353
		800	649	258	206
Net gain/(loss)		400	212	26	(44)

Exhibit 14.15 Easymoney: Gains/losses from cash holding activities

depreciation charge to reflect the effect of the fall in the purchasing power of money on the historical cost of this asset, as follows:

	Year			
	1	*2*	*3*	*4*
	£	£	£	£
Opening balance	4,000	3,000	2,000	1,000
	× (110/100)	× (120/110)	× (125/120)	× (130/125)
=	4,400	3,273	2,083	1,040
Additional depreciation	400	273	83	40

Easymoney's profits for the four years can then be restated as in Exhibit 14.16.

However, the story is not yet complete. Exhibit 14.16's adjustments reflect the effect of inflation within each year. Thus Easymoney is £662 'better off' at the end of year 1 than at the beginning, £641 'better off' at the end of year 2 than at the beginning, etc. However, these annual results are not comparable since, because of inflation, a pound earned at the end of year 1 is not the same as a pound earned at the end of year 2 etc. To allow inter-period comparisons a further adjustment is necessary to allow for differences in purchasing power between the years. The necessary adjustments to allow such inter-period comparisons are shown in Exhibit 14.17.

These adjustments assume that, for instance, year 1 profit is earned on the last day of year 1 and that it is desirable to convert it to its equivalent money value at the end of year 4. Similarly year 2 profit is converted to its equivalent money value at the end of year 4 etc. Allowing for rounding errors in the conversions, the profit total in year 4 spending power (£2,876)

	Year				
	1	*2*	*3*	*4*	*Total*
	£	£	£	£	£
Per Exhibit 14.12	662	702	739	775	2,878
Effects of changes in purchasing power (inflation) within each year:					
1 additional depreciation	(400)	(273)	(83)	(40)	(796)
2 holding money items	400	212	26	(44)	594
	662	641	682	691	2,676

Exhibit 14.16 Profit adjusted for within-year purchasing power changes

			Year		
	1	*2*	*3*	*4*	*Total*
	£	£	£	£	£
Profit	662	641	682	691	2,676
	× (130/110)	× (130/120)	× (130/125)	× (130/130)	
	782	694	709	691	2,876

Exhibit 14.17 Profit adjusted for between-year purchasing power changes

checks with the profit total, also in year 4 spending power, shown by Exhibit 14.12 (£2,878). Hence total profit is unaltered by the conversions but the trend of continuously improving profits shown by Exhibit 14.12 (£662 → £775) no longer holds since Exhibit 14.17 shows a profit drop (£782 → £691).

SUMMARY

Companies for whom a principal business activity is the holding of money items should reflect the impact upon this activity of changes in the purchasing power of money. This impact is in two parts. First there is the impact of changes in purchasing power within each year. This adjustment (Exhibit 14.16) is made to each year's profit to reflect the gains or losses from money holding activity during the year. Secondly, there is the impact of changes in purchasing power between years. This adjustment (Exhibit 14.17) is made to each year's profit in order to restate profits in pounds of comparable purchasing power. Hence this adjustment is important when making inter-period comparisons.

Easymoney not only holds money items, it also holds equipment in connection with an operating lease. In Exhibit 14.16 an adjustment for depreciation has been made to reflect the impact of changes in general purchasing power (inflation) upon the historical cost of this asset. However, the main thrust of the final section of this chapter has been to highlight the impact of inflation on money items, using a financial services company as the illustration.

SELF-STUDY EXERCISE 14.1

BOS

BOS is a bank whose results for the three years 19X1, 19X2 and 19X3 are as follows:

	Profit statements		
	19X1	*19X2*	*19X3*
	£	£	£
Interest receivable	1,380	2,176	2,755
Investment income	21	26	26
	1,401	2,202	2,781
Interest payable			
to depositors	(983)	(1,677)	(2,193)
to loanholders	(36)	(57)	(58)
Net interest income	382	468	530
Charge for bad debts			
Specific	(35)	(67)	(181)
General	(14)	(23)	(21)
Net interest income after bad debts	333	378	328
Other operating income	136	179	218
	469	557	546
Operating expenses	(291)	(342)	(409)
Operating profit	178	215	137

	Balance sheets		
	19X1	*19X2*	*19X3*
	£	£	£
Advances to customers	10,706	14,364	17,269
Cash and investments	3,076	3,708	4,439
Property at valuation	291	323	387
	14,073	18,395	22,095
Current, deposit and other accounts	12,377	16,377	19,899
Other liabilities	418	480	490
Loans	452	642	657
Shareholders' funds	826	896	1,049
	14,073	18,395	22,095

Shareholders' funds reconcile with operating profit as follows:

	19X1	*19X2*	*19X3*
	£	£	£
Opening shareholders' funds	772	826	896
Operating profit	178	215	137
Dividends, tax	(143)	(167)	(113)
Surplus on revaluation of properties	19	22	29
Share capital issued			100
Closing shareholders' funds	826	896	1,049

Required:

1 A financial analysis of BOS's performance during the period 19X2 and 19X3, based on the information provided. For computational convenience you may calculate ratios using opening balance sheet figures. This is equivalent to an assumption that all of each year's transactions take place on the last day of the year.

2 What further information from management would you find most useful in order to assess the performance and prospects of BOS?

3 You are now advised that the index of general purchasing power during the period 19X1 to 19X3 has moved as follows:

1 January	19X1	103.7	19X1
1 January	19X2	111.8	19X2
1 January	19X3	120.2	19X3
31 December	19X3	130.9	

What impact does this information have on your financial analysis conducted in answer to (1) above for the years 19X2 and 19X3?

CHAPTER 15

Strategic activity

INTRODUCTION

This chapter illustrates how financial statements reflect corporate strategy. Three companies – Faith plc, Hope plc and Charity plc – commence manufacture of the same product on the same day using identical machinery. However, their corporate strategies differ and their business activity and hence financial statements reflect these strategic differences. Faith's strategy is to build market share through a large marketing effort, keeping price competitive and production volumes high to meet demand. Charity's strategy is to concentrate on productive excellence keeping unit costs low and using its productive ingenuity to develop a more sophisticated version of the product. Its present product is able to carry a price premium because of its perceived quality. However, the price premium has tended to depress sales volumes. Hope's strategy is 'middle of the road'. It competes with Faith on price but does not maintain the same marketing effort. It pays some attention to production costs, keeping them lower than Faith but not as low as Charity.

The three companies also differ with respect to their financial structures. Faith is the most adventurous, obtaining its productive machinery on a finance lease. Hope is financed 50 : 50 by share capital and loans, whilst Charity is entirely financed by share capital. It will be seen that Faith's choice of finance allows it to provide relatively large returns to its shareholders. Part of Faith's strategic thinking is to achieve a high share price underwritten by high returns. This will enable it to pursue takeover targets through the issue of further shares. (Potential interference by the Monopolies and Mergers Commission is not considered!) Faith's strategy is financially ambitious, acquisitive and market led. At the other end of the spectrum Charity's strategy is financially cautious, production oriented and product led.

THE FAITH, HOPE AND CHARITY CASE STUDY

As previously stated, Faith plc, Hope plc and Charity plc commence manufacture of the same product on the same day. Each has invested in £90 of identical machinery with an expected life of three years or 300 units (whichever comes first). There is no expected residual scrap value. Each company starts with £10 of working capital and the financing structures are as follows:

1 *Faith:* Share capital of £10 and a financing lease for the machinery. The terms of the lease require Faith to pay an annual rental of £36.20 at the end of the first, second and final years. The implicit finance charge is 10%.

2 *Hope:* Share capital of £50 and a secured long-term loan of £50. The loan carries an interest rate of 10%.

3 *Charity:* Share capital of £100.

During the first year of operations the manufacturing records of the companies are as follows:

	Units produced	Units sold	Average unit cost of material and labour	Average selling price
Faith	120	120	£1.00	£1.60
Hope	100	80	£0.90	£1.60
Charity	75	60	£0.70	£1.70

Assume there are no other expenses except that Charity has spent £9 on attempting to develop a more sophisticated version of the product, and Faith has spent £10 on marketing.

The historical cost results: sales and cost of sales

Exhibit 15.1 gives the historical cost profits for Faith, Hope and Charity in the first year of operations. Sales (line 1) are easily calculated as *units sold* times *average selling price*. Similarly the labour/material element of cost of sales (line 2) is calculated as *units sold* times the *average unit cost of material and labour*. It is important to note that cost of sales reflects the units sold and not the units produced. Rather more difficult is the calculation of overheads to be included in the cost of sales (line 3) and this calculation is given in Exhibit 15.2.

In the Faith, Hope and Charity example the only production overheads are the depreciation of the machinery, and in line with SSAP 9 such overheads are to be included in stock as a product cost on the basis of 'normal' levels of production. It is often difficult to determine what is a 'normal'

		Faith	Hope	Charity
		£	£	£
Line no.				
1	Sales	192	128	102
	Cost of sales			
2	Labour/materials	120	72	42
3	Overheads	36	24	24
		156	96	66
4	Gross profit	36	32	36
5	Selling	10	Nil	Nil
6	Operating profit	26	32	36
7	Interest/R&D	9	5	9
8	Net profit	17	27	27

Exhibit 15.1 Historical cost profits

	Faith	Hope	Charity
Unit cost	90	90	90
	300	300	225
Units sold	× 120	× 80	× 60
Units in stock	× Nil	× 20	× 15
COS	36	24	24
Stock	Nil	6	6
Closing stock			
Overheads	Nil	6	6
Labour/materials	Nil	18	10.5
		24	16.5

Exhibit 15.2 Overheads into cost of sales and closing stock

level of production. In this example it is assumed that first year production levels will continue, even though, for Hope and Charity, such an assumption may not be plausible in the long run unless sales improve. Faith is producing 120 units per annum and will therefore hit the 300 units life expectancy for the machine rather than the three year limit. Overheads calculated on a per unit basis are £90/300, being machine cost divided by total output. In the first year Faith sells 120 units and hence the overhead component of cost of sales is £90/300 × 120 = £36. Faith has no year end stocks. Hope will, on the basis of current production levels, hit the three-year life expectancy simultaneously with the 300 unit limit, and hence the total output will be 300 units. Consequently the overhead component of stock is £90/300 per unit. First year sales are 80 units and hence the overhead element of cost of sales is £80 × 90/300 = £24. Closing stock is 20 units with an overhead element of £20 × 90/300 = £6.

Charity will hit the three-year life expectancy ahead of the three-year limit and hence total output will be 225 units giving a unit cost for overheads of £90/225 = £24. The overhead element of first year cost of sales is £60 × 90/225 = £24 and for closing stock it is £15 × 90/225 = £6.

Gross profit, operating profit and net profit

Line 4 of Exhibit 15.1 gives gross profit from which selling expenses (there are no administration expenses) are deducted to give operating profit (line 6). Operating profit is reduced by interest charges and in the case of Charity, research and development, to give net profit.

The interest of £9 charged to Faith (line 7) represents the effective rate of interest on the opening capital supplied to Faith in the form of lease finance. The full schedule of interest and repayments under the terms of the lease is calculated in Exhibit 15.3.

Returning to Exhibit 15.1, £5 of loan interest (line 7) is charged to Hope and the £9 charged to Charity is in respect of development expenditure. Charity would be allowed, under SSAP 13, to capitalize that development expenditure if, but only if, the outcome of the project can be assessed with reasonable certainty and its commercial viability established. Even then Charity's directors are allowed to write off the development expenditure if they so wish.

Year	Opening capital £	Interest £	Payment £	Closing capital £
1	90	9	36.2	62.8
2	62.8	6.3	36.2	32.9
3	32.9	3.3	36.2	Nil

At the end of year 1, the amount owing of £62.8 is split as follows:

		£
Owing within 1 year	36.2 − 6.3 =	29.9
Owing outside 1 year		32.9
		62.8

Exhibit 15.3 Lease payments for Faith

Looking at Exhibit 15.1 it is useful to distinguish lines 1 to 6 which form the operating section of the profit statement from lines 7 and 8 which together show how the operating profit has been applied (1) to development of new products (R&D), (2) as a return to loan capital (interest), and (3) as a (potential) return to share capital (net profit). Lines 7 and 8 explain the applications of the operating profit. It should be noted that this treatment of R&D does not conform with the presentation requirements of the current Companies Acts and accounting standards. These require that research and development expenditure (unless capitalized) is written off as an operating expense. Much depends upon whether the R&D expenditure is designed to keep pace with the competition and allow Charity to maintain its market share. If this is the case it should be treated as an operating expense necessary if Charity is to sustain its existing level of business. Alternatively the R&D expenditure may be an attempt to develop a product not being developed by the competition and therefore providing Charity with the opportunity to enhance its business share. Such expenditure is more akin to a speculative investment and could be regarded as an allocation of profit made on behalf of the shareholders.

Companies are naturally reluctant to reveal the nature and extent of R&D being carried out and this raises the interesting issue of whether Charity should be required to reveal its R&D expenditure to its competitors by highlighting it in the financial statements. Under SSAP 13, Charity is required to disclose its R&D expenditure.

INTERPRETING THE HISTORICAL RESULTS

Financial performance

It is seen from line 8, Exhibit 15.1 that Hope and Charity produce the same historical cost profits of £27 in their first year of operation but that Faith's profits are lower at £17. However, the three companies have different financial structures and their profits provide a different proprietorial return in each case depending upon the proprietor's interest. The proprietorial returns are calculated as follows, expressed as profit per pound of proprietorial investment:

$$\textit{Faith} \qquad \textit{Hope} \qquad \textit{Charity}$$

$$\frac{17}{10} = 1.7 \qquad \frac{27}{50} = 0.54 \qquad \frac{27}{100} = 0.27$$

It is seen that the proprietorial return is higher, the lower the proportion of finance provided by the shareholders and hence the higher the proportion provided other than by shareholders. The proportion of a company's long-term finance supplied other than by shareholders' funds is known as the company's gearing.

Faith has the highest gearing (90% of its capital is provided by lease finance) and gives the highest proprietorial return. Hope has a gearing of 50% and Charity no gearing at all. In our example the higher the gearing, the higher the return to the proprietor.

It should also be noticed that Faith is the most sensitive of the three companies to changes in operating performance. For example, if cost of sales had been 20% higher all round, profits (losses) would have been:

	Faith	Hope	Charity
	£	£	£
Net profit	17.0	27.0	27.0
20% COS (i.e. profit reduction)	31.2	19.2	13.2
Profit reduction as a % of original net profit	184%	71%	49%

It is seen, therefore, that Faith has given its proprietors the highest return on what is the riskiest investment. However, that high return has been earned ex post and to that extent Faith has proved to be the best performer to date from a proprietorial point of view. It is seen ex post that Faith's intended strategy of providing high proprietorial returns has been achieved through its high gearing.

Productive performance

The productive performances of these companies can be investigated by examining the ratio of gross profit to sales. The ratios are as follows:

	Faith	Hope	Charity
Gross profit percentage	18.75%	25%	35.3%

Charity is seen to be the most productive in the sense of having the highest gross profit percentage. Of course it is also the least productive in terms of volume. An examination of the three companies' unit costs reveals that Charity is by far the best performer in respect of labour/materials, but that its low volumes make it expensive in terms of unit overhead cost. The unit cost structures are:

	Unit costs		
	Faith	*Hope*	*Charity*
	£	£	£
Labour/materials	1.0	0.9	0.7
Overheads	0.3	0.3	0.4
	1.3	1.2	1.1

At present volume levels Charity's advantage in labour/materials more than outweighs its disadvantage in terms of per unit overheads. Charity's overhead unit cost could be reduced by expanding volumes although this could conceivably result in less efficient production in terms of labour/materials. Charity is not getting its fixed assets to work as hard as those of Faith and Hope. This is reflected in the companies' respective fixed asset turnover figures. Fixed asset turnover can be calculated by dividing the depreciation element in cost of sales into sales. The figures are:

	Faith	*Hope*	*Charity*
	£	£	£
Sales	192	128	102
Depreciation (overhead) in cost of sales	36	24	24
Fixed asset turnover	5.33	5.33	4.25

However, overall Charity's strategy of being the low cost producer has been achieved. Charity's gross profit percentage is also helped by the fact that its product carries a 10p price premium in the market. This premium reflects the perceived quality of Charity's product – quality achieved as a result of its concentration on production.

Marketing/selling performance

Faith's strategy involved capturing a large market share and that has been achieved. It has involved marketing expenditures of £10. Hope is offering its product at the same price as Faith but without an equivalent marketing effort and it has only achieved sales of 80 units as against 120 units for Faith. Faith's marketing has therefore boosted sales by $40 \times 1.60 = £64$ and profits by $40 \times (1.60 - 1.30) = £12$. Since the marketing expense was £10, marketing has made a marginal contribution to Faith's profit of £2.

However, the success of the marketing effort should not be judged solely in terms of its short-term contribution to profit but also in terms of its longer-term contribution to the strategic objectives of Faith.

Cash flows

The cash flow statements are given in Exhibit 15.4 on the assumption that all sales and expenses are for cash.

It is seen from Exhibit 15.4 that Faith has the highest cash from operations (£62) but the lowest net increase in cash (£25.8) due to the large repayment under the terms of the lease. Faith needs to pay particular attention to operating cash flow projections since each year it has to meet a large lease repayment and given its high gearing there may not be much scope for bank borrowings. However, Exhibit 15.4 does not suggest that Faith has so far failed to generate adequate cash and there is therefore little reason to change the assessment that Faith has been the best performer to date from a proprietorial point of view. In each case there is adequate cash flow to allow the company to pay its net profit to shareholders by way of dividend if it should choose so to do. Cash shortage can adversely affect a company's operations in the short term and therefore cash must be monitored and controlled by management. However, generally it is profit rather than cash flow which is considered to be the better overall indicator of performance. The reason is that profit represents the increase in the

	Faith	Hope	Charity
	£	£	£
Share capital paid in	10	50	100
Loans received		50	
Paid for machine		(90)	(90)
Opening cash for operations (working capital)	10	10	10
Sales	192	128	102
Purchases/labour	(120)	(90)	(52.5)
Marketing	(10)		
Cash from operations	62	38	49.5
Repayment/interest/R&D	36.2	5	9
Cash flow during year	25.8	33	40.5
Closing cash	35.8	43	50.5

Exhibit 15.4 Cash flow statements

fund of all the company's assets, whereas cash flow represents the increase in the fund of one particular asset, cash.

Overall performance is concerned with the increase in the total fund of assets under a company's control rather than with increases in the fund of any single asset (cash flow) or subset of assets. However, a shortage of a particular asset can cause serious operational difficulties.

Balance sheets

The main problem affecting the preparation of the balance sheet is the treatment of the finance lease. Under SSAP 21 the asset purchased using lease finance is shown in the opening balance sheet at what it would have cost if purchased for cash. It is subsequently depreciated on the basis of usage, and at the end of the first year has an unexpired historical cost of £90 − £36 = £54. The finance lease is shown in the opening balance sheet as a source of finance for the purchase price of the asset. This source of finance, as shown in Exhibit 15.3, is subsequently increased by interest and reduced by repayments. At the end of the first year the outstanding finance is £62.8 which can be split depending on the timescale of the repayment into that repayable within or outside one year. Faith's balance sheet at the end of the first year is:

Resources	£	
Tangible assets		
Plant and machinery (90 − 36)	54.0	
Current assets		
Stock	Nil	
Cash	35.8	(see Exhibit 15.4)
	89.8	
Sources of finance		
Repayable within 1 year		
Finance lease	29.9	(see Exhibit 15.3)
Repayable after 1 year		
Finance lease	32.9	(see Exhibit 15.3)
Capital and reserves		
Share capital	10.0	
Profit and loss account	17.0	
	89.8	

The reader is invited to test his/her balance sheet preparation skills by completing the end of first year balance sheets for Hope and Charity. The answers are given in Exhibit 15.6 at the end of the chapter.

AN ALTERNATIVE PERSPECTIVE

To date the analysis of performance has relied upon sets of financial statements prepared

1 on a historical cost basis;
2 complying with relevant accounting standards such as SSAP 9 (treatment of production overheads) and SSAP 21 (treatment of Faith's finance lease); and

3 adopting the conventional operations versus financing perspective.

An alternative perspective is to substitute an analysis of operational versus holding activities for the more conventional operational versus financing approach. The results would then be as shown in Exhibit 15.5.

The key to the operating versus holding split is to assume that use of the machine can be obtained for an annual rental of £36.2 as per Faith's lease agreement. This rental is treated as operating expenditure for all three companies, and asset-holding income for Hope and Charity both of which hold the machine. A further feature to the operating/holding split is the treatment of interest. Faith is financed to the extent of the £10 required for operating. Interest, assumed to be at 10%, is therefore charged on this sum against operations. Hope and Charity are financed to the extent of £10 for operations and £90 for machine purchase. They are therefore each charged interest of £1 against operations and £9 against holding the machine. For all three companies interest charged against both operations and holding activity is treated as income for a separate financing activity. The expense charged against this financing activity is in respect of interest paid on outside loans. This only affects Hope.

From Exhibit 15.5 it is seen that Faith's operating activity is in absolute profit terms almost on a par with that of Hope (£17.6 against £18.8) although behind Charity if Charity's R&D expenditure is added back to Charity's profit (£17.6 against £22.8). When profit from operating is

	Faith	Hope	Charity
Operations activity	£	£	£
Sales income	192	128	102
Machine rental	43.4*	36.2	36.2
	148.6	91.8	65.8
Labour/materials	120	72	42
	28.6	19.8	23.8
Selling/R&D	(10)		(9)
Interest**	(1)	(1)	(1)
Profit from operating	17.6	18.8	13.8
Holding activity			
Rental income	Nil	36.2	36.2
Depreciation		(30)	(30)
Interest**		(9)	(9)
Loss from holding	Nil	(2.8)	(2.8)
Financing activity			
Interest income	1	10	10
Interest expense		(5)	
Profit from financing	1	5	10
Combined profits	18.6	21.0	21.0
Proprietorial return	1.86	0.42	0.21

* Machine rental is three years at £36.2 = £108.6/2.5 = £43.4 since the total expense is £108.6 from which benefit is anticipated over 2.5 years.
** Interest is apportioned on the basis that £10 cash is required for operations.

Exhibit 15.5 An alternative perspective

compared to sales, the relative productive efficiencies are revealed as follows:

	Faith	Hope	Charity
	£	£	£
Profit from operating	17.6	18.8	22.8*
Sales	192.0	128.0	102.0
Profit/sales (%)	9.2	14.7	22.4

*Adding back R&D.

Both Hope and Charity incur small losses (£2.8) on their holding activity whereas Faith is not engaged in this activity at all. The implication is that

Hope and Charity would have been better advised to follow Faith and lease their machines. The income from financing activity reflects in each case the level of finance supplied by the shareholders. In each case the return from the financing activity is 10%.

THE FUTURE

The most significant point about Faith, Hope and Charity is that whilst Faith is to date the best performer from the point of view of the proprietor, Faith is also the highest cost producer and therefore the lowest performer from the point of view of productive efficiency. This was seen from Exhibit 15.1 by comparing the ratio of gross profit to sales for the three companies as follows:

	Faith	Hope	Charity
Gross profit/sales as a percentage	18.75%	25.0%	35.3%

The most productively efficient is Charity. Charity is also the only one of the three companies paying attention to new product development. However, Charity has set its price higher than the competition and has low volumes. In addition it is, arguably, undergeared. This reflects the fact that Charity has a strategy focused on productive efficiency and new product development rather than selling or finance.

The least productively efficient is Faith. However, Faith sells aggressively and has captured 46% of the market. It has also taken advantage of *relatively* sophisticated financing arrangements by finance leasing its assets. This reflects the fact that Faith has a strategy focused on selling and finance rather than productive efficiency. Its market share may allow it to dominate the market, squeezing out Hope and Charity. Its high proprietorial returns will be popular in the stock market, allowing it to expand and if necessary target other companies for takeover.

Charity is just such a target. Its low proprietorial returns might make it less popular with the stock market unless its potential as a takeover target creates interest. The accounting standard on development expenditure does not help Charity since it has to write off such expenditure until it is a demonstrable commercial success. This reduces profits making it more vulnerable to takeover and more attractive as a takeover target provided the new product has some chance of commercial success. Charity could also be valuable to Faith for the productive skills of its managers, an area in which Faith is weak. An alternative scenario might be a defensive merger between Hope and Charity.

If the selling and financial management at Charity were to be strengthened the picture could change significantly. Charity has the best margins and hence the opportunity to increase its market share. It can also improve its proprietorial returns through increased gearing, and it has a new product under development.

The outlook for Hope is uncertain. It does not appear to have the boldness of Faith's strategy, nor the productive excellence of Charity. Improved selling and financial management at Charity, or a takeover of Charity by Faith, would leave Hope in a very weak position.

The discussion demonstrates how proprietorial return can be achieved through selling and finance rather than productive excellence. This may not be good for the economy since resources and market share should flow to the most efficient producer.

SELF-STUDY EXERCISE 15.1

Pin and Stripe

During the year ended 31 December 19X0, Pin plc and Stripe plc are in direct competition in a market in which they are the only two producers. Details of the two companies during 19X0 are as follows:

	Pin	Stripe
19X0 sales (units)	750	600
Plant purchase date	1.1.X0	1.1.X0
Plant original cost	£18,000	£6,000
Plant capacity (units)	1,000	600
19X0 production (units)	800	600
19X0 opening stock (units)	Nil	Nil
19X0 selling price (unit)	£24	£24
19X0 per unit production cost:		
Labour	£2	£6
Material	£2	£6
Depreciation	£6	£2
	£10	£14
19X0 administration (fixed cost)	£200	£200
19X0 selling and distribution expenses per unit	£2	£2
19X0 promotional expenditure	£400	£100

Each company has financed its plant by a share issue of £2,000 plus a 10% bank loan for the remainder. The bank loans are repayable in five years' time. Assume no interest is earned on net cash receipts from operations.

Required:

1 Prepare historical cost profit statements for Pin and Stripe for the year ended 31 December 19X0. Ignore dividends and taxation.

2 Prepare operating cash flow statements, showing cash receipts and payments, for Pin and Stripe for the year ended 31 December 19X0, assuming there are no debtors or creditors.

3 Prepare historical cost balance sheets for Pin and Stripe as at 31 December 19X0. Ignore dividends and taxation.

4 Discuss briefly the advice you would offer to the managing directors of Pin and of Stripe assuming (a) the total market looks set to grow, and (b) the total market looks set to decline.

	Hope £		Charity £	
Resources				
Fixed asset				
Cost	90		90	
Depreciation	(30)	[100 × 0.3]	(30)	[75 × 0.4] *
	60		60	
Stock				
Labour/materials	18		10.5	
Overhead	6		6	
	24		16.5	
Cash	43		50.5	
	127		127.0	
Sources of finance				
Share capital	50		100	
Retained profit	27		27	
Shareholders' funds	77		127	
Loan capital	50		Nil	
	127		127	

* It should be noted that expiry of the machine (depreciation) is driven by production rather than sales.

Exhibit 15.6 End of first year balance sheets

CHAPTER 16

Segmental activities

INTRODUCTION

The accounting standard on segmental reporting (SSAP 25) explains the need for segmental information in the following terms:

> Many entities carry on several classes of business or operate in several geographical areas, with different rates of profitability, different opportunities for growth and different degrees of risk. It is not usually possible for the user of the financial statements of such an entity to make judgements about either the nature of the entity's different activities or their contribution to the entity's overall financial results unless the financial statements provide some segmental analysis of the information they contain. The purpose of segmental information is, therefore, to provide information to assist the user of financial statements:
>
> (a) to appreciate more thoroughly the results and financial position of the entity by permitting a better understanding of the entity's past performance and thus a better assessment of its future prospects; and
>
> (b) to be aware of the impact that changes in significant components of a business may have on the business as a whole.

To a significant extent this book has been devoted to the identification of different activities within a business so that the performance and contribution of those activities to the business from both shareholder and economy-wide perspectives can be understood. Distinctions have been made, for instance, between operations and financing, between operations and holding activities, and between production and other functional activities. There has also been a recognition that the provision of a particular product constitutes a business activity and that multi-product businesses are therefore engaged in multiple activities. It follows that a study of segmental reporting provides an appropriate penultimate chapter. Segmentation has been one of the book's major themes.

The accounting standard on segmental reporting does not by any means deal with all of the distinctions covered in this book. However, it requires segmentation for differences in the geographical regions in which a company operates and differences in classes of business. A geographical segment is an individual country or group of countries, whereas a class of business is a separate product or service or a group of related products or services. Key financial information such as profits, turnover and capital employed should be shown for each segment by way of a note to the financial statements. The standard indicates that different classes of business may arise due to differences in:

1 the nature of the products or services;

2 the nature of the production processes;

3 the markets in which the products or services are sold;

4 the distribution channels for the products;

5 the manner in which the entity's activities are organized;

6 the legislative framework under which different parts of the business operate (e.g. a banking or insurance section).

This chapter consists of a case study of two companies – Gourmet and Formula – who operate in the same geographical areas and who, on the face of it, are engaged in the same business activities. Those activities are the provision of hotel and associated restaurant facilities. However, the case study examines how differences in the nature of the products of the two companies and the way they are marketed lead to quite different requirements in respect of the segmentation of their results.

THE GOURMET AND FORMULA CASE STUDY

Gourmet Hotels Limited own a mini chain of three hotels in different cities – they are called the Crown, the Lion and the Unicorn. Each hotel runs a gourmet restaurant with its own individual style of cuisine. Each hotel does its own marketing and in general there is a minimum of head office control or direction except that there is a requirement for each hotel to submit monthly accounts showing separately the trading results of the restaurant and the hotel. As it happens each hotel has geared its marketing effort towards promotion of its gourmet restaurant. Marketing costs have been as follows:

	£
Crown	15
Lion	20
Unicorn	20
	55

Historical cost sales and profits for 199X *before* charging for marketing costs are:

	Crown		Lion		Unicorn		Total	
	Sales	Profits	Sales	Profits	Sales	Profits	Sales	Profits
	£	£	£	£	£	£	£	£
Hotel (excl. rest.)	360	60	180	15	300	50	840	125
Restaurant	90	30	90	30	30	5	210	65
	450	90	270	45	330	55	1,050	190

Further investigation reveals that the Lion has a reputation of being a restaurant rather than a place to stay. The Unicorn has no shortage of residents but they are generally tourists unprepared for gourmet prices. Most of its residents eat elsewhere in the city. Market research of customers of the Crown, however, shows that the gourmet restaurant is an attraction to those booking rooms.

Formula Hotels Limited is a rival chain of three hotels and it has hotels of similar size but in different cities to those of Gourmet. The hotels are known as Formula 1, 2 and 3. The hotel and restaurants are run to a formula and menus, prices etc., are strongly controlled from head office. Moreover, marketing services are provided centrally by head office. The Formula brand image is marketed centrally as providing a service of recognizable standard and quality. Total marketing costs are £90.

Formula hotels have a separate division based at head office to promote use of the hotels at the weekends at a discounted rate and markets them under the brand name 'Weekend Experience'. It has its own marketing budget and during 199X it spent £15. 'Weekend Experience' obtains its discount from the hotels on the condition that Weekend's customers also eat in the hotel restaurant.

The historical cost profits for 199X of Formula hotels *before* charging marketing costs are as follows:

	Hotel excl. restaurant		Restaurant		Total	
	Sales	Profit	Sales	Profit	Sales	Profit
	£	£	£	£	£	£
Formula 1	260	52.5	90	17.5	350	70
Formula 2	260	45	90	15	350	60
Formula 3	260	45	90	15	350	60
	780	142.5	270	47.5	1,050	190
Weekend Experience	300	35	100	15	400	50
	1,080	177.5	370	62.5	1,450	240

Further investigation reveals that the higher margins achieved by Formula 1 reflect a shortage of hotel accommodation in that city. Assume that Gourmet and Formula have the same capital employed and capital structures.

Required:

1 Illustrate the various ways in which Gourmet Hotels Limited could prepare segmental information for inclusion in its published accounts and discuss the merits of each option. Include in your discussion consideration of whether and how marketing expenses should be disclosed.

2 Discuss the issues surrounding the identification of business segments within Formula Hotels Limited and prepare an appropriate note giving segmental information in Formula's published accounts.

3 Discuss briefly the future prospects for Gourmet and Formula.

DISCUSSION OF GOURMET

Different approaches to the problem of segmentation in the published accounts of Gourmet include:

1 to treat hotels and restaurants as separate activities;

2 to treat hotels, restaurants and marketing as separate activities;

3 to treat each hotel as a separate activity;

4 to treat each hotel and each restaurant as a separate activity;

5 to treat each hotel, each restaurant and each marketing effort as a separate activity.

Option 1

Treating hotels and restaurants as separate activities gives the following note in the published financial statements:

Note 1
The company operates hotels and restaurants situated within those hotels. The contribution of hotels and restaurants to turnover and profit has been as follows:

	Turnover £	Profit £
Hotels	840	125
Restaurants	210	10
	1,050	135

In this presentation marketing cost has been charged against the restaurant activity. The presentation has the merit of simplicity and reflects the fact that the hotel and restaurant businesses (of Lion and Unicorn at least) have a large measure of independence from each other. They have quite different customer bases and serve different markets which may in turn be driven by different factors. It would be possible for one market to improve in terms of turnover and/or profitability much more than the other, thus generating the need for the results to be segmented in order to judge (1) how the current results have been achieved and (2) future prospects. If the hotel and restaurant businesses always moved in step in response to the same underlying factors then segmentation would not be necessary.

Option 2

Treating hotels, restaurants and marketing as separate activities gives the following note:

Note 2
The company operates hotels and restaurants situated within those hotels. The contribution of hotels (excluding restaurants) and restaurants to turnover, profit and marketing expense has been as follows:

	Turnover £	Marketing expense £	Profit £
Hotels	840	0	125
Restaurants	210	55	10
	1,050	55	135

This presentation has the merit of focusing on the key issue of marketing. It shows that the restaurant business has had the direct benefit of £55 of marketing effort whereas hotels received no direct marketing support. In the case of Crown, where the hotel and restaurant businesses appear to have a high level of interdependence, room lettings may have benefited indirectly from the marketing of the restaurant. This, however, is not apparent from the note. The argument for disclosing the level of marketing expense is that marketing is a significant independent variable in a causal relationship with the success or otherwise of the restaurant and hotel businesses. Disclosures about marketing (including the level of expenditure) are therefore important to an understanding of those businesses.

Option 3

Treating each hotel as a separate activity gives the following note:

Note 3
The company operates three hotels, the Crown, the Lion and the Unicorn, which have contributed to turnover and profit as follows:

	Turnover	*Profit*
	£	£
Crown	450	75
Lion	270	25
Unicorn	330	35
	1,050	135

This presentation has the merit of reflecting the organizational structure operating within Gourmet whereby each hotel has a large measure of managerial autonomy. It also reflects the fact that the three hotels are operating in three quite distinct markets both geographically and in terms of what the market is demanding. For instance, from the question, it is clear that Crown's market demands a mix of hotel accommodation and gourmet restaurant facilities, whereas Unicorn's is primarily demanding hotel accommodation with 'non-gourmet' eating.

Option 4

Treating each hotel and each restaurant as a separate activity gives the following:

Note 4
The company runs three hotels and operates three gourmet restaurants

situated in those hotels. The contribution of the hotels (excluding restaurants) and restaurants to turnover and profit has been as follows:

	Crown		Lion		Unicorn		Total	
	Turnover	Profit	Turnover	Profit	Turnover	Profit	Turnover	Profit
	£	£	£	£	£	£	£	£
Hotel	360	60	180	15	300	50	840	125
Restaurant	90	15	90	10	30	(15)	210	10
	450	75	270	25	330	35	1,050	135

This note has the merit of allowing the reader to understand the nature of the three different markets in which the Crown, the Lion and the Unicorn are operating. It can be seen, for instance, that Crown customers spend £4 on room accommodation for every £1 in the restaurant whereas the equivalent figures for the Lion and the Unicorn are £2 to £1 and £10 to £1. The position is that the Crown has by far the best balance between its room letting and restaurant businesses and that as a result it has the highest turnover and the highest profits.

Option 5

Option 5 treats each hotel, each restaurant and each marketing effort as a separate activity. Arguably to try and add information on marketing expense to the information already contained in Note 4 above results in a somewhat unwieldy matrix of information. It is therefore suggested that the marketing expense is analysed in a separate statement as follows:

Note 5
Each hotel has geared its marketing effort towards the promotion of its gourmet restaurants. Marketing costs have been as follows:

	£
Crown	15
Lion	20
Unicorn	20
	55

The breakdown of marketing expenditure, in association with the information given in Note 4, allows judgement to be made of the quality or effectiveness of the marketing expenditure. Clearly marketing expenditure is more cost-effective when the restaurant and room letting businesses are interdependent. In such circumstances promotion of the gourmet restaurant will enhance business in both the restaurant and the hotel. This has been the effect of Crown's marketing effort but the same effect has not been achieved by Lion or Unicorn, where the restaurant and hotel businesses have been less interdependent. The marketing of the restaurants of Lion and of Unicorn has in any event been less successful than the marketing of Crown's restaurant. Whilst Crown's restaurant made £1 of profit for each pound of marketing, the equivalent figures for Lion and Unicorn are 50p and a loss of 75p.

It should be noted that the benefits of a good marketing campaign can be felt for some time after the campaign has ended and been paid for. Normal accounting practice, however, is to accept all the expense in the year of the campaign irrespective of whether any benefit is expected in subsequent years. It is, therefore, possible that some of the effects of the marketing campaigns may yet show in increased profits.

DISCUSSION OF FORMULA

Formula differs from Gourmet in being tightly controlled from the centre, with standard products being offered throughout the hotel chain. Whereas Gourmet may be characterized as a series of investments by head office, Formula is a much more integrated business and consequently the general case for segmental reporting is perhaps not as strong since segmental reporting would not reflect the organizational culture. The principal issues are:

1 Should Formula 1's results be shown separately?

2 Should 'Weekend Experience's' results be shown separately?

3 Should the results of the hotels and the restaurants be shown separately?

4 Should marketing be treated as a separate activity?

Issue 1

The case for showing Formula 1's results separately rests on its greater profitability than Formula 2 or 3 and this in turn reflects the greater opportunities afforded by its market. The higher margins of Formula 1 reflect a shortage of hotel accommodation in the market in which it competes. Whether this greater profitability justifies a separate business segment is open to question. Its greater profitability has increased company profits by £10 (from £90 to £100) when compared with the profits of Formula 2 or 3. This increase is just about sufficiently material to justify Formula 1 being treated as a separate segment. Nevertheless the directors of Formula will not be keen to publish Formula 1's results separately since its profitability may encourage new hoteliers to contest Formula 1's market.

Issue 2

Whereas Formula 1, 2 and 3 are providers *and* retailers of hotel and restaurant services, 'Weekend Experience' is a retailer only and specializes in the weekend market. Moreover, the fact that 'Weekend Experience' has its own marketing budget suggests a certain limited degree of organizational independence. There is therefore a strong case to suggest that treating 'Weekend Experience' as a separate segment reflects both market and organizational realities. The weekend market in which 'Weekend Experience' specializes has quite different characteristics to the weekday market and can be booming when the weekday market is in decline, or vice versa. There is therefore a level of market independence between the 'Formula' and 'Weekend' businesses. This is backed up by a certain amount of operational independence. 'Weekend' can fix its own prices, negotiate its own marketing budget and negotiate discounts with the Formula hotels.

For their part Formula hotels are free not to sell through 'Weekend' but to use other retailers. It is the *degree* of independence that the 'hotel' and 'Weekend Experience' businesses have from each other which determines the need for them to be treated as separate segments in the published financial statements.

Issue 3

Throughout Formula Hotels 1, 2 and 3, the ratio of hotel (room letting) sales to restaurant sales and hotel profits to restaurant profits are constant. This supports the view that Formula's hotel and restaurant businesses are highly integrated and with a high level of interdependence. In these circumstances there is little justification for separate reporting of the hotel and restaurant results even though their respective profitabilities are different. Of course, the experience of Gourmet Limited suggests that the high level of integration and interdependence is not inevitable but is a reflection of the way Formula runs its affairs. The question arises as to whether better results could be obtained by allowing hotels and restaurants to develop as quite different businesses. This question can only be answered in the aggregate by comparing the results of Formula Limited with aggregated hotel and restaurant results of Gourmet. To compare Formula's restaurant or hotel results separately with those of Gourmet would not be comparing like with like. For instance Formula's restaurant menu and prices may be tailored to the requirements of the hotel tenants whereas those of Gourmet may (as in the case of Lion) be geared to more lucrative non-resident business. This could lead to Formula's restaurant business appearing to perform less well than the better restaurants in the Gourmet chain. However, the effects of restaurant menu and pricing policies on the hotel business more generally also need to be considered. In the case of Lion, for instance, there is evidence that the restaurant has prospered at the expense of the hotel.

It should be noted that there is no case for splitting Weekend's results into hotel and restaurant segments since the nature of Weekend's contract with the hotels prevents it from splitting the room letting and restaurant products, which it must therefore both purchase and sell as a package.

Issue 4

In Formula's business the level and quality of the marketing is a major determinant of Formula's turnover and profit. To a significant extent, turnover and profit are dependent upon the marketing activity. Marketing is the independent variable whilst turnover and profit are the dependent variables in an essentially causal relationship. In these circumstances information about the marketing activity, including the level of expenditure, is needed to understand how the business results have been achieved.

Excluding 'Weekend Experience' which has its own marketing budget, marketing support is directed towards Formula's image of providing both hotel rooms and meals at consistent quality and prices. Thus marketing supports a 'standard' product available at all Formula hotels (subject to a small premium at Formula 1). Given the integrated nature of the Formula business it may be better to charge marketing against the combined income of the three Formula hotels rather than to charge each hotel with the common marketing costs according to an (arbitrary) allocation process.

Any attempt to generate an 'internal' market in which individual hotels 'buy' marketing services from head office will run into 'free rider' problems since any purchase by one hotel will automatically benefit other hotels in the chain who are not contributing to the purchase. In these circumstances each hotel's management will hold off purchasing marketing services for their hotel in order to see if they could 'free ride' on the back of purchases made by other hotels in the chain. The cumulative effect would be total marketing expenditure at well below optimum levels. Given the nature of Formula's business it follows therefore that the scale and nature of the marketing effort should be controlled centrally. Any attempt to recover central expenses from the individual hotels is more akin to a tax than it is to a charge for a service.

Formula Limited's published accounts

The discussion of the issues suggests that:

1 Formula 1's results should be separately disclosed;

2 Weekend Experience's results should be shown separately;

3 the results of the hotels and restaurants should *not* be shown separately;

4 marketing expenditures by Formula and by Weekend Experience should be disclosed but the marketing expenditure should not be allocated to individual hotels or subdivided between hotels and restaurants.

A possible note is as follows:

The company operates two divisions:

(a) *Formula* which runs three hotels (Formula 1, 2 and 3); and

(b) *Weekend Experience* which sells weekend getaway packages at Formula hotels. Contributions to turnover, profit and marketing expense are as follows:

	Turnover £	Profit £
Formula 1	350	70
Formula 2 and 3	700	120
	1,050	190
Formula's marketing		90
Formula's profit		100
Weekend Experience	400	50
Weekend's marketing		(15)
	1,450	135

THE FUTURE

Gourmet has returned profits of £135 on a turnover of £1,050 and has therefore used up resources of £915. Formula has returned the same profit of £135 apparently on a turnover of £1,450. However, on reflection this turnover figure includes sales by Formula to Weekend Experience and hence overstates sales by Formula Limited as a whole to outside customers. Suppose the detailed profit statement for Weekend Experience is as follows:

	£
Sales	400
Purchases from Formula hotels	(300)
Administration	(50)
	50
Marketing	15
Profit	35

It is seen from this profit statement that the inter-segment sales/purchases between Formula hotels and Weekend Experience are £300. This amount should be deducted from £1,450 to give sales by Formula Limited to outside customers of £1,150. It follows that the expenses of Formula Limited excluding inter-segment purchases are £1,015, being £1,150 − £135. Assuming that the two companies are similar in terms of capital employed and capital structures then it is seen that Gourmet has been the more efficient operator in terms of resources consumed (£915 consumed as against £1,015).

Gourmet's aggregate profitability, however, masks a wide variability of performance by the individual hotels. Gourmet's management must try to improve performance of Unicorn's restaurant and Lion's hotel. This requires understanding of Unicorn's and Lion's businesses and how they differ from Crown's. The strength of Gourmet's decentralized structure is that different hotels should be encouraged to respond to local market conditions in their own way. Lion may wish to market its hotel in order to combat the perception held locally that it is principally a restaurant. The Unicorn represents a more difficult problem. Its customers do not want a 'gourmet' restaurant and yet the 'up-market' restaurant is the chain's hallmark. The key options appear to be:

1 sell Unicorn on the grounds that it does not fit in with the chain's strategy of offering gourmet facilities, or
2 replace the gourmet restaurant with a more down-market facility, or
3 do option (2) above in the short term (to improve profitability) with a view to subsequent disposal.

If there is a decision to dispose of Unicorn then Formula is a possible buyer.

Compared to Gourmet, Formula aims to be a higher-turnover, lower-margin business with turnover supported by a higher level of marketing effort. It is also riskier. Gourmet's experience suggests that the markets in which Crown, Lion and Unicorn operate have a measure of independence from each other. Hence the greater degree of segmentation required for Gourmet reflects the fact that Gourmet is operating in a wider variety of markets and is therefore spreading its risk to a greater extent than Formula. As previously noted, Formula is more expensive than Gourmet in terms of resources consumed. This might adversely affect the productivity of the economy as a whole since the same resources given to Gourmet would, prima facie, have generated higher sales and profits. However, this inefficiency may not be apparent to shareholders (provided that both companies have the same capital employed and capital structure) since shareholders will observe both companies earning the same profits on the same capital employed. If the capital allocation mechanisms at work within the economy attempt to channel funds to those management's which offer the best return on capital employed, then productive efficiency is not necessarily achieved.

The nature of Formula's business drives it towards expansion. Since it offers a standard product a better return can be obtained on its marketing effort (assuming that the marketing is national rather than local) by offering that standard product in as many outlets as possible.

An important strategic issue facing the Formula board of directors is whether to allow, in future, Weekend Experience to market hotels outside the Formula chain. Should it, for instance, be allowed to market Gourmet hotels at the weekend? Such a development would cost little extra but would help Formula diversify its business which would become less dependent on the popularity of the Formula hotel. However, it might have the effect of diverting weekend business away from the Formula hotels. Strategically the main constraint facing Formula is likely to be the finance necessary for the hotel expansion implicitly required for its standard product, high marketing business. A development of Weekend Experience has the potential advantage of improving profits without invoking this financial constraint.

SUMMARY

The accounting standard on segmentation argues that 'although it is possible to identify certain characteristics that differentiate between business classes, no single set of characteristics is universally applicable nor is any single characteristic determinative in all cases'. It follows that the identification of different products for segmental reporting purposes is a subtle process intimately linked to an understanding of the business. Segmentation needs to follow 'the contours' of the business. The cases of

Gourmet and Formula highlight this. Ostensibly both companies provide the same services in the same places. However, there are differences in the packaging and nature of the product, differences in the intended market and differences in the organizational structures. These serve to justify differences in the segmentation of the results. Formula is effectively delivering the same product at different sites. Marketing is not site distinctive and is therefore managed centrally. Individual hotel managers have to follow the company 'formula' closely. Their primary responsibility is to ensure operational (productive) efficiency and compliance with company procedures. Hence the organizational structures are moulded by the product and its intended appeal. The appeal is a standard and reliable product wherever it is consumed.

Formula's organizational structures do not suit the development of a distinctive, individualistic and possibly high-class product. Such a product is more compatible with the greater autonomy given to managers in Gourmet. Such autonomy leads to a greater variety in performance at the level of the individual hotel/restaurant. However, in the case study (though not necessarily in real life) it leads Gourmet to a better overall performance than Formula in terms of return on resources consumed. Gourmet's marketing is site-specific and designed to underwrite the appeal of each restaurant as unique and distinctive. It is managed locally in response to local tastes and market conditions. Clearly the company exists to provide certain services centrally but these are probably limited to finance and personnel matters such as training and career development.

To summarize the discussion of this chapter, Gourmet's array of product characteristics, intended markets and organization structures requires a greater degree of segmentation than does the more rigid business of Formula. The performance of individual sites in the Formula chain need only be separately reported by exception, i.e. when their profitability is out of line. In general similar sites will be expected to produce similar performances and need not be examined in detail. The level of aggregation, however, may well differ between whether the information is being generated for Formula's directors or for outside shareholders. In general internal management will, for control purposes, require the more detailed knowledge of the business based on a more fine grained analysis of results across different sites. The information which investors need in order to make proper decisions about their involvement with an entity is the same in kind, but not in volume, as the information which management need to run it.

Segmentation is an issue addressed by a number of accounting standards apart from SSAP 25. In particular the accounting standard on reporting financial performance (FRS 3) requires the performance of continuing businesses to be reported separately on the face of the profit statement from the performance of discontinued businesses. It is this segmentation which forms the basis of the following self-study exercise.

SELF-STUDY EXERCISE 16.1

The XtraOrdinary Company Limited

The 19X1 profit statement and accompanying notes (1 and 2) of the XtraOrdinary Company, along the lines required by FRS 3, is as follows:

THE XTRAORDINARY CO. LIMITED
19X1 profit statement

	£	£
Turnover		
Continuing operations	14,000	
Discontinued operations	3,000	
		17,000
Cost of sales		(8,800)
Gross profit		8,200
Net operating expenses		(1,740)
Operating profit		
Continuing operations	7,660	
Discontinued operations	(1,200)	
		6,460
Provision for closure costs of		
discontinued operations		(2,250)
Profit on ordinary activities		4,210

Note 1

	Continuing	Discontinued	Total
	£	£	£
Cost of sales	4,940	3,860	8,800
Net operating expenses			
Selling and distribution costs	1,050	220	1,270
Administrative expenses	350	120	470
	1,400	340	1,740

Selling and distribution costs for continuing operations include £250 bad debt provision in respect of a major customer in financial difficulties.

Note 2
Statement of total recognized gains and losses

	£
Profit for the financial year	4,210
Unrealized surplus on revaluation of properties	1,000
	5,210
Prior year adjustment	(500)
Total gains and losses since last report	4,710

The prior year adjustment relates to a change in the accounting policy for development costs which are now written off as incurred.

Further information

Discussion with the directors of XtraOrdinary reveals that the financial statements reflect the following:

1 It has been decided to change the accounting policy for development costs, which are shown in the 19X0 balance sheet at £500. The new policy incorporated into the 19X1 accounts is to write off development costs.

2 A major customer has collapsed and a bad debt provision of £250 has been made as a consequence. Annual sales to this customer in financial difficulties accounted for £500 profit per annum in each of the last three years. There is little prospect of any replacement business. The customer belonged to the continuing activities.

3 At its last meeting before the end of 19X1, the board of XtraOrdinary decided to close down a major division with immediate effect. Anticipated costs associated with the close-down are estimated at £2,250. The division has been generating losses of £1,200 per annum.

4 A revaluation of XtraOrdinary's buildings shows a 'one-off' unrealized surplus of £1,000 which the directors have incorporated in the financial statements as part of a statement of gains and losses, shown separately from the profit statement. The surplus relates to buildings used in the continuing activities.

Finally you are advised that the 19X1 expenses of XtraOrdinary, exclusive of bad debts, are as shown in the following matrix:

	Production	Distribution	Administration	Total
	£	£	£	£
Staff	800	400	200	1,400
Depreciation	1,600	350	150	2,100
Raw materials	6,050	270	120	6,440
Decrease in finished goods/work in progress	350			350
	8,800	1,020	470	10,290

Required:

1 Calculate the expected 19X2 operating profits for XtraOrdinary assuming:

   (a) the staff pay rise for 19X2 is expected to be 5%;

   (b) the directors have launched an exercise to trim administration costs by 20% at end of 19X2 'prices';

   (c) no new activities are expected to be undertaken in 19X2;

   (d) there are no anticipated changes in repeatable revenues and expenses other than those given in (a) and (b) above.

2 Detail any assumptions you have made to allow you to answer part 1 above.

3 Comment on the usefulness of the FRS 3 format for presenting the XtraOrdinary Company's performance and prospects.

K

CHAPTER 17

Implementing strategy: coordination and mobilization

INTRODUCTION

Selecting the organization's strategy is crucial, but so is the implementation of the chosen strategy. To implement strategy, functions must be coordinated and the commitment of functional heads to the strategy must be mobilized. In particular the support of those responsible for the key functions in which the organization seeks a competitive advantage may be generated through their involvement in the development of both the strategy itself and a plan for its implementation. This chapter's case study concerns a university which is committed to a strategy of expanding student numbers. The objective of the case study is the preparation of the annual budget for the university's forthcoming financial year. This budget fulfils a number of roles, and in particular it can act as a plan for the organization, enabling it to implement the chosen strategy. A plan establishes a set of coordinated instructions for functional heads and provides a yardstick against which performance can be assessed.

THE UNIVERSITY OF ABC CASE STUDY

The case study is set in the University of ABC which has one department of 100 students and five academic staff. The case takes the form of a meeting of five senior university personnel (the executive committee) plus an outside consultant to determine the university's budget for 19X2 and to consider the need, if any, for longer-term changes in the budgeting arrangements. The meeting is chaired by the university's Chief Executive Officer (CEO). Thus the case takes the form of a role play in which the class is divided into groups of six and the following roles are allocated within each group (in the event of a smaller group not all roles need be allocated):

Chief Executive Officer (CEO)
Head of Administration (HA)

UNIVERSITY OF ABC
Financial result for 19X1

	Actual £000	Budget £000
Student income 100 @ £2,000	200	220
Academic salaries 5 @ £20,000	(100)	(120)
Departmental grant	(15)	(5)
Administrative salaries 4 @ £15,000	(60)	(45)
Accommodation (all accommodation is rented)	(50)	(30)
Administrative running expenses	(5)	(3)
Interest on bank overdraft £100,000 @ 10%	(10)	(5)
Annual (deficit)/surplus	(40)	12

Explanation of financial results

Why shortfall on student income?
  We anticipated 110 students.

Why academic salaries down?
  One member of staff left.

Why departmental grant up?
  Allocated £10,000 for casual teaching.

Why administrative salaries up?
  Decision to appoint Director of Student Recruitment (DSR).

Why accommodation up?
  Additional space hired for new director and £17,000 charged for new lecture theatre fittings purchased during the year. These had been omitted from the budget.

Where did authority to appoint/purchase come from if not in budget?
  Appointment of DSR recommended by external consultant. Poor accommodation identified by Director of Recruitment as priority area.

Why administrative running expenses up?
  Links to new appointment.

Why has interest gone up?
  Interest is charged on the overdraft at the year end. Overdraft at year end is £47,000 higher than planned. 10% on £47,000 = £4,700 (approximately £5,000).

Exhibit 17.1 Memorandum from the Chief Financial Officer

1 The Director of Student Recruitment considers that recruitment is the key function, and he wants to run his own show. He feels that he should have a separate budget from Administration. This is resisted by the Director of Administration. However, the DSR has been given responsibility for recruitment from 19X2 onwards.

2 The Head of the Academic Department considers the university is unnecessarily burdened with administration. He considers his student:staff ratio (SSR) of 20 (100 students to 5 permanent staff) is far too high to allow scholarship and development of courses. He considers that he should have his own departmental profit and loss account and that this would show:

	£000
Income	200
Salaries	(110)
Grant	(5)
Surplus	85

A very healthy position compared to the university's deficit of £40,000.

The university is financed by the government on the basis of a fee per student. The basic fee is £1,500 per student, but if the university is rated highly for its research and scholarship an additional £500 per student is awarded providing a student fee income of £2,000 per student. At present the university is rated highly for research and scholarship.

The HOD argues that 25% of the student income is supposed to finance research by staff but that teaching pressures are too high to allow research to take place. He says that his research rating is at risk and hence the 25% to cover research might be removed from future student fees by the funding body. If so this would take effect for 19X3. Furthermore, the HOD argues that the replacement of permanent academic staff (one full-time academic staff member left at the beginning of 19X1) by short-term contracted (casual) staff is detrimental to the department's research since such casual staff have little research experience.

3 The Head of Administration feels that control should remain at the centre and does not wish much power to be devolved to the Head of the Academic Department. The Chief Financial Officer reports to him and this allows the HA to be influential in the choice of budgeting and accountability arrangements. At present the only budget head not controlled by the Head of Administration is the departmental grant which is controlled by the HOD.

4 The External Consultant has been hired to make recommendations regarding the organizational processes of the university. His initial report identified the need to increase volumes and recommended the appointment of a Director of Student Recruitment.

5 The Chief Financial Officer's main concern is to improve the financial health of the university by reducing the overdraft and interest burden as quickly as possible. He argues that the university must budget for a healthy surplus.

Exhibit 17.2 The role plays

Chief Financial Officer (CFO)
Head of Academic Department (HOD)
Director of Student Recruitment (DSR)
External Consultant (EC)

Exhibit 17.1 is an explanation of the university's 19X1 financial results circulated by the Chief Financial Officer, whilst Exhibit 17.2 gives the background to the role plays.

Case study requirement

The Chief Executive Officer for each group is required to pull together a budget for 19X2 which is supported by his senior team. The budget should be presented to, and challenged by, the class as a whole.

PRESENTING THE BUDGET

There is no single answer to this case study but Exhibit 17.3 provides one possible solution. It is written in a format which gives the surplus of income over academic expenses (akin to gross profit), from which are subtracted marketing expenses and administration expenses to give a surplus (akin to operating profit) before charging the financing cost of interest. The budget is prepared on the basis of an additional 40 students and two additional full-time academic staff. It is assumed there is no need for further casual teaching or for further investment in lecture theatre fittings. It is further assumed that the increased student numbers can be accommodated within the present capacity of the rented accommodation and that two-thirds of the total accommodation cost relates to academic activity.

CHALLENGING THE BUDGET

The first task is to challenge the competence of the strategy itself. Will expansion of student numbers improve the financial health of the university without a consequent deterioration in the quality of teaching and research? If financial health and quality are in conflict then the strategic choice of expansion will be highly unpopular with those committed to the qualitative rather than financial dimensions of the university's activity. The position is even more complicated if the university's reputation for teaching and research is an important element in attracting students. However, in the case study expansion need not necessarily put a strain on

			£000
Student income 140 @ £2,000			280
Academic salaries 7 @ £20,000		140	
Departmental grant		5	
Accommodation (Note 1)		22	167
Academic surplus			113
Marketing			
Salaries		15	
Running expenses		2	
Accommodation (Note 1)		3	
		20	
Administration			
Salaries	45		
Running expenses	3		
Accommodation (Note 1)	8	56	76
Surplus before interest			37
Interest (10% on £100 − £37)			6
Net surplus			31

Note 1

In this budget proposal the accommodation costs are calculated as follows:

	£000
19X1 actual cost	50
Lecture theatre fittings included in the above*	(17)
19X2 budget cost	33
Attributable to academic activity (2/3)	22
	11
Attributable to DSR*	3
Attributable to administration	8

* 19X1 actual cost was £20,000 over budget of which £17,000 was lecture theatre fittings written off. The remaining £3,000 over budget is attributable to accommodation needed for the newly appointed Director of Student Recruitment.

Exhibit 17.3 Suggested budget proposal for 19X2

quality. For example, one additional academic will have a marginal annual cost of £20,000 but will, without a deterioration of the student : staff ratio, permit a further 20 students at £2,000 a time, giving an income of £40,000 and a surplus of £20,000 towards overheads. Implementation, of course, is dependent on there being no shortage of suitably qualified staff or students.

The second challenge is to the competence of the decision to appoint a Director of Student Recruitment. The appointment costs an extra £20,000 per annum being:

	£000
Salary	15
Accommodation	3
Running expenses	2
	20

As previously identified, an additional 20 students must be recruited to provide a surplus of income over academic salary costs sufficient to pay for the DSR appointment. Hence the appointment begins to make sense if the budgeted increase in student numbers is in excess of 20. The budget proposed in Exhibit 17.3 is for an additional 40 students and therefore meets this requirement.

A third challenge relates to achievability. Have the constraints on implementation been identified and recognized in the budget? Possible constraints are:

1 inability to recruit extra students;

2 inability to recruit extra staff;

3 non-availability of extra accommodation;

4 capacity of central administration;

5 unwillingness of the university's banker to continue with the overdraft.

In the case study the key constraint has been identified as the recruitment of extra students. This is the rationale behind the appointment of the Director of Student Recruitment, but can the DSR achieve the intended increase of 40 students? He/she should be questioned closely on this. What does the DSR see as the main impediment to achievement of the task? What are the key selling points for the University of ABC? Lecture theatre accommodation was identified as substandard and £17,000 of improvements undertaken. What else needs to be done? Is a separate marketing budget required? If so, what would it be spent on? Given the centrality of student recruitment it seems sensible to grant the DSR's request for a separate budget from Administration.

A fourth challenge relates to acceptability. Has the Chief Executive Officer secured support for the budget from his or her senior team or are key functional heads, such as the head of the academic department, dissatisfied? The CEO must be firm, show leadership, and take decisions in the interest of the university as a whole. Inevitably this will lead to some disaffection, but if the CEO is skilful in the management of people, then the prospects for achievement are enhanced significantly. A spirit of compromise is sometimes necessary. It should be noted, for instance, that in the Exhibit 17.3 budget, the CEO has attempted to take some pressure off the academic department by accepting the HOD's argument in favour of full-time rather than casual academic staff. However, the HOD has lost the benefit of the casual teaching which provided some compensation in 19X1 for a 20 to 1 SSR (based on permanent staff numbers). To explore acceptability each functional head can be questioned by the class about the impact of the budget on their particular function. In addition, key outsiders such as the university's bankers should be approached to ensure that they are satisfied with the budget.

This chapter's case study has explored the tensions between heads of functions such as production (HOD), marketing (DSR) and administration (HA). The chapter concludes with a suggested second role-play exercise to be carried out by university personnel. This exercise deals with the tensions between two academic (production) departments. These departments are in competition for students and for staff resources but they also need to cooperate in the provision of a joint degree covering both departments' subject areas.

CASE STUDY EXERCISE 17.1

During 19X2 the Chief Executive Officer, on the recommendation of the Director of Student Recruitment, decides to increase the number of academic departments to two, effective at the beginning of 19X3. The DSR has identified the university's limited range of subjects as a major constraint on student recruitment. The new department takes one member of staff (a key researcher) from the existing department and hires three new staff members including a departmental head. The new appointments include two with considerable research reputations. However, it proves harder than expected to attract students to the new department.

During 19X3 the financial results for the two departments (Old and New) are as follows:

	Actual	
	Old	*New*
	£000	£000
Students 140 @ £2,000	280	
40 @ £2,000		80
Academic salaries 6 @ £20,000	(120)	
4 @ £20,000		(80)
Departmental grants	(5)	(5)
Academic accommodation (rented)	(22)	(10)
Academic surplus contributing to overheads	133	(15)

The Old department (O) teaches subject A.
The New department (N) teaches subject B.

For 19X3 the university offered a degree in A, a degree in B and a joint degree in AB. Student numbers are as follows:

		Departments	
	Total	*Old*	*New*
A	120	120	
B	20		20
AB	40	20	20
	180	140	40

The expansion of student numbers has been accommodated by taking on additional rented accommodation. Assume that this additional accommodation has the capacity to cope with an additional 120 students, whereas in 19X3 it was only required to cope with an additional 40. Further assume that the Director of Student Education has identified the university's research reputation as one of the major selling points for attracting students.

The next research ratings exercise is due in 19X5. Both departments are currently rated '2' and the fee per student depends on the rating as follows:

Rating	1	2	3
Fee	£2,500	£2,000	£1,500

Required:

The circumstances of the case are that department O and department N have been asked to prepare their budgets for 19X4. Departmental meetings are held to determine the budget 'bids' and the supporting case.

The departmental heads then present their respective bids to an executive committee who must decide on the departmental budgets, bearing in mind the university has decided that it needs an overall contribution from academic departments for 19X4 of £160,000. (As an alternative the case can be played with the university looking for a contribution of £120,000 in 19X4, i.e. a similar contribution as for 19X3.)

Groups should be established to role play the departmental meetings and the meeting of the executive committee chaired by the Chief Executive Officer.

Solution to
self-study exercise 1.1

Parts 1 and 2

THE WOODEN STOOL COMPANY — Accounts for 19X2

Assets			Liabilities		
Transactions	£	Total £000	Transactions	£	Total £000
Bank		(42)	**Tax payable**		40
OB £4,000	(9) 150,000		OB £30,000		
(1.1) (30,000)	(13) (6,000)		(1.1) (30,000)		
(1.2) (20,000)			(10) 40,000		
(2.1) (15,000)					
(4) (50,000)			**Creditors**		70
(6.1) (45,000)					
(6.2) (30,000)			OB £40,000		
			(3) 80,000		
			(4) (50,000)		
Equipment		20			
			Dividend payable		25
OB £15,000	2.2 (5,000)				
(2.1) 15,000	(7.1) (5,000)		OB £20,000		
			(1.2) (20,000)		
			(12) 25,000		
Premises		40			
			Loan		60
OB £45,000					
(7.2) (5,000)			OB £60,000		
Raw material stock		40			
			Equity		
OB £20,000	(5) (60,000)				
(3) 80,000			**Capital**		40
Finished goods stock		50	OB £40,000		
OB £25,000	(7.2) 5,000				
(2.2) 5,000	(8.2) (125,000)*		**Retained profit**		78
(5) 60,000					
(6.1) 45,000			OB £9,000	(11) (10,000)	
(6.2) 30,000			(8.1) 275,000	(12) (25,000)	
(7.1) 5,000			(8.2) (125,000)*	(13) (6,000)	
			(10) (40,000)		
Debtors		225	**Reserves**		20
OB £100,000	(9) (150,000)		OB £10,000		
(8.1) 275,000			(11) 10,000		
		333			333

* *Unit cost of sales calculation:*
Year 2 production of 6,000 stools costs:

	£
Use of premises	5,000
Use of equipment	10,000
Wages	45,000
Other overheads	30,000
Raw materials	60,000
	150,000

The unit cost of each item is 150,000/6,000 = £25 (unchanged from year 1).

Part 3

THE WOODEN STOOL COMPANY
Balance sheet at 31.12.X2

			£000
Fixed assets			
Premises			40
Equipment			20
			60
Current assets			
Raw material stock		40	
Finished goods stock		50	
Debtors		225	
		315	
Current liabilities			
Bank	42		
Trade creditors	70		
Tax payable	40		
Dividend payable	25	177	
Net current assets			138
			198
Long-term liabilities			
Bank loan			60
NET ASSETS			138
Represented by:			
Capital			40
Retained profits			78
Reserves			20
SHAREHOLDERS' FUNDS			138

Part 4

THE WOODEN STOOL COMPANY
Profit statement for 19X2

	£000
Sales	275
Cost of sales	125
Gross profit	150
Interest	6
Profit before tax	144
Taxation	40
Net profit	104
Transfer to reserves	10
	94
Dividend proposed	25
Retained profit for 19X2	69
Retained profit brought forward from previous year	9
Retained profit carried forward	78

Cash flow statement for 19X2

		£000
Cash inflows from operations		
Receipts from customers		150
Cash outflows from operations		
Payments to wood suppliers	50	
Payments of wages and overheads	75	
		125
Operating cash flow		25
Tax and finance payments		
Payment of tax	30	
Payment of dividends	20	
Payment of interest	6	
		56
Cash flow after finance payments		(31)
Purchase of fixed assets		15
Cash flow for 19X2		(46)
Opening balance		4
Balance carried forward		(42)

Part 5

THE WOODEN STOOL COMPANY
Financial ratios

		19X2	19X1

ROTA
$$= \frac{\text{Net profit plus interest}}{\text{Assets}} \times 100 = \frac{110}{(60 + 315)} \times 100 \qquad = 29.3\% \quad 21.5\%$$

Profit margin
$$= \frac{\text{Net profit plus interest}}{\text{Sales}} \times 100 = \frac{110}{275} \times 100 \qquad = 40\% \quad 30\%$$

Asset productivity
$$= \frac{\text{Sales}}{\text{Assets}} \times 100 = \frac{275}{375} \times 100 \qquad = 73.3\% \quad 71.8\%$$

Expense analysis 1
$$= \frac{\text{Cost of sales}}{\text{Sales}} \times 100 = \frac{125}{275} \times 100 \qquad = 45.5\% \quad 50\%$$

Expense analysis 2
$$= \frac{\text{Tax}}{\text{Sales}} \times 100 = \frac{40}{275} \times 100 \qquad = 14.5\% \quad 20\%$$

Fixed asset turnover
$$= \frac{\text{Sales}}{\text{Fixed assets}} = \frac{275}{60} \qquad = 4.6 \quad 2.5$$

Current asset turnover
$$= \frac{\text{Sales}}{\text{Current assets}} = \frac{275}{315} \qquad = 0.87 \quad 1.01$$

Debtors turnover
$$= \frac{\text{Sales}}{\text{Debtors}} = \frac{275}{225} \qquad = 1.2 \quad 1.5$$

No. of days sales in debtors
$$= \frac{\text{Debtors}}{\text{Average daily sales}} = \frac{225}{275/365} \qquad = 299 \quad 243$$

Stock turnover
$$= \frac{\text{Cost of sales}}{\text{Total stock}} = \frac{125}{90} \qquad = 1.4 \quad 1.66$$

No. of days sales in stock
$$= \frac{\text{Stock}}{\text{Average daily cost of sales}} = \frac{90}{125/365} \qquad = 263 \quad 219$$

Creditors turnover
$$= \frac{\text{Purchases}}{\text{Creditors}} = \frac{80}{70} \qquad = 1.1 \quad 1.5$$

No. of days purchases in creditors
$$= \frac{\text{Creditors}}{\text{Average daily purchases}} = \frac{70}{80/365} \qquad = 319 \quad 243$$

Current ratio	$= \dfrac{\text{Current assets}}{\text{Current liabilities}} = \dfrac{315}{177}$	$= 1.78$	1.66

Quick ratio	$= \dfrac{\text{Current assets} - \text{Stock}}{\text{Current liabilities}} = \dfrac{(315 - 90)}{177}$	$= 1.27$	1.16

Gearing	$= \dfrac{\text{Long-term loan}}{\text{Long-term loan plus equity}} \times 100 = \dfrac{60}{60 + 138} \times 100$	$= 30.3\%$	50.4%

ROSF	$= \dfrac{\text{Net profit}}{\text{Shareholders' funds}} = \dfrac{104}{138} \times 100$	$= 75.4\%$	66.1%

Note

This solution follows the practice of the text in taking the balance sheet numbers required to calculate ratios, from the *closing* (i.e. year end balance sheet). Alternatives are to use *opening* balance sheet numbers or the *average* of the opening and closing balance sheet numbers. Theoretically the average gives the most appropriate result, but calculating ratios on the basis of the opening or closing balance sheet figures is computationally easier.

INDEX